D0374937

The Good Cook's Book of Oil & Vinegar

Other Books by Michele Anna Jordan

More Than Meatballs

The Good Cook's Journal

The Good Cook's Book of Mustard

The Good Cook's Book of Salt & Pepper

The Good Cook's Book of Tomatoes

Vinaigrettes & Other Dressings

The World Is a Kitchen

Lotsa Pasta

VegOut! A Guide Book to Vegetarian Friendly Restaurants in Northern California

The BLT Cookbook

San Francisco Seafood

The New Cook's Tour of Sonoma

Pasta Classics

California Home Cooking

Polenta

Pasta with Sauces

Ravioli & Lasagne

A Cook's Tour of Sonoma

The Good Cook's Book of Oil & Vinegar

ONE OF THE WORLD'S MOST DELICIOUS PAIRINGS, WITH MORE THAN 150 RECIPES

MICHELE ANNA JORDAN

Foreword by M. F. K. Fisher

Photographs by Liza Gershman

Skyhorse Publishing

Originally published in 1992 by Addison-Wesley Publishing Company.

10 9 8 7 6 5 4 3 2 1

Library of Congress Cataloging-in-Publication Data is available on file.

Cover design by Erin Seward-Hiatt
Cover photo credit Liza Gershman

Print ISBN: 978-1-63220-587-2
Ebook ISBN: 978-1-63450-014-2

Printed in China

Plant a vineyard for your children and an olive grove for your grandchildren.
—An old Italian saying

for Lucas, my one and only grandchild

&

for California's olive oil and vinegar pioneers, especially Ridgely Evers & Colleen McGlynn of DaVero, the Sciabica Family, Bruce Cohn, Greg Hinson of O Olive Oil, and Yvonne & Jerg Hall of Terra Savia/Olivino

Table of Contents

Foreword

Comparisons are said to be odious, but I would not find it odious at all to have anything that I have written about either oil or vinegar compared with this book, In other words, Michele Jordan and I seem to agree and I am proud to admit it.

Of course, I don't recognize many of the private product names given and I admit to real ignorance about the uses of fruit or berry vinegars. I do know and love anything connected with *aceto balsamico*, which for some reason I have never thought of as being especially exotic.

I also confess to a complete ignorance of using pure virgin olive oil for anything except lubricating the umbilical cords of new babies, until I was perhaps in my early teens and my mother had finally stopped reproducing. It was about then that my grandmother Holbrook died too, and the scrubby little two-ounce bottle of olive oil, which had stayed on a shelf in the medicine cabinet, was correctly moved to a shelf in the kitchen cooler. It automatically became a quart bottle or a two-quart tin. In other words, I am an addict but not a snob.

I am very glad to be in the good company of Michele Jordan. I suppose we are both more addicts than snobs, but neither of us cares one whit. I think Michele uses both oil and vinegar more in cooking than I do, but that's all right too since we both know what oil and vinegar are for: They are as necessary to us as water, or almost. And that is as it should be.

M. F. K. Fisher
Glen Ellen, 1991

Acknowledgments

A huge *mille grazie* goes out to the staff at Skyhorse Publishing, especially editor Nicole Frail but also the entire production team whose names I do not know, for such fine work and astonishing patience as I powered through *The Good Cook's* series, sliding at the last possible moment to the finish line. What a whirlwind it has been.

Thanks, as well, to L. John Harris, who shepherded the first edition of this book into print.

And thanks one more time to photographer Liza Gershman, who worked under extremely difficult time constraints to produce these beautiful photographs. And to the team who helped during those crazy sessions, thank you! Kelly Keagy, you are a rock in the best possible way and I deeply appreciate your support and understanding. Deborah Pulido, you helped in so many ways but it was your tender caring for my little dachsies Joey and Lark that touched my heart. Thank you.

Chef Evan Euphrat of Knife for Hire and Sara Ely, thank you huge bunches for saving the day on barely a moment's notice. Sara, you have a remarkable eye and true talent for styling and staging. Evan, you are a blast in the kitchen!

Fabiano Ramaci, what a treasure you are. I thank you for your warmth, your friendship, your hard work on behalf of this book and for your delicious oils and wines.

Ridgely and Colleen of DaVero, what can I say? I love you both and love your olive oils, your wines, your tasting room, your ranch, your wisdom, your talent, your common sense, and, most importantly, your willingness to share it all with me.

Thanks, once again, to Cultivate, a lovely kitchenwares store in Sebastopol, for the loan of linens and props.

And to my dear friend and landlady, Mary Duryee, from the deepest recesses of my heart and soul, *thank you, once again, for everything.*

Finally, to my daughters Gina and Nicolle, my grandson Lucas, my son-in-law Tom, my friends James Carroll and John Boland: *Look! I have come through!* Thank you so very much.

Introduction to the Second Edition

In a very specific way, the publication of the first edition of this book was a study in bad timing. I completed the manuscript in the fall of 1991 and as it wound its way through the editing and publication process, with printed galleys and such going back and forth via snail mail, the California olive oil renaissance was simmering just beneath the awareness of all but a very few people, specifically the late Lila Jaeger, software entrepreneur Ridgely Evers, and a few others. Email communication was still a couple of years in the future and the Web had opened to the public that summer, in August, 1991, and was still an electronic Wild West, sparsely populated and all but impossible to navigate. Websites? *We don't got no stinkin' Website.*

The book, my second, hit the shelves of book stores—there was no amazon.com yet—in October. In November, everything in California changed, thanks, to a large degree, to Bruce Cohn of B. R. Cohn Winery.

Bruce's wife at the time was fed up with olive stains on her carpets, tracked in from ripe olives that fell from the ancient trees that came with the estate, Picholine trees planted sometime in the mid 1880s and left untended for decades. The green olives would hang until they turned black and fell to the ground, there to be trampled, crushed, and carried inside on the bottoms of everyone's shoes.

So Bruce decided to harvest the olives and have them pressed into oil, which he then bottled in beautifully etched bottles.

It was a lovely oil, lean and bright on the palate, with a pleasing trail of pepper in the back of the throat. The race was on and California was poised to catch up with Italy, something I had not seen coming when

I wrote that the oils of my home state were good but not great. When I was a speaker on the topic of olive oil at the Fancy Food Show in San Francisco, the large room was packed to capacity, and when it came time for comments and questions I might as well have been standing there naked, as I don't think I could have felt any more humiliated than I did as one person after another took me to task for my comments about California's nascent industry.

At least the book isn't about just olive oil, I thought to myself, and was pleased when the book went through several printings.

And now, here we are, nearly twenty-five years later. The California industry has blossomed, established itself as a world class producer, and begun to struggle with some difficult realties that have nothing to do with the quality of its oil, which is as good as any produced anywhere.

The other major change is the Internet itself and the ease with which we can find products that once required a major scavenger hunt. Looking for roasted pumpkin seed only? I found it only in France in 1990 but now there are several websites that sell it. On and on it goes, our changing world and its kaleidoscope of delicious inspiration, so close at hand.

Introduction to the First Edition

"Oil and vinegar?" said a friend who is a musician. "Is that a book about men and women?"

I was astonished by her comment, probably the most interesting comment I heard when mentioning this book, but conceded that I could see her point. Opposites in nearly every way, oil and vinegar in one form or another have been companions since the beginning of our own history, a culinary parallel to that most pervasive of all unions of opposites, male and female. It was not a comparison that had ever occurred to me and I still laugh when I remember the sincerity and assuredness that accompanied her statement. But who is the vinegar, I wondered, and who, the oil? Regardless, look at this book as a celebration of their marriage.

The need for a cookbook like this one becomes apparent every time I mention the topic. Except for the single exception above, people respond, "Oh, yes, a book on salad dressings." That these wonderful and varied ingredients, a panorama of flavors and textures and aromas, are viewed in most people's minds nearly exclusively as components of salad dressings is revealing. Chefs rely on the qualities and nuances of vinegars and oils to inform diverse cuisines, and yet there is a void in our culinary literature. The topic is not widely addressed. Certainly, salad dressings are one of the important and delicious results of mixing together an oil and a vinegar. These mixtures add spark not only to salads, but also to seafoods, meats, vegetables, pastas, and grains. There are other blends that are equally delicious and important: marinades, for example, and emulsified sauces such as mayonnaises and aïolis. As I have researched the topic, developed many recipes, and discovered others, I have realized just how diverse and delicious a subject this is.

Both oil and vinegar are simple, essential foods that have been with us for thousands of years, ingredients many of us eat daily, that appear in a multitude of recipes in all cuisines the world around. There are technical journals that speak to the scientific and medical communities, and there are slim pamphlets put out by producers of various oils and vinegars. There are a few small booklets that contain a great deal of misinformation about vinegar. A slim volume, *Oil, Vinegar, and Seasonings*, appeared in early 1991 but again, with limited scope. Olive oil stands alone in its legacy of literary inspiration; there are three substantial works on the topic, including *The Feast of the Olive* by Maggie Klein, a lovely book that has influenced me greatly.

I found no basic text that covered the broader subject of oils or vinegars in general, no cookbook that treated the ingredients comprehensively. I have attempted to make a start, offering here not only what I view as the essential information, the tools for navigating the vast pantry of oils and vinegars now readily available to the home cook, but also many of my favorite recipes, dishes that would either not exist or be drastically different were it not for a special quality contributed by a favorite vinegar or a distinctive oil.

It is not possible to discuss specific foods without addressing the issue of personal biases. This book reflects mine in many ways. First and last, I write about the things I love, in this case the olive oils and the vinegars that do the right thing when they cross my lips. Yes, I am an addict when it comes to things culinary and I think that is as it should be. We have to eat, and I believe we might as well make it as much a thrill as possible. I love a good olive oil so much that I am not averse to taking a healthy swig directly from a bottle of the best. It is this enthusiasm—obsession, if you prefer—that shapes my approach.

I do not expect everyone to respond as I do and you should keep my personal preferences in mind. When I tell you about my favorite olive oil or talk about my reasons for liking toasted sesame oil, I am in part revealing a purely subjective reaction. For flavor, I most often prefer unrefined olive oils from the heart of Tuscany, "big" oils with lots of peppery fire slipping down the back of my throat. When I can find it, I relish the intensity of the extra virgin olive from Poggio Lamentano, the only olive oil I have come across that dates its production. Ardoino offers several wonderful olive oils from the Italian Riviera, and I'm especially fond of the Biancardo, a late-harvest, light golden oil that is both intense and delicate, delicious drizzled on poached seafood or a baked potato. It is not made every year, but only when weather conditions have been such to allow it. I have had exquisite oils from Antinori, though I have also tasted oils of that brand that I have not cared for. When I must use an oil from a major producer, I favor Sasso or Monini extra virgin olive oils, which have a consistently pleasant taste at a reasonable price. Sasso or Ardoino pure olive oil is well suited to high-temperature cooking, when the flavors of more delicate oils would be compromised. I find the other major brands unacceptable. Although I feel disloyal saying so, I prefer European olive oils to those produced in California. Very good oils are produced from the olive groves of California, but not great oils. Nick Sciabica & Sons, in the Central Valley, produces consistently high-quality California olive oils, and their Sevillano Fall Harvest is lovely, but even at their best they do not compare with the finest Italian and French oils. As better and better oils begin to arrive from Spain, we will be offered a larger range of high-quality oils. My recent discovery of Spectrum Naturals' unrefined corn oil was an exhilarating surprise: corn oil so full of the flavor of real corn! The increased availability of unrefined oils that retain their natural aromas and flavors is great news for cooks.

I take a more subtle approach to my vinegars, preferring acidity no higher than 6 percent, or 6.5 percent if it is a particularly rich vinegar. I like a red wine vinegar in which the character of the wine still shines through, and prefer the clear, light Champagne vinegar to other white wine vinegars. With berry vinegars, the richer the better, and again, that frequently implies low acid. Kozlowski Farms berry vinegars, made near my home in Sonoma County, have only 4.5 percent acidity and allow the rich flavor of the berries to dominate. I find balsamic vinegar delightful, use it frequently, and hope someday to possess a little of the true aceto balsamico tradizionale, whose story I find so intriguing. Personal preferences do not, however, make it impossible to judge objectively. There are standards of quality, absolutes of freshness, and standards of production and storage that we can all use to ferret out our favorites in a vast and confusing marketplace. One can distinguish the quality of a food or a particular product while not necessarily favoring it for personal use. Thus, I present to you here, not only my own favorites, but also what I hope will be guidelines for finding your own.

PART 1
All About Oils

Rarely a day goes by that a home cook doesn't reach for some sort of oil, for sautéing, for frying, for lubricating sliced eggplant or steak before tossing it on the grill, for dressing a salad. We shake toasted sesame oil over rice, dip bread in olive oil, add a little walnut oil to wild rice salad. Some of us rub coconut oil into our hair to condition it and slather olive oil on our skin for the softness it conveys.

But, what, exactly, is oil?

The answer is simple: Oil is a fat. The distinction that places oil in its own category is its melting point. In both common and scientific usage, almost all fats that are solid at room temperature are considered fats, and those that are liquid at room temperature, oils. This distinction generally follows the divisions between animal and vegetable, too. Animal fats, such as butter, lard, beef suet, and duck fat, remain firm at room temperature; most of the familiar vegetable fats—fruit oils, seed oils, nut oils—are easily poured. A few vegetable fats—coconut, palm, and dendê—remain solid at room temperature.

In cooking, a fat has two primary functions: to lubricate and to transfer heat. Some specialty oils, notably olive oil, toasted sesame oil, and some of the nut oils, have a third function: They impart flavor. With so many oils available on the market these days, each subject to a wide range of nutritional and culinary claims, it is important to develop a basic understanding of them.

Fats and oils, members of a group of biological compounds called lipids, are triglycerides. They are composed primarily of glycerol and hydrocarbon chains called fatty acids. Saturated fats have mostly short and medium hydrocarbon chains; fats are composed mostly of long ones. Detailed knowledge of the chemistry of fat is not essential to the understanding of its nutritional and culinary functions, but it can be helpful.

Fat, carbohydrates, and protein are the three macronutrients in the human diet, each one with specific functions. The primary functions of fat are the storage of energy and the distribution of nutrients. Fats contain more than twice as much energy as carbohydrates and thus are an efficient way for an animal to carry along an extra source of fuel. A good example of this can be found in birds, especially geese, that migrate a great distance. In anticipation of their long flight, geese overfeed, which in turn enlarges their livers, where the extra fat is stored, and allows them to fly great distances without stopping to graze. More than two thousand years ago, ancient Egyptians discovered that the liver of these geese was delicious: Foie gras, fattened liver, was found before it was farmed.

Fats contribute a pleasing richness to the foods we eat and give us a feeling of satisfaction, of being full, thus preventing the quick return of hunger. The body assimilates fat more slowly than other nutrients and this accounts for both our feelings of satisfaction and our sustained energy. It was not easy for early humans to acquire necessary fat and those who craved it and were successful at finding it passed on their hardwiring to their offspring. As with salt, we need fat and so we crave it.

Today, our cravings can work against us, leaving us, in part, vulnerable to producers of packaged foods and fast foods who understand these truths. Add fat and salt—sugar, too, but that's another topic—and we'll come back for more. This reality is one of the best arguments for cooking from scratch, at home, with whole and wholesome ingredients.

Fats & Nutrition

Very little is known about the health effects of transforming millions of confident, healthy people into cholesterol neurotics. And there is even evidence to suggest that stress and worry about anything—including fats in the diet—can itself raise blood cholesterol levels.

Robert Ornstein and David Sobel,
Healthy Pleasures, Addison-Wesley, 1989

Because fats are abundant in the modern world, we now either take them for granted or eschew them. The 1980s and 1990s were filled with hysteria about fat, and zero-fat diets became distressingly trendy. If we were nutritionally correct, we were told, if we had will-power, we would avoid the oh-so-attractive culinary bad boy. Enjoying fats, even enjoying one's food, was viewed as a sign of weakness, and "if it tastes good, it's bad for you" became, once again, a popular slogan. As I was promoting the first edition of this book at specialty food shows, I was frequently attacked for my "dangerous" stance that fat is not our enemy and was told more than once that I was both causing and promoting cancer. When I gave a restaurant specializing in no-fat cooking a less-than-positive review, I was reprimanded by the owner, who declared, in a letter to the editor, that "this food is not supposed to taste good, it's supposed to be healthy."

Really? How long would any species last if eating, if sustaining one's self, were unpleasant? Puritans not withstanding, we'd die out in a generation. We'd have never come so close to ruling the world.

Photo provided by Ridgely C. Evers

But the pendulum always swings and swinging it is, in a good direction, back towards acknowledging the value of fats in human health, dispelling myths and reclaiming the best fats. The shift began years ago, first with scientific studies that contradicted the demonization of both fats and dietary cholesterol and soon with the work of such organizations as the Weston A. Price Foundation, founded by Sally Fallon and Mary G. Enig. Fallon's book, *Nourishing Traditions: The Cookbook that Challenges Politically Correct Nutrition and the Diet Dictocrats* (New Trends Publishing, 1999, 2000), was followed soon by *Politically Incorrect Nutrition: Finding Reality in the Mire of Food Industry Propaganda* (Square On Publishers, 2004) by Michael Barbee and *The Good Fat Cookbook* (Scribner, 2003) by Fran McCullough. These books are well-researched, well-written, and informative resources, with detailed information about how fats function, why they are so important, how and why we have been mislead about cholesterol, and which fats are the best.

There is now wide agreement that butter, whole milk, whole milk yogurt, real ice cream, eggs, chocolate, red meat, bacon, and lard are among the foods we should eat, not avoid. We can enjoy nuts and nut oils, avocado and avocado oil, olives and olive oils. Our concerns should shift away from mass-produced foods grown, raised, or produced with chemical additions and towards cleaner foods from natural sources, including grass-fed, pastured, and truly organic. How do you know? To whatever degree possible, eat as close to home as you can and when you can't, know your farmers and ranchers. These days, with farmers, ranchers, and other producers a click of a mouse away, it's easy.

As I was completing this revised edition, new federal nutrition guidelines declared that dietary cholesterol—a component of saturated fats—so recently one of our scariest nutritional boogiemen, is no longer a concern. Even saturated fat itself is receiving a big national nod of approval. *Bring on the butter, the lard, the bacon, the expeller-pressed organic coconut oil!*

Olive Oil—The Golden Glory of Civilization

O Love! what hours were thine and mine,
In lands of palm and southern pine,
In lands of palm, of orange-blossom,
Of olive, aloe, and maize and vine!
—Alfred, Lord Tennyson, "The Daisy"

Ahh, the beguiling little olive. No other fruit, not temptation's famous apple, not even the beloved grape, has served humanity so well, for so long, and in so many ways. The olive tree, *olea europaea*, with its silvery halo of leaves and gnarled trunk, has been cultivated for at least five thousand years. A native of the Middle East, the long-lived olive tree spread throughout the Mediterranean and only climate stilled its reach; it can withstand a few days of freezing temperatures but it does not thrive in hard winters. There are trees today in southern Europe thought to be more than two thousand years old.

In ancient times, the olive was valued primarily for the oil within it, which was used as fuel for light, as a lubricant, as a medicine and a tonic, to make soap, and to anoint humans at birth, at baptism, at death, and at ascension to the priesthood and the throne. Today, we press out the oil, of course, and use it in both cooking and ritual anointment and we also eat the olive itself, plunking it into Martinis, grinding it into tapenade, stuffing it into sausages, and enjoying it neat. But it is the juice of the olive, its oil, that most fascinates and inspires us.

One of the most intriguing qualities of the olive is that the fruit is inedible without some sort of processing to tame its bitter glucosides—birds don't eat olives for this reason—yet the oil needs only to be separated from the fruit to delight us. And delight us it does, in myriad ways.

When I returned from my first trip to Italy in the spring of 1990, I was laden with several liters of golden-green olive oil from Tuscany. I hobbled

The First Olive Tree

The first olive tree is said to have been planted during a dispute between Athena and Poseidon for the possession of the Acropolis. Athena claimed that she could give greater benefits to her people. Poseidon, when he struck a rock with his trident and a spring began to flow, hoped to prove her wrong. She planted an olive tree beside the spring, the gods acknowledged her gift, and she kept possession of the temple. Thus the first olive tree grew at the center of the Acropolis in the center of Athens, the very heart of Greek civilization.

onto the plane, trying to appear as if my carry-on luggage actually met the weight requirements. I am lucky that the overhead compartment did not collapse and drown me in a bath of oil. Those precious bottles made it back intact and were my balm and my solace in the days following my return when all I wanted to do was head back over the Atlantic. Instead, I ate grilled bread drizzled with the best of the olive oil, drank red wine, and longed for Tuscany, where olive trees anoint the countryside with their rustic, silvery beauty. I didn't know then that before long, the place I call home, Sonoma County in Northern California, would mirror that landscape, though primarily with young trees, not yet twisted and gnarled as they are in so many of Van Gogh's famous paintings.

An olive branch placed above the door will drive away evil spirits and keep husbands faithful, the Spanish say.

Olive oil is not the only oil in the world, of course, but it is the most versatile, the most varied, the most interesting and the best. No other oil has the range of flavor from dozens of varieties of olives, each with its own unique flavors and textures. Back in 1990 when I set out on my research, I was guided simply by curiosity and what I discovered affirmed

Olive oil is sacred, infused with spiritual qualities by religions throughout the world. It is the ritual oil of the Catholic Church, where it is blessed in a special mass each year. Olive oil was used to anoint Queen Elizabeth II, the baptized infant nephew of Michael Corleone in *The Godfather*, and President John Kennedy as he lay stricken in Parkland Hospital in Dallas in 1963. It has been used throughout the ages in religious ceremonies and rituals and to provide illumination in the dark of night. It is the miracle of olive oil and how a day's worth of it lasted eight days that is celebrated during Chanukah. No other oil has such a scope of meaning, or such a spectrum of flavor, which is influenced by variations in the variety, the soil in which it is grown, the climate, and, according to some, the temperament of the producer.

my particular passion. No other oil engages the emotions, or evokes such reverence, as the oil, or juice, of the olive.

"Olive oil is interesting because it is very special," Darrell Corti told me when I visited him at Corti Brothers, his family's market, in Sacramento in 1991.

"In fact, it is sacred, probably more sacred than wine. It was used for anointing, for light, for flavoring," he added.

You Take Olives and You Press Them

Part of the beauty of olive oil is its simplicity, its perfection in its natural state. As Darrell Corti says, you take olives and you press them, a fact that has led to the comment that olive oil is found, not made. It is a little more complex, but not much, for olive oil is simply the juice of the olive, at its best when it is first pressed out of the fruit.

"Making good extra virgin olive oil is really easy," Ridgely Evers, one of California's contemporary olive oil pioneers, says as he looks back to the early days of the state's renaissance.

"We thought it would be really hard but it isn't."

Olive oil, to a very large degree, is made in the grove, where things must go right, from early spring, when tiny flowers must be pollinated, through the fall, when a long moderate growing season will encourage the olives to develop full flavors before they ripen. When all the right conditions coalesce, a producer's job is fairly simple: Pick the olives at the right moment, preferably when there is a blend of mostly green with some ripened fruit, get the fruit to the mill right away so that the olives do not heat up and begin to ferment, and get the oil out of the fruit by the best method available. Opinions vary, of course, as to what the best method is but no matter how it is done, the olives must be washed, crushed, and mixed and the oil must be separated from the vegetable matter and bitter juices.

Of course, what, exactly, is planted is crucial to an oil's character. Some regions make oil from a single variety. France, for example, is known for its Picholine olive and the suave oils it produces. In Tuscany, field blends are more common, with orchards containing a mix of four or five varieties, each selected for its unique qualities and all harvested together to create a full-flavored oil.

The best oil olives are small. California's signature olive, the Mission, planted by Spanish padres as they journeyed from San Diego north, is a multipurpose olive, best suited, perhaps, to the table but also a good late-harvest olive for oil that lends itself to crushing with a wide range of citrus. Europe's enormous Cerignola, like the Mission, is best cured and enjoyed at the table, though it, too, is now grown for its oil in California, though not widely.

The mix of green and black is crucial to an olive's character. Green olives have less oil but lower acidity and better flavor, with that characteristic pepper-like heat at the back of the throat that aficionados love. Oil from green olives is less viscous, less "oily," too. Ripe olives contain more oil but higher acid and less flavor. Understanding what balance of green and ripe olives will produce the most delicious oil is a crucial part of the art of making olive oil for flavor. Olive oil for cooking doesn't need such careful orchestration; it makes sense to wait until the yield is as high as possible.

The traditional method of harvesting is slow and expensive. Olives are simply picked by hand, each one pulled individually from its branch. Many large producers wait until olives are ripe before harvesting, not just because of the higher yield but also because the olives can be beaten and shaken down onto tarps or nets placed underneath the trees. Olives harvested in this way do not produce the finest of oils, as their taste is compromised by ripening and by bruising.

The simplest method of crushing olives is with a granite stone and throughout the Mediterranean you can see ancient stones, blackened by centuries of use. Larger producers have their own mills and process their own olives as well as those of smaller farmers in the region. California producers function this way, too, with the established mills offering production services to nearby producers.

After olives are crushed, the paste is mixed for upwards of an hour, a process that allows the oil to coalesce into larger and larger globules, which makes it easier to press. After malaxation, as the mixing is call, the pulp is spread onto mats—once made of straw, now typically made of nylon—stacked on top of one another with metal discs between the layers and pressed, with tons of pressure applied by a screw or hydraulic press. The oil must then be separated from the vegetable water, a process typically accomplished with a centrifuge.

At this point, extra virgin olive oil is at its peak of flavor. It will never be better than at this moment. However, if bottled right away, the oil is quite unstable, with flavors that will deteriorate quickly, within a few months. The standard practice is to hold the olive oil in large tanks for a few months, a period of rest that results in a longer life for the olive, before bottling.

An Olive Sampler

There are hundreds of cultivars of the olive, some suited to the table, some to oil, a few to both. It can be challenging to sort them out not only because there are so many but also because the same cultivars sometimes have different names in different countries. This sample of olives from around the world focuses on those varieties with an established history in an area. In California, for example, there are now dozens of varieties, near groves planted by recent pioneers, and passionate farmers hoping to ride the wave of contemporary fascination with olive oil, yet just four varieties have a long history in the Golden State.

California:	Mission, Manzanilla, Sevillano, Picholine
Italy:	Frantoio, Leccino, Pendolino, Moraiolo, Agogia, Rosciolo, Raggia, Nicastrese, Biancolilla, Coratina, Taggiasca, Cerignola
Spain:	Arbequina, Manzanillo, Sevillano, Gordal, Picual, Racimal, Argudell, Verdillo, Nevadillo blanco, Blanqueta, Hojiblanca, Rojal
France:	Aglandau, Bouteillan, Olivière, Pigalle, Pendoulier, Cailletier, Moiral, Picholine, Lucques, Niçoise, La Tanche
Greece:	Caronaiki, Daphnoelia, Mouratolia, Carydolia, Stravolia, Kalamata, Koroneiki
Portugal:	Gallego, Verdeal, Cordovil, Carrasquenha, Redondil, Madurai
Libya:	Enduri, R'ghiani, Rasli
Tunisia:	Ouslati, Meski, Cornicabra
Turkey:	Sam, Girit, Hurma

This traditional method of production is quickly being replaced by the new horizontal decanter method, a continuous system of production that some advocates—especially those who use it—claim results in a finer oil. Certainly, the possibility of contamination by odors in the air or by a worker's unclean hands is eliminated. (Olive oil is unstable and will pick up scents in the room where it is made. This presented a problem in the days when the large stone presses were driven by horses. Today the entire process can take place away from such potential influences, away from light, away from any possible interference.) The process can and often does result in high-quality oils. Critics of the horizontal decanter method of production point out that, inevitably, pits and leaves are crushed in the process and contribute to the final taste of the oil. I wonder, too, how much character we can expect from all that stainless steel, from that clinically sterile room? What is the temperament of the machinery? What do we lose as we become more efficient?

Grades of Olive Oil

There was a scandal a few years ago when it was discovered that adulterated olive oils were being dumped on the American market, which did follow the International Olive Oil Council's standards. A crisis in trust ensued and soon a book, *Extra Virginity: The Sublime and Scandalous World of Olive Oil* (W. W. Norton & Company, 2011) by Tom Mueller, exposed the corruption and fraud in the industry. Yet this exposé was nearly as poorly timed as the first edition of this book and its take on California olive oil, as California's Department of Food and Agriculture adopted standards that were even more stringent than those of Europe.

The new regulations serve the consumer well, as the category of "light" and "lite" oils has been eliminated, as has "pure," as a designation. All California olive oils—with certain exemptions for very small producers—must now be tested to confirm it is what its label says, 100 percent extra virgin olive oil that has not been diluted with inferior oils or chemicals.

Determining true quality among olive oils is difficult for the consumer. Because of the ambiguity in labeling requirements, ferreting out an authentic extra virgin oil from among the industrially produced oils is not a simple task, although there are a few guidelines that help. First of all, keep in mind that it is the smaller farmers who are making oil in the traditional manner of simply removing the juice from the fruit with a stone press. Because of the time-consuming process and limited production, these true extra virgin olive oils are expensive. That consideration immediately rules out, for authenticity, any inexpensive oil labeled as "extra virgin." Price is, however, no longer a guarantee of quality in olive oil. Larger producers, cultivating the lucrative gourmet market, are selling inferior oils that have been refined and bolstered with the addition of some cold-pressed oil at high prices. Some of these oils are perfectly satisfactory; a few have a pleasing taste of olives and an acceptable texture; the best have their place in a pantry, where they should be used when the flavor of olive oil is necessary but will not be the dominant factor. Some are unpleasant, bland, oily, and occasionally even rancid.

The true extra virgin olive oils—the specialty oils from Tuscany, Liguria, Provence, and California—should be used as condiments for the flavors they impart, not for the ability to lubricate or transfer heat. If you can buy directly from a small producer, which has become much easier in the age of the Internet, do so.

Testing for Virginity

Place a small amount of olive oil in a glass bowl and refrigerate it for a few days. If it becomes crystalline, the chances are good that it is a true extra virgin olive oil. If it forms a block, it is most likely chemically refined oil that has had some first-pressed oil added. A buttery consistency indicates pit, or sansa, oil.

Olive Oil & Health

In the ancient world, olive oil was used on wounds to promote healing, for cleansing the skin, and for soothing it after the burning and drying effects of sun and wind. It was used on hair to make it shine and was taken as a tonic for many ills, including insomnia, nausea, and ulcers. Olive oil is said to prevent dandruff and wrinkles. There are even claims that olive oil slows the aging processes of both the brain and the body's tissues and organs. Many of these ancient treatments have stayed with us, evolving into folk remedies that are still used in many parts of the world. The golden glory of civilization, olive oil has been used since earliest time to enhance life on all levels. Today, we know it best for its marvelous culinary properties and the current claims made about its health benefits.

With growing concern over heart disease, scientists have examined those cultures where incidence is low. It is common knowledge now that the Mediterranean diet has produced an extremely low rate of coronary disease in that region, especially compared with rates in northern Europe and the United States of America. The areas with the lowest incidence of heart disease and cancer are those where the diet is closest to what it has been for millennia, when 80 percent of a day's calories came from grains and olive oil.

Health claims about particular foodstuffs can be both overwhelming and confusing, and it seems to be part of the American spirit to embrace fad after fad, abandoning one for the next to come along with its miraculous claims. Olive oil has the blessing of the ages.

A California Olive Oil Sampler

California has come of age when it comes to olive oil. It is now well established that it can and does produce world class olive oil. The finest are best purchased directly from their maker, easy to do in the Internet age, as many premium producers have no or limited distribution. There are many benefits of buying directly from a producer. First, you are guaranteed that the oils have been handled properly. Additionally, the full purchase prices goes to the producer, not to distributors and retailers. Given the grim economics of growing olives and making olive oil in Northern California, many of the best producers are shifting to direct-to-consumer marketing, with online sales and olive oil clubs, which function much as wine clubs do.

Extra virgin olive oil should be stored away from heat and light. Although a well-made and properly stored oil may last for years without turning rancid, flavors are never better than when the oil is just pressed. Use new oils within a year of production; just when you are running low, the year's first oils, Olio Nuovo, should appear.

These oils represent the best of the best California has to offer. Contact information, including website addresses, are in Resources, pages 392 to 394.

B. R. Cohn Olive Hill Estate Picholine Extra Virgin Olive Oil

DaVero Dry Creek Estate Extra Virgin Olive Oil
DaVero Dry Creek Estate Meyer Lemon Olive Oil
DaVero Olio Nuovo
Club Nuovo

McEvoy Ranch Extra Virgin Olive Oil, Traditional Blend
McEvoy Ranch Extra Virgin Olive Oil, Limited Edition

The Olive Press Sonoma Valley Blend Extra Virgin Olive Oil
The Olive Press Club

O Ultra EVO Extra Virgin Olive Oil
O Meyer Lemon Olive Oil

O Organic Extra Virgin Olive Oil
O Tahitian Lime Olive Oil
(widely distributed)

Round Pond Premium Italian Extra Virgin Olive Oil
Round Pond Premium Spanish Extra Virgin Olive Oil
Round Pond Meyer Lemon Olive Oil

Terra Savia Classic Tuscan Extra Virgin Olive Oil
Terra Savia Pure Moraiolo Extra Virgin Olive Oil
Terra Savia Pure Leccino Extra Virgin Olive Oil
Terra Savia Olio Nuovo

The Fly in the Oil

As the new edition of this book goes to press, new trouble is brewing in the world of olive. In 2014, Italy lost an enormous portion of its harvest to the Mediterrean olive fly. Recently, experts recommended that enormous orchards in Puglia in the south of Italy and in a few other regions be destroyed.

The fly is now in California, too, arriving in Los Angeles a few years ago. It had a devastating impact on many groves in 2014, a year that was troublesome for other reasons, too. It was a hot summer and fall and the olives ripened early, before wine grapes were harvested. Most of the year's crop of oil olives were harvested ripe, resulting in a softer, golden oil, rather than a peppery green oil.

What impact will the olive fly have on California's industry? It's hard to say. The fly has no natural predators and environmentally friendly solutions have not proven particularly effective. The only approved treatment, spinosad, is toxic to pollinators and so is not a viable solution.

The fly is tenacious and there are five generations during a single growing season. Females sting the olives and deposit an egg, which becomes a maggot that then eats its way out of the olive, rendering it unsuitable for production. A farmer cannot simply abandon a crop that has been infected with flies because unharvested olives make comfy omes for the flies, creating an enormous problem in the following year.

The University of California Davis Olive Center is working on the problem of the fly but exactly what the solution will be or what its long-term impact on California and Italy's olive oil industry will be, no one knows.

There is another challenge to California's producers of ultra-premium olive oils, the ones from groves in Marin, Sonoma, Napa, and Mendocino Counties, where a moderate climate produces the finest oil olives. It is not possible, given the cost of land and labor, to be a profitable venture. At the time the California renaissance began in the early 1990s, the price of premium Italian olive oils was at an all-time high. California's pioneers based their financial projections, at least in part, on these figures.

But the high prices were an anomaly, based on a hard frost that was thought to have killed thousands of the best olive trees in Tuscany. There was not a lot of premium Italian extra virgin olive oil in the wake of the killing frost. Italian producers began planting enormous groves and by the time they matured—it takes fifteen years for an olive tree to hit its stride—the ancient trees had come back. Prices plummeted, which had an impact on California's producers who needed to compete with Italian oils, hard to do if they priced themselves out of the market.

Many of California's best olive oil producers—DaVero, McEvoy, and Terra Savia, for example—have planted vineyards, which are much more profitable than olive groves.

WHAT IS MARGARINE?

Why does margarine exist? A French invention of the early 1800s, margarine was being produced in large quantities in the United States by 1880. For decades, there was great resistance to its use, especially by the dairy industry, and it was not until 1950 that government restrictions and heavy taxes were lifted. Until 1967, it was illegal in Wisconsin to sell margarine, which is naturally white, that had been dyed yellow.

Ostensibly a substitute for butter and relied upon during dairy shortages during World War II, margarine is made of vegetable oil that has been artificially saturated through a process of hydrogenation to make it stable at room temperature. The process is similar to the method used for making plastics, and, as we now know, artificially hydrogenated foods function in our bodies like plastics. Margarine and other artificially saturated fats are trans-fats and it has long been understood that they are quire harmful to human health. There is no safe amount.

Today, most margarine brands have eliminated trans-fats. That said, they are still a substitute for butter, which is one of the best fats there is, especially when it is made using milk from cows that graze on organic grass. *Ain't nothing like the real thing.*

What will become of the scores of new groves, many still immature, that punctuate the back roads of Northern California? In early 2015, many are for sale and the future of California's olive oil industry is in question.

Still, California olive oils offer something to Americans that European oils don't: freshness. Because olive oil does not benefit from aging, the sooner it is enjoyed, the better it is.

Perhaps no greater change has taken place since I wrote the first edition of this book than how we think of fat and dietary cholesterol.

Photo provided by Ridgely C. Evers

Storage of Oils

All oils should be kept away from heat and light. A cool, dark cupboard is the best environment for oils when they are not sitting on your work counter. Tinted glass, porcelain, or stainless steel are the best materials for containers; oils should never be stored in plastic or in reactive metals. Extra-virign olive oil must be protected from light and is typically packaged in dark glass; if it is in clear glass, be suspicious of it unless it is further packaged in a box, as several ultra-premium olives oils are. Certain oils—walnut and hazelnut oils, for example—are unstable with delicate flavors that deteriorate quickly and should be refrigerated.

Manufacturing of Oils

Many plants contain oil, some in the seeds, some in the nuts, and others—olive oil, avocado oil, coconut oil—in fruit. For the oil to be made available for cooking and other uses, it must be extracted either by a mechanical process or with the use of chemicals. Oils that are extracted mechanically and go through no further processing are typically called unrefined oils; oils that are extracted with chemical solvents are known as refined oils. Unrefined oils provide the highest overall quality and the fullest, most complex taste, but both can have a place in our pantries.

Unrefined Oils

The function of unrefined processing is to expel the oil from its raw material by mechanical means with minimal heat. "Cold-pressed," a term once common on oil labels, is misleading and rarely used today. The only oil that is actually pressed cold is olive oil and then only by smaller producers. Other sources of oils—nuts, seeds, and grains—are cleaned mechanically and then heated. The oil may be warmed as high as 160 degrees and then pressed out mechanically. These oils can be labeled "100 percent expeller pressed." Olive oil, once the pulp has been crushed and the oil pressed out, may be centrifuged to separate it from the juices it releases or it may be left to settle, the olive rising above the liquid.

Unrefined oils typically have a richer appearance than their refined cousins, as well as more flavor and aroma. They also contain essential nutrients and vitamins that are removed in refining.

Although not all unrefined oils are used for their taste, all oils that are valued for their flavors are unrefined.

Unrefined oils typically have a lower smoke point than refined oils and are not suitable for high-temperature cooking. They should be stored away from heat and light.

Photo provided by Ridgely C. Evers

Refined Oils

Most oils, especially those from large producers, are chemically extracted by a process that uses solvents made from petroleum. After the raw material is cleaned and crushed, a solvent is applied to draw out the oil. Once the solvent has extracted the oil from the raw material, the fluid is boiled to evaporate the solvent. The oil then must be refined. Many expeller-pressed oils are also later refined. Oils produced by both methods of extraction—expeller and solvent—are subjected to identical methods of refining. An oil's label is not required to identify the type of extraction.

The process of refining strips an oil of its color, its scent, and most of its nutrients. A process called degumming removes the lecithin, chlorophyll, vitamin E, and minerals. The addition of an alkaline solution removes any other substances that linger through the first step of refining. Diatomaceous earth is added to bleach the oil, and then the oil is steamed to deodorize it. Finally, the oil goes through a process called winterizing, during which it is cooled and filtered to remove any material that may cause cloudiness at low temperatures. Although refined oils have a place in the world of cooking, their functions, just like their flavors, their nutritional values, and their aromas, are limited. I rarely, if ever, use them.

Fruit Oils

In addition to olive oil, two other important oils come from fruit: avocado oil and coconut oil.

Avocado oil is produced primarily in California and New Zealand, in a process similar to that used to make olive oil, which makes sense, given that the oil is contained in the fruit of the plant. After avocados are peeled and pitted, the flesh is crushed and mixed at a warm temperature, which facilitates the release of the oil, which is then pressed. It has a healthy nutritional profile, as do other fruit oils, and does not need to be refined. Because of its high smoke point, avocado oil is used in certain specialty food products, including high-end potato chips. It does not, however, retain much characteristic flavor. Use it whenever you want a mildly flavored oil.

Coconut oil, once scorned as all but poisonous because of its high percentage of saturated fat, is now praised and prized as a healthful oil. Once impossible to find in the United States, we can now find several brands—organic and expeller pressed—in the marketplace.

When I traveled to Malaysia in 1998 to research peppercorn farms in the state of Sarawak on the island of Borneo, I had just begun to hear whisperings about the health benefits of coconut oil. It was a good source of nutrients for individuals with HIV and AIDS, I'd been told, and made a mental note to look into it when I had time. One day in Kuching, I was riding in the back seat of a town car with the the general manager of the Pepper Marketing Board, Anandan Abdullah, on the way to lunch. Somehow, a question of age came up and he asked me how old I thought he was. I looked at his flawless skin framed by glistening black hair and ventured what I thought was a conservative guess.

"About 28 or 29," I suggested, afraid I may be insulting him.

He laughed, loud and long, and then told me he was 54, with nearly grown children.

"It's our coconut oil," he explained, "it is so good for you."

Photo provided by Ridgely C. Evers

I returned home and it wasn't long before I began to see coconut oil on the shelves of our supermarkets. Word was out.

Coconut oil goes through a similar process as both olives and avocados. The fruit is ground or shredded, pressed, and separated from its liquid. There are many variations of this basic process, some that involve chemicals and result in refined coconut oil, others that preserve the high levels of antioxidants for which this oil is praised. Coconut oil is good for stir-frying and quick sautéing but should not be used for deep-frying or other high-temperature cooking, as it has a low smoke point. It does not contribute much flavor but instead has a clean, almost neutral taste.

Dendê oil, also a type of fruit oil derived primarily from the African oil palm, is not widely available. Extracted from the fruit of the palm, not its seed, the unrefined oil is a rich-orange red and contains high levels of beta-carotene. It is used in traditional Brazilian cuisine.

Oil from its seed is known as palm kernel oil.

There is serious concern over the environmental impact of both dendê and palm kernel oil, based on the destruction of enormous portions of rain forests in both Malaysia and in Indonesia, which in turn has resulted in decreased habitat for endangered species, including the beloved orangutan. Monoculture, whether of soy, corn, grapes, olive trees, or palm trees, is not a sustainable practice and it is important, I believe, to be vigilant and not support products that put the planet and its creatures at risk.

Nut Oils

Peanut oil is probably the most familiar of all the nut oils. In its refined form, it has just a slight hint of peanut flavor and is one of the most commonly used oils, the choice of many chefs whose specialties include Creole, Cajun, and oriental cuisines. Unrefined, it has a long and pleasant aftertaste of raw peanuts. Almond oil, because it retains a strong

taste of almonds, is used most frequently in baking. Although it has a high smoke point, it is not widely used in general cooking. In recent years, oils from pine nuts and pistachio nuts have been produced. They are, however, not widely available, and are extremely expensive. Both oils are intensely flavored, with a distinctive scent and taste, and should be used sparingly. The pine nut oil is pale, and the pistachio nut oil is a rich, deep green.

For a nut oil to have its characteristic flavor and aroma, the nuts must be roasted before they are pressed. Oils made from raw nuts are flavorless; they have a number of uses but food is not typically one of them. Oils made from good-quality nuts that have been roasted with care offer a vast range of flavors and culinary possibilities. The most flavorful nut oils, pressed from hazelnuts and walnuts, are produced in Europe. Because walnut trees thrive where olive trees do not, the regional cuisines of certain areas of France and Italy are rich with the oil of the walnut. Vinaigrettes made with walnut oil and sauces featuring walnuts abound. If olive oil is the oil of the Mediterranean, walnut oil has long been known as an oil of France. In her book *The Cooking of South-West France,* Paula Wolfert tells of several old mills that are still making delicious walnut oils by the old method. One of them, Moulin de la Tour in Sainte Nathalène, near Sarlat in the Dordogne, is over four hundred years old and is one of only four in France still open to the public. Only fifteen such mills remain in France today.

At Moulin de la Tour, walnuts are cracked open and gently crushed by a stream-driven mill. After crushing, the nuts are heated in a wooden caldron to 120 degrees and then pressed out directly into the 150-quart bottles the mill produces twice a week.

Seed Oils

Many plants have oil-rich seeds, but not all yield an edible oil; most of our most common oils have been with us for centuries. In ancient times, oils were drawn from what was at hand. In Greece, olive oil, walnut oil, and oil from the opium poppy were used. In Africa and Mesopotamia, olive oil and sesame oil were used. Argan oil was and still is used in Morocco. In Egypt, flax seed oil and radish seed oil were common. Asian oils included soybean, rice bran oil, and coconut palm and in the Americas groundnut (peanut), corn, and sunflower seed oil were used. In certain parts of South America and Africa, dendê oil shaped the native cuisine.

Sesame seeds probably provided the world's first source of oil, as olives are limited by their geographic requirements. Sesame, with its short growth cycle, can thrive almost anywhere. The seeds themselves are oily and it would not have taken early humans—restricted to a simple process of expelling oil by mechanical means—long to discover that the oil could be pressed out of the seeds fairly easily. Today, we associate sesame oil, especially toasted sesame oil, with Asian cuisines.

Oil made from pumpkin seeds is particularly delicious, especially if the seeds have been toasted. It is, however, difficult to find in this country. Small amounts are produced in Europe and some makes its way to specialty retailers in the United States but not a lot. If you find it, use it as a condiment, drizzled over a winter squash soup, perhaps, with some toasted pumpkin seeds scattered on top.

Corn oil is one of the most common oils, particularly here in the United States where over 70 percent of the world's supply is produced. Nearly all corn oil is refined. Unrefined corn oil is absolutely delicious but it is quite unstable, going rancid quickly, and is all but impossible to find.

Other seed oils—rapeseed, which produces canola oil; grape seed; safflower; sunflower; cottonseed—are mild, almost to the point of having no taste. These oils do not contribute flavor, they do not have desirable nutritional profiles, and most experts do not recommend them, nor do

I. Cottonseed oil, once commonly used in commercial food production and long used in generic vegetable oils, contains the highest level of residual pesticides of any of the edible oils; it is best avoided. Soybean oil is best avoided, too, as it foams at high temperatures and is grown using genetically modified seed.

In saying this, I am, in spirit, taking a page out of Thomas Hardy's playbook and standing up, so to speak, to be shot. The great British novelist eventually sat down and stopped writing his extraordinary but disturbing novels and turned, for the last decades of this life, to poetry. I will, no doubt, be scolded for dismissing some of these oils but my commitment is to you, dear reader, and I offer you my best and most honest advice.

Flavored Oils

Oils with added flavor have become extremely popular, with scores of options in the marketplace. Oils, typically olive oils, combined with garlic, basil, sage, chilies, and citrus—lemon, Meyer lemon, lime, blood orange, clementine, citron, and grapefruit—are readily available.

The best are those made using fresh ingredients combined with fresh olives at the time of production. It is a fragrant joy to be in a mill as lemons, say, and olives are being crushed together; the aromas that fill the room and hold you in their embrace are so lovely, nearly intoxicating. *When do we eat?*

During the process, the essential oils in the rinds of the fruit are released and merge with the oil when it is pressed and the juices settled out or spun off. What remains is a smooth, integrated oil with a bright dimension of fruit. Meyer lemon olive oil is the most popular among both producers and consumers and I find it the most versatile. Next is lime olive oil, with its delicious savory possibilities. Blood orange olive oil is quite good, too, but it introduces a whisper of sweetness which is not always what you want.

O Olive Oil & Vinegar, based in Sonoma, California, produces some of the finest flavored oils and vinegars in the world, using California's signature olive, the Mission. The Mission olive does not produce a particularly complex olive oil—it is sweet and buttery, without the lively peppery flavors of so many other varietals—and it is ideal in combination with other flavorings. O Fresh Basil Olive Oil employs the same technique used with citrus; fresh sweet basil is crushed with the olives, infusing the oil with the herb's essential oils. O Roasted Garlic Olive Oil combines slow-roasted garlic with its Mission olive oil, producing a lovely condiment oil.

Many chefs and enthusiastic home cooks prefer to add a spritz of juice or minced herbs instead of using a flavored oil and it is important, I think, to understand that these oils won't make your cooking *better.* The reason to buy them—they tend to be pricey—and to use them is because you like them. It is important, too, not to hoard them. Use them up so that their flavors don't drop off.

Photo provided by Ridgely C. Evers

Photo provided by Ridgely C. Evers

Essential Oils

Some culinary oils are used not for their cooking properties and not for their ability to transfer heat or lubricate pieces of food, but for the flavors they impart. These are the essential oils, lemon oil, cinnamon, oil, bitter orange oil, black pepper oil. They are pure oils removed from their source material by a process of distillation, extraction, or expression. They impart concentrated aromas and flavors and are used widely in baking and in other types of cooking to impart an intensity of flavor to foods in which a juice or spice would not be appropriate.

Experimented with essential oils can be fun and rewarding, though be warned that they can be very intense and should be used sparingly, drop by drop. I most enjoy black pepper oil and occasionally add less than a drop—it is quite powerful—to a dish with a range of peppery flavors.

What about other flavored oils? Oils infused with hot chilies make great condiments, especially on pizza, certain types of sandwiches, and many Asian dishes. They are very easy to make at home (see pages 302 to 304).

Most other flavored oils are produced using extracts and flavorings; if you have a sensitive palate, you'll notice this. A prime example is truffle oil, which has no truffle in it at all, just a chemical equivalent. Its popularity is nearly ubiquitous these days, especially among restaurant chefs. But not all agree it's a good thing. Chef Ken Frank of La Toque in Napa, California, who hosts an annual truffle festival, says truffle oil "stains the palate" and should never be used. I agree.

Oil Tasting

It is important to be familiar with the taste of the oils that you use, and to understand the best ways of tasting and evaluating a variety of oils. This will give you more control over your cooking and will lead to a better intuitive sense of which products to use. Most of us are not in the habit of opening the cupboard for a little nip of oil, so the process of tasting needs some explaining.

On pages 386 to 389 you'll find tasting forms on which you can describe characteristics of specific oils and note your preferences. Tasting oils is hard work for our palates, and I do not recommend that you taste more than seven or eight at one time. Two or three are enough for the novice.

To taste an oil, pour a small quantity into a clear glass—a wine glass works perfectly. Smell the oil and note the aroma. Rub a little into the back of your hand and smell it again. Can you identify the raw material from which the oil was made? It will be most noticeable in unrefined oils, which are the best to taste. It makes little sense to taste refined oils, though everyone should be able to identify a rancid oil.

Pour a little oil onto a plastic spoon, take it into your mouth, and hold it there briefly, breathing in slightly. As you swallow, note the way it slides down the throat and the degree to which it coats the tongue. Between tastings, cleanse the palate with a celery stick or a piece of bread and a drink of mineral water. If the consumption of oil by the spoonful is particularly objectionable to you, soak a cube of bread in the oil and then taste it. It will not yield as immediate a taste of the oil, but the method is preferred by some.

A high-quality oil will not be overly oily nor coat the tongue with fat. It will have a pleasing, fresh taste and a rich texture. If an oil is rancid, you should be able to detect it immediately. It will have an off taste, something that is obviously unpleasant that cannot be ascribed to individual preference. Rancid oils are often described as having a painty smell and a scratchy taste, sensed quickly on the tip of the tongue. They can produce gastrointestinal discomfort similar to that caused by foods cooked in overheated oil. Such oils should be discarded or, if recently purchased, returned to the market for a refund.

With oils other than olive oils, tasting is a matter of acquainting oneself with an oil's characteristics. Hazelnut oil, for example, should taste clean with a long finish of hazelnut flavor.

Because of the diversity of olive oils, it makes sense to group them together, all from a single region, perhaps, or all of a similar price range. It makes no sense to compare, say, a $10 oil with a $40 oil or a French oil with one from Spain.

If you are especially fond of olive oils, it makes sense to taste them regularly. Preferences for olive oil are very subjective. You will probably find your preferences changing as you become more knowledgeable. Flavors can vary from year to year, as well.

Experts on olive oil can discover a panorama of details about an oil from a single taste. The type of olive is indicated by the color, and the first sip frequently reveals the country and region of origin, whether or not the oil is truly extra virgin, and if it is made by a small or large producer. An experienced taster can also tell if leaves of the olive tree made it into the crush. Even these experts exhaust their palates after tasting seven or eight oils.

Menu for an Olive Oil Tasting

For each taster provide:
One plastic spoon, several celery sticks, cubes of sourdough bread, a large glass of unflavored mineral water, evaluation forms, and a pencil.

On the common table place:
The bottles of olive oil to be tasted, eight-ounce wine glasses to be filled with between one and two inches of each oil, the glasses being arranged in front of their corresponding bottles, and extra bottles of chilled mineral water.

PART 2
All About Vinegar

Vinegar is ubiquitous. It appears in nearly every pantry the world over, although its type and flavor, its regulation and uses, even the shape of its container, may change with its location. So universal is vinegar in recipes that it is all but taken for granted. In cookbooks, you'll rarely find it indexed, and when you do, only a few of the recipes in which it is an integral part are listed. Vinaigrettes will appear, as will vinegar pie and perhaps fruit vinegars, but vinegar will have made its aromatic, acidic appearance in many more recipes than those listed.

Because vinegar has long been a household word and product, we tend not to think about it much, or at least not until quite recently. But an understanding of vinegar, what it is exactly and what variables influence its production, is useful to anyone interested in food. Once you have a basic understanding of vinegar, you can choose comfortably among the many vinegars available in the marketplace, or make an intelligent effort to produce vinegar at home.

What Is Vinegar?

Simply put, vinegar is a tangy liquid produced by a secondary fermentation, the action of a species of bacteria known as acetobacters. Acetobacters feed on alcohol—the first fermentation, when yeasts produce alcohol as they digest sugar—and create acetic acid, which gives vinegar its sour taste.

Our word "vinegar" comes from the French *vinaigre*, which means, literally, sour wine. In the United States, only vinegar made from the juice

of apples can be called, simply, vinegar. If made from other substrates, such as wine, there must be an identifying adjective.

In Italy, vinegar is known as *aceto*, for the bacteria that produce it rather than for the results of production.

It's fairly easy to understand what type of vinegar is used in specific regions of the world. If you know the types of fermented alcohol indigenous to an area, you can make an educated guess about the vinegar you will find there. In wine-producing regions, it will be wine vinegar. Not surprisingly, Champagne vinegar, white wine vinegar, and red wine vinegar are all common in France. Italians typically use red wine vinegar and, to a lesser degree, white wine vinegar. Spain is well known for both its fortified wines and its sherry vinegars. The English, a beer- and cider drinking people, use malt vinegar and cider vinegar much more than wine vinegar. Malt vinegar also appears in the cuisines of Germany and eastern Europe, where beer has long been a favored beverage. Japan makes extensive use of rice vinegar, acidic companion to their sake, an intoxicating beverage made from fermented rice. China and Southeast Asia, where rice is also widely consumed including in fermented beverages, use rice vinegar, too.

In the United States, where cider was an early ubiquitous beverage, vinegar is, by definition, apple cider vinegar.

The Legal Definition of Vinegar in the United States

All types of vinegar must contain a minimum of four grams of acetic acid per 100 cubic centimeters and all must be a product of alcoholic fermentation and the subsequent acetic fermentation of one of the following liquids:

The juice of apples: vinegar, cider vinegar, apple cider vinegar
The juice of grapes: wine vinegar
Dilute distilled alcohol: spirit, distilled, or grain vinegar

An infusion of barley malt or cereals, the starch in which has been converted by malt: malt vinegar
Sugar syrup or refiner's syrup: sugar vinegar
A solution of glucose or dextrose: glucose vinegar

(Source: University of California, College of Agriculture, Circular 334, January 1934.)

The First Vinegar Was Found, Not Made

By the time humans began making a written record of their activities, vinegar had been a part of life for a long time. Some of the first written records refer to both wine and vinegar made from dates as common in Babylonia as long ago as 5000 B.C. Because the production of alcohol and acetic acid occurs naturally, it seems safe to speculate that vinegar was around long before that. Its actual discovery was likely accidental: Someone tasted a liquid, wine left uncovered, perhaps, or a syrup that had fermented out in the open, and found it good. There is evidence that commercial production was extensive by 2000 B.C., and that the addition of flavoring agents—herbs, spices, and fruits—was common practice even then.

The Versatility of Vinegar

We may keep vinegars in our pantries and reach for them as we are cooking, but they have many uses beyond the flavors they impart.

- Tobacco odors can be eliminated by placing a bowl of distilled vinegar in the offending room.
- To remove lime deposits from your tea kettle, fill it with water and half a cup distilled vinegar and boil it gently for twenty minutes. Rinse it well before using.

- A teaspoon of vinegar can save an overly salty soup, sauce, or stew. Simply stir in the vinegar and a bit of sugar to balance the acid.
- A teaspoon of vinegar in poaching water will help keep eggs well formed. Use a mild, neutral-tasting vinegar or tie the flavor of the vinegar to other flavors in the meal.
- Regret that bumper sticker you put on in the fervor of the moment? A few applications of white vinegar should remove it.

Throughout history, vinegar has had medicinal as well as culinary uses. It has served as an elixir and as a tonic in times of poor health and as a hedge against disease during epidemics. Vinegar was extremely valuable as a preservative before modern methods of refrigeration were developed and it is still essential for canning and pickling.

How Vinegar Is Made

Although vinegar has been actively produced for thousands of years, the first modern method of commercial production began in France about five hundred years ago in the city of Orleans, in the Loire Valley west of Paris, after which the method takes its name. The Orleans process, or slow method as it is also called, was the only way vinegar was produced commercially until the development of the generator method by Hermann Boerhaave, a Dutch technologist. The Orleans method is slow because as the substrate sits in its barrel only a small surface area is exposed to oxygen. The acetobacters act slowly to digest the alcohol. There is no heat involved in the Orleans method, so the subtle flavors of the original material are not altered or destroyed. But because the producers of Orleans-style vinegars are aiming for quality, part of the difference in their products can be attributed to the superior raw ingredients they begin with and the care that goes into production.

Tis melancholy, and a fearful sign
Of human frailty, folly also crime,
That love and marriage rarely can combine,
Although they both are born in the same clime,
Marriage from love, like vinegar from wine—
A sad, sour, sober beverage—by time
Is sharpen'd from its high celestial flavor,
Down to a very homely household savor.

Lord Byron, *Don Juan*

There were two problems with the early Orleans method of production. One was that it was inherently slow, a problem for which there was no solution save patience. The other was more urgent. Frequently the vinegar mother would grow to an enormous size in the vinegar barrel, crowding the vinegar and oxygen and slowing production. The formation of a thick mother can still be a problem today, although most producers seek strains of bacteria that have a minimal tendency to form a mother. In 1868 Louis Pasteur perfected a method of keeping the mother afloat with a wooden raft. Although Pasteur may not have realized it at the time, this technique would result in a superior vinegar. A submerged mother is dead and contributes a taste of decay to the vinegar.

Because the Orleans method is so slow, it was inevitable that new methods would be developed. The generator process, the first alternative to the slow method, is a technique by which the vinegar is dripped or manipulated in some way to increase the surface area exposed to oxygen so that the acetobacters feed upon the alcohol more quickly. When the process was first developed, a variety of structures were made to facilitate it, but all had a similar function. Some sort of material—frequently wood shavings or branches, but also charcoal, corn cobs, chunks of pottery, and various other materials—was packed into an enclosed cylinder and the substrate was circulated through it.

Meet the Vinegar Man

Here comes the vinegar man
To help all his vinegar fans
Here comes the vinegar man
To make this a vinegar land
It's the man of the hour
With his great sour power
In his vinegar dressings
He brings us great blessings

L.J. "The Vinegar Man" Diggs

I came across Lawrence Diggs, who long ago claimed "The Vinegar Man" as his moniker, in the early 1990s, as I worked on the first edition of this book. His exuberance for vinegar, his passion, is boundless. He devoted four years of his life to studying and researching vinegar and in 1989 self-published *Vinegar: The User-Friendly Standard Text, Reference and Guide to Appreciating, Making and Enjoying Vinegar*. It is an exhaustive account of vinegar and its making throughout history.

All these years later, Lawrence's enthusiasm has not ebbed. He maintains a Website, vinegarman.com, and his book is still available through the site, along with dozens of other books about vinegar.

The original generator, or fast, method has evolved into a completely automated process that converts the substrate into vinegar in about twenty-four hours. The Frings acetator has brought speed and efficiency to the vinegar industry and is currently used for most commercial vinegar production. In a highly aerobic environment, the substrate is kept at the optimum temperature for the function of the acetobacters, and the level of acidity is closely monitored.

As America's appetite for artisan foods began to blossom in the early 1970s, a few producers began to examine the possibilities of older hands-on

GABBIANO
Aceto
Balsamico

techniques, including the Orleans method of producing vinegar. First on the commerical scene may have been Kimberley California, founded in 1975 in San Francisco. Today, the company makes five vinegars using the Orleans method, with organic wines as substrate. After aged wine is inoculated with an actively fermenting vinegar and a commercial mother, the solution ferments in barrels until it reaches 6.5 percent acidity, a process that can take up to a couple of years. It is then bottled and corked. In 2000, the company added a balsamic vinegar, which ages for five years.

Today, there are dozens of small producers offering beautifully made Orleans-method vinegars. You'll find the best sources for these vinegars

Balsamic Vinegar & the Alchemy of Time

from a pamplet by the Consortium of Producers of the Traditional Balsamic Vinegar of Modena, 1988

In Modena, in the attics of ancient buildings, they have been making a vinegar for centuries. A vinegar, or rather a liqueur, which demands an entire life from those who make it.

Vincenzo Buonassisi

It's something capable of raising the dead.

Luigi Mani

close to home, at farmers markets, at specialty shops that feature local products, and, sometimes, at local wineries.

Aceto balsamico tradizionale is to vinegar what extra virgin olive oil is to oil: It is provocative, inspiring, diverse, and delicious beyond its traditional functions. Balsamic vinegar stands alone in the culinary world as a rich, dark, luscious substance that has a taste, a history, a process of production, and a price that set it apart from any other vinegar. Aceto balsamico is produced solely in one region of northern Italy, but that geographical limitation is the only variable that is not challenged when enthusiasts discuss their favorite versions. Balsamic vinegar—its production and aging, its taste, its judging, its marketing—evokes the same pride and fervor as do the olive oils from the Mediterranean's prime olive-growing regions.

If you have picked up a bottle from your grocer's shelf recently, paying a price most likely under twenty dollars, you might wonder what all the fuss is about. Some brands have wonderful flavors but it is difficult to imagine offering large sums of money for another taste. So, whence this mystique, these exotic claims?

First of all, few people outside the region of production have tasted true balsamic vinegar. Most of what is brought to this country is an officially sanctioned substitute. The supply of the true vinegar cannot keep up with the demand. Production remains the very slow, laborious process it has been for centuries, and to change it would be to change the very nature of the vinegar itself, thus creating something other than true, or traditional, aceto balsamico.

Emilia-Romagna spans nearly the enitre width of the Italian peninsula, stretching from the Adriatic Sea to within a few miles of the Gulf of Genoa. It is to the heart of this northern Italian region that we must go to discover true aceto balsamico tradizionale, the secret treasure of Modena and Emilia.

It appears that the vinegar was produced as early as the eleventh century, when records show that Duke Boniface of Canossa presented a barrel of it as a coronation gift to the Holy Roman emperor, Henry III, in 1046. The great ducal family of the region, the Estes, served it as a cordial and gave it as gifts to the important statesmen of Europe. It was also used as a tonic for protection against the plague. After the decline of the Este family, the vinegar was rarely exported beyond the region's boundaries and production gradually diminished. It remained prized in regional households, a well-kept Modenese secret, and it was not until the late 1970s that signs of a revival appeared and imitators proliferated. Even as the reputation of the foods of the region grew—prosciutto and Parmigiano-Reggiano, for example–aceto balsamico remained relatively obscure. Until recently. Now some version of it is everywhere, in supermarkets and specialty stores, on both down-market and high-end restaurant menus, in pantries throughout America.

But what is it, exactly?

True balsamic vinegar, a thick, rich liquid, is a product of time, temperature, and attention. It is valued for its exquisite aromas and the flavors that develop during aging, differences so distinct, so singular, that they defy comparison with other vinegars. It is always sweet and always a little sour, but its exact nature is an individual expression of its producer. Preferences vary throughout the region and it is common to hear passionate arguments between aficionados in Modena, who prefer the drier version produced there, and aficionados in Emilia, who claim that their sweeter versions are superior.

The vinegar gets its start in the vineyard. The white Trebbiano is the most commonly used grape, although Malvasia, Occhio di Gatto, Spergola, and the more common red Lambrusco have all released their juices to become aceto balsamico. After ripe grapes are crushed and the stems removed, the resulting must—unfermented juice of pressed grapes—sits until the first signs of fermentation. It is then filtered and the liquid is simmered in copper caldrons over wood fires until reduced by about 40 percent. The liquid is placed in demijohns or small stainless steel vats and, come spring, the juice is inoculated with an old vinegar and begins the first of a series of transfers to progressively smaller wooden barrels known as the *batteria*. As summer approaches and the temperature of the reduced liquid begins to rise, two processes occur nearly simultaneously: Alcoholic fermentation occurs as yeast turns the sugar to alcohol, and acetic oxidation takes place as acetobacters change the alcohol to acetic acid. It is this wood aging, a labyrinthine process that would thwart all but the most dedicated, that shapes the character of this mysterious elixir.

As historical records as early as the thirteenth century document, this process traditionally takes place in the attic, where temperatures fluctuate with the extremes of the season. The intensity of the heat of a summer day, at which time the chemical activity is at its peak, and the near freezing nights of winter, when the chemical activity is still, are both essential for the slow processing of the vinegar.

Originally, aceto balsamico tradizionale was made by women. The batteria was often a part of the dowry, and artworks dating from the thirteenth century depict women in their attics tending the wooden casks. A batteria is dated and vinegars produced from a particular batteria bear that date. Thus, when you see an aceto balsamico tradizionale dated 1650, that date refers to the beginning of the particular batteria that produced the vinegar. The older the batteria the more precious, and thus the more expensive, is the vinegar.

The liquid is shifted, generally once a year, through the range of seasoned casks of diminishing sizes. Oak and chestnut are the most common woods, though cherry, locust, ash, alder, mulberry, and juniper are used as well, each variety of wood making its imprint on the final flavor. With an evaporation rate of 10 percent a year, a hundred liters of must become, twelve years later, a mere fifteen liters of vinegar. Most often further aging and, hence, further evaporation, is required. We begin to understand the high retail cost, over $150 for a 100ml bottle.

In response to the phenomenal new interest in balsamic vinegar, and the predictable surge of imitators, the Italian government has bestowed its recognition and blessing upon the dark, rich liquid by offering an official designation for vinegars of a certain quality. *Denominazione di origine controllata* (DOC), parallel to the French *appellation controlée*, recognizes the geographical areas and methods of production and aging in a way previously offered only to wines. For a vinegar to qualify it must be from Modena or neighboring Reggio nell'Emilia. It must be made not from wine but from cooked grape must according to the traditional method.

Absolutely no flavorings or other ingredients can be added and the vinegar must be aged for a minimum of twelve years.

The licensing of the special vinegar is controlled by the Consortium of Producers of the Traditional Balsamic Vinegar of Modena. To receive the government sanction of DOC, the vinegar must be submitted to the official board of tasters for approval. About one third of the vinegars submitted each year receive the designation, and generally those approved are between twenty and thirty years old. The twelve-year-old vinegars are thought to be too young and immature in flavor.

With the introduction of the DOC designation came officially required packaging as well. The amount of approved vinegar that a producer wishes to sell is delivered in bulk to the consortium, where it is bottled in specially designed, 100-cc bottles and closed with the consortium's official wax seal. It is then returned to the producer, who labels it, always including the required "aceto balsamico tradizionale di Modena" designation and the date of the batteria. The bottles come in two shapes, one with the vinegar from Reggio nell'Emilia, the other holding the Modenese vinegar.

Like the very best olive oils, traditional balsamic vinegar is a condiment, not a cooking agent. The very oldest and finest is reserved for drinking or for flavoring well-aged wine vinegar. The use of traditional balsamic vinegar as an elixir is not as common as it once was, although a dash in cocktails and other iced drinks is still considered delicious and refreshing. Many think even that is a waste, so precious has the concoction become, though I can attest to the delight of a few droplets in a glass of sparkling wine.

If the dark liquid is used on salad, it is in combination with olive oil and another vinegar. It may be added to mayonnaise for flavor. In cream and butter sauces for both vegetables and seafood, especially for steamed mollusks and crustaceans, a few drops of an old, true balsamic vinegar magically transforms the dish. An extravagant cook may add a liberal splash to tomato sauces and meat ragouts to intensify their flavors, and Parmigiano-Reggiano cheese melted with white truffle shavings is heavenly when sprinkled with the vinegar.

The government's aim when it offered the DOC designation to the vinegar was to distinguish the true aceto balsamico tradizionale from the imitators that have flourished. As knowledge of aceto balsamico has spread beyond its native Modena, demand has soared and the decline in production has slowly begun to reverse. Still, because of the aging required, there is not enough to satisfy the demand. Thus, we find an aged wine vinegar that has been fortified with caramelized sugar, herbs, and other flavorings legally described as Aceto Balsamico di Modena. Detractors call it aceto industriale, but this pleasant vinegar has given most of the outside world its first taste of "balsamic vinegar," and still constitutes much of what is available and affordable in this country today. Four brands are imported from Italy, although they are bottled and sold under a variety of specialty labels. The key distinction between these vinegars and traditional balsamic vinegar is the term "tradizionale." Although similar labeling restrictions do not apply in the United States, it is easy to distinguish the authentic substance. Disregard all of the claims and confusion, ignore all the labels that scream at us from the grocer's shelves, it is really quite simple to determine if you are holding the real thing in your hands. First, it must be in one of the two types of approved glass bottles and have the consortium's seal. Anything sold in quantities over 100 cc, or 3.3 ounces, is fraudulent. Second, true aceto balsamico is extremely viscous, a dark brown liquid that coats the neck of the jar when turned on its side. When righted, it slowly oozes down the glass, all thick and syrupy and voluptuous. The contents of a bottle of vinegar that has been turned and then righted that splash happily back into place will not be the traditional vinegar of Modena. You can also recognize the authentic by its price; it is exorbitantly expensive, selling for well over a hundred dollars even for the younger versions.

Like cheese and wine, aceto balsamico is said to reflect the character of its maker. "Violent people make violent vinegar; sweet old people make sweet old vinegar," claims Glauco Smadelli, a producer, a taster, and

> Modena's vinegar is the result of the alchemy of time. Thus when you taste an ancient balsamic vinegar, you have the immediate pleasure of the taste but you also receive a revelation of the magic that lies in the sequence of toppings up and the dedicated attention of the craftsman. You will detect all this in a thousand and one shadings of flavor, and your enjoyment of them and appreciation will make you part of the art and wisdom of those who have preceded us down the years.
>
> Renato Bergonzini, from a Consortium of Producers of the Traditional Balsamic Vinegar of Modena pamphlet, 1988

a family doctor, who added, "and it might even be said, though more so in the past than now, that noble people make noble vinegar because they had the best of materials to work with."

Domestic Balsamic Vinegar

It was inevitable that someone outside of Italy, of Europe, would attempt to make balsamic vinegar and it's not much of a surprise that it took hold in California, specifically in Northern California's wine country. Around the time that the first edition of this book was published, rumors began circulating that two chefs with shiny new wooden barrels in descending sizes were trying their hand at making the elixir that had, so recently, but little more than a rumor itself. I tasted one and then another and before long, other versions began appearing in specialty shops and soon on supermarket shelves. Now there are too many versions to count, some flavored with all manner of fruits, the most popular of which seems to be figs.

About this same time, a small company in Mendocino County began making apple balsamic, a thick golden liquid that was nearly as close to syrup as it was to vinegar. Before long, white balsamics began appearing. They, too, are everywhere now.

What's the deal? Are they the real thing?

Yes and no.

Aceto balsamico tradizionale is made only in Modena and Reggio Emilia and I don't believe it can be duplicated elsewhere, at least not in my lifetime and quite possibly never. Part of its taste is the taste of age and of history. The very best ones are cured in barrels that have been used not for decades but for centuries. These vinegars are in uniform 110ml bottles, one shape in Modena, another in Reggio Emilia, and bear the official seal of the consortium of producers. Before they can be bottled, they must be tasted and approved for release. This vinegar is the rarest of the rare and in a category of its own. You don't use it by the cupful or even by the spoonful; rather, it is dispensed in droplets, using an eyedropper. It is not for cooking, not for vinaigrettes, and not for splashing onto roasted strawberries.

When it comes to other balsamic and balsamic-style vinegars, there is no reason they can't be made successfully anywhere. There are great versions from Italy and excellent versions from California, some imported in bulk and bottled under a California label and some made here and aged in oak.

There may be some advantage to the ones made in California, as high levels of lead have been found in some Italian balsamic vinegars.

When it comes to white balsamic, I think it is misnamed. A key characteristic of both true balsamic and its less expensive cousins is caramelization, which darkens even the whitest grapes. White balsamic is sweet and a tad tart but lacks the sultry quality contributed by the caramelization process.

The reason to use any balsamic vinegar, including white, is because you like it. I can't recommend it over other vinegars and believe it belongs in its own category. Its uses arc limited, at least for my palate. I don't typically want a layer of sweetness in savory foods and balsamic vinegars are, by definition, sweet. I think they show themselves to the best advantage in desserts. If you like a sweet flourish in your salads, pastas, soups, and stews, you'll want to try as many of these as you can—some stores have tasting bars—until you find your favorites.

Making Vinegar at Home

It's easy to make vinegar at home. It's hard to make vinegar at home. Don't do it. Why wouldn't you do it? Start with fruit, start with fruit juice, begin with wine, beer, or cider. When it comes to making vinegar, advice from experts varies widely.

A friend crushes pears and quince in a big crock, covers them, and months later, *Voila!*, she has wonderful fruit vinegar. A chef collects leftover wine in a small tabletop barrel and in a few months has the best vinegar he has ever tasted. I collect wine in a gallon jug, inoculate it with a favorite vinegar, one that has not been pasteurized, and pour it down the drain a couple of years later.

So many elements go into the crafting of vinegar that it is both easy and difficult, dependent on everything from your ingredients, your equipment, and your environment to your temperament and, perhaps most importantly, your passion. If you are driven to produce great vinegar, you will find a way.

There is plenty of help in the marketplace these days, as fermentation of all kinds has become increasingly popular.

If you want to try your hand at making vinegar, the guidelines set down by the United States Department of Agriculture (USDA) in 1924 offer step-by-step advice that begins with the juice of fresh fruit, not alcohol. The instructions were written during Prohibition so the government could hardly recommend beginning with wine or beer. And one must wonder, too, how many thousands of citizens found the guidelines most useful for the first, alcoholic, fermentation, not the second.

The Official Home Vinegar Production Guidelines, University of California 1924

When you begin, make certain that all of your equipment, your workspace, your utensils, your hands, and your clothes are absolutely clean. The vinegar itself should never come in contact with metal. Use cheesecloth, paper, or plastic to strain the liquid. When bottled, use corks to close rather than metal screw tops.

Fill a four-gallon stone or glass jar about two-thirds full of unpasteurized grape juice or the juice of crushed fruit such as grapes, apples, pineapple, or pears. Mix a cake of compressed yeast with a small amount of the juice and add it to the jar. Cover with several layers of cheesecloth to keep out dust, insects, and other contaminants in the air. Keep the jar in an easily accessible, warm, dark area. Stir it daily, breaking up any surface crust formation. This will help prevent mold and ensure a complete fermentation. This process will take about six days.

Strain the fermented liquid through cheesecloth and return it to the jar. Inoculate with a good vinegar that has not been pasteurized, using one quarter the amount of the juice. Cover with cheesecloth and let the mixture sit in a dark, warm place until the alcohol has been converted to acetic acid. Depending on the room temperature, this process can take from a few weeks to a few months. For informal vinegar making, it is not necessary to test for acid content. Rely upon your palate to tell you when your vinegar is complete.

When you are satisfied with the taste of your homemade vinegar, you should strain it through a paper coffee filter and bottle it. Used wine bottles, especially 350ml bottles, are perfect for storing homemade vinegars. Close with a cork.

The bacteria in the vinegar may continue their activity after filtering and bottling. For this reason, you may wish to heat your vinegar to 160 degrees to kill the vinegar culture. This informal pasteurization will discourage the formation of a mother, though [the vinegar] should be bottled before it cools significantly to decrease the possibility of contamination with new acetobacters. Do not heat the vinegar past 160 degrees F., or the acetic acid will begin to evaporate and there will be a loss of strength, aroma, and flavor.

If you would prefer to begin with a substrate that is already fermented, red wine will yield better results than white wine. White wine contains considerable sulfur dioxide, which inhibits the growth of the essential acetobacters.

How Strong Is That Vinegar?

The strength of a vinegar depends upon how much acetic acid it contains, an amount that is expressed either as a percentage or grain. Vinegar with 6 percent acetic acid is 60 grain. The higher the percentage or grain, the stronger the vinegar. Vinegars must be at least 40 grain and are rarely above 90 grain, or 9 percent, which itself is fairly uncommon; most commercial vinegars weigh in around 6 percent. For preserving, a minimum acidity of 5 percent is necessary. For other uses, taste is the main consideration. The stronger the acidity, the more it dominates, eclipsing the flavors of the substrate. For this reason, consideration should be given to acidity when choosing vinegars for cooking. Most vinegars have their acidity listed on their labels.

Recipes rarely list optimum acidity, just as most—and, in my opinion, the best—don't give precise amounts for salt and pepper. Taste as you cook and let your preferences guide you, though there are times when it is important to known a bit more than simply what you like. This became very clear to me as I was working on my first cookbook and received a call from an editor who had just made my Raspberry Hollandaise. It was good, she said, but too tart; might I consider reducing the *amount* of vinegar? Checking the label, I discovered that I had been making the sauce for years with a low-acid, 4.5 percent raspberry vinegar from a local producer;

she had used a 7.5 percent raspberry vinegar from France. Not only was her hollandaise quite acidic, but also was less fragrant and less voluptuous, as the acidity eclipsed both flavors and aromas. Since then, I indicate the recommended acidic level for a particular dish when it is a crucial factor.

Flavored Vinegars

Vinegar with flavors beyond its substrates has a history that goes back thousands of years, though their contemporary diversity and proliferation on supermarket shelves make them seem like a new trend. California cuisine may get the credit—or blame, depending on your point of view—for raspberry vinegar but it has been common in France for centuries. The marketplace is filled with vinegars to satisfy almost any preference, with vinegars flavored with every herb, every spice, and every fruit imaginable, or almost. I haven't yet seen durian-flavored vinegar but perhaps it is on its way.

Among flavored vinegars, raspberry vinegar is probably the oldest, most common, and most readily available. Excellent brands abound in the marketplace and are available to the home cook without much of a chase. Blueberry vinegar is also fairly common and quite delicious. When I want a strong berry flavor, I prefer low-acid varieties made with black rather than red raspberries: They have a richer, more voluptuous flavor. Raspberry vinegars are produced by several domestic companies and are also imported from France. Kozlowski Farms in Sonoma County, California, makes outstanding low-acid berry vinegars, both red and black. If you prefer higher acidity, I recommend either B. R. Cohn raspberry vinegar or a French one, from either Le Vinaigre or Velux, both of which have enough true raspberry flavor to stand up to the higher acidity. If you find a vinegar with good flavor but a level of acidity too sharp for your palate, the addition of a small amount of wine will mellow it.

There is one excellent reason to make your own berry vinegar: a berry patch that produces more than you can eat. Raspberries and blueberries

Best Uses for Vinegar

Type	Price	Best Uses
Aceto Balsamico Tradizionale	Extremely Expensive	As a condiment
Balsamic	Inexpensive to Moderate	As a condiment, vinaigrettes, sauces, marinades
Black	Inexpensive	Chinese & other Asian cooking
Cane	Inexpensive	Filipino cooking
Champagne	Moderate	Vinaigrettes, fruit vinegars
Cider Shrubs	Inexpensive to Moderate	Preserves, pickling, chutneys, dressing, sauces
Distilled	Inexpensive	Cleaning; certain traditional recipes
Fruit	Moderate	Vinaigrettes, dressings, sauces
Malt	Inexpensive	As a condiment, pickling, ketchup
Red Wine	Inexpensive to Expensive	Vinaigrettes, dressings, sauces, spiced vinegars, emulsions
Rice	Inexpensive to Moderate	Asian cuisines, sauces, with seafood
Sherry Vinaigrettes	Moderate to Expensive	Spanish cooking, soups, sauces
White Wine	Inexpensive to Expensive	Vinaigrettes, sauces, emulsions, herb vinegars, fruit vinegars

are expensive, and with all of the excellent raspberry vinegars available commercially, it is generally less costly to buy a vinegar you like than to make one, unless you can make it with your own berries. If you are lucky enough to live in an agricultural area, you might be able to buy flats of berries cheaply enough to make a batch of vinegar each year. It is worth the effort to make your own if you can do it inexpensively but it is also a comfort to know that there are many good commercial versions available.

When it comes to other flavored vinegars, some are are lush and rich, full of good, true flavor. Others, made not with actual foods but instead with chemical flavorings, are not so fine. Let taste guide you. Specialty markets often offer tastes of the products they carry and if you find one you love, enjoy it. If you're searching for something specific and have been disappointed by your options, try making it yourself. Making flavored vinegars is much more predictable and much easier that making vinegar itself. You'll find details on how to do this, along with suggestions for what make the best-tasting flavored vinegars, on pages 305 to 313.

Vinegar Tasting

Vinegar tasting might strike the novice as a strange thing to do. After all, vinegar, unlike wine, is not something we drink for pleasure or for quenching thirst. But what other way is there to find vinegars you like except to taste and compare them?

I have tasted vinegars formally, high up in the Italian hill town of Volpaia, for example, where the American writer John Meis arranged a special preview of the flavored vinegars made at Castello di Volpaia. Seven different vinegars were poured from fresh bottles into seven wine glasses, and we sipped and compared and refreshed our palates with bottled spring water. We tried to identify the different components that contributed to the complex blends known as erbe, spezie, orto, fiori, and fresco. The highlight of the tasting was, for me anyway, when our guide took us to the tiny production facility a few kilometers away and opened the spigot on one of the aging and flavoring tanks. The orto—or vegetable garden—vinegar was about four months into its aging process and, much to my delight, one sip revealed that the first flavor to develop was garlic. It was a joy on the palate, and the finished product was delicious, too, if somewhat mellower and more balanced than that first powerhouse sip. I have also tasted vinegars informally, licked from the palm of my hand where a friend has poured the sample of a personal favorite.

What to look for in vinegar is very much what to look for in wine. A vinegar should be pleasing to the eye, with clearness and clarity. The aroma should be clean—if it is very strong, you will detect that immediately because your head will go back. We react to the scent of acetic acid, just as we do to the scent of alcohol. There should be no hint of decay. In general, vinegars do not smell like the grape varieties they are made from, with the exception of Pinot Noir and Muscat, which have a high residual fragrance. The vinegar should taste pleasing and full, not just acidic, and it should have body, depth of flavor, and character. Consider the aftertaste. Is it pleasant? Does it linger?

When tasting for comparison, choose vinegars of a similar type. For example, taste a selection of unflavored red wine vinegars in a range of acidic levels. Taste and compare several raspberry vinegars, judging them for their bouquet and fruitiness. It makes little sense to taste a variety of vinegars with unrelated qualities, unless you simply want to become acquainted with their flavors.

Vinegar may be tasted straight, diluted, and on sugar cubes. To taste a vinegar straight, you simply pour a small quantity into a glass—a wine glass works perfectly. After looking at it in the light and smelling it, take a small sip, holding it in your mouth for a few seconds and swallowing it slowly. Before tasting the next vinegar, cleanse and relax your palate with a drink of unflavored mineral water and a small piece of celery or bread. Repeat the process until you have tasted all your vinegars. This method allows you to taste the vinegar directly at its full intensity, but it is hard on the palate and difficult to keep your taste buds open during the assault of so much acetic acid. I do not recommend your tasting more than five or six vinegars by this method at one seating.

A method that is easier on the palate is to dilute one teaspoon of vinegar with two tablespoons of good bottled water. Your palate does not wear out so quickly nor do you get the full intensity of the flavor. This is a good method if for some reason you find yourself needing to taste many vinegars.

A third method is dramatic and at least one expert on vinegar, Dante Bagnani, considers it purely for show. Others recommend it, and I think it is a good idea when a large group is tasting. It uses fewer glasses and less vinegar and the palate does not shut down. To taste with sugar cubes, place the vinegars to be tasted in wide-mouthful wine glasses or small Mason jars. Most sugar cubes are made to dissolve quickly; you should use Domino cubes for vinegar tasting. Each taster dips a sugar cube quickly into the vinegar and then sucks the vinegar out of it. There is a hint of sweetness but not an overwhelming amount, and the taste buds generally stay perky through eight or nine tastes. A fresh sugar cube should be used for each vinegar and discarded after tasting the vinegar.

Menu for a Vinegar Tasting

For each taster provide:

One Domino sugar cube for each vinegar that will he tasted, large glass of water, several saltines or breadsticks, an evaluation sheet (see page 390) and pencil, and a napkin.

On the common table place:

Bottles of vinegars to be tasted, eight-ounce wine glasses filled with between one and two inches of the vinegars, the glasses being arranged in front of their corresponding bottles, and pitchers of water.

Cooking with Vinegar

Sometimes vinegar is the centerpiece of a recipe, in a bright vinaigrette, perhaps, or a mignonette. Its distinctive qualities give the dish its character and shape. All sorts of pickled fruits and vegetables, condiments as diverse as ketchup, prepared mustards, Tabasco sauce, chutneys, and salsas rely on vinegar for their nuances of tartness and pleasing sour flavors. Sometimes vinegar itself is the condiment; I can't imagine, for example, enjoying pot stickers without a little black rice vinegar for dipping.

Sometimes vinegar is a deeper component, a supporting player brought in early in the show, perhaps in a marinade or as one of many elements in a sauce, such as in Chicken au Vinaigre (page 248), a traditional dish from Orleans, France. Its touch then is more subtle, indirect, and its acidity and particular flavor help to shape the building blocks of a dish. It may not be distinctly recognizable in the final product, but its contribution is nonetheless essential to the outcome.

When using vinegar in a marinade, you must understand its function. Acids denature, or cook, protein. When you submerge a piece of protein, a chicken breast, let us say, into pure vinegar, the acetic acid goes to work immediately on the cellular structure of the protein. Your chicken will be "cooked," that is, the protein will be denatured, quickly, and it will be dry, with an unpleasant texture. Because this is not the result any cook wants, wet marinades should almost always be a combination of oil, acid, and seasonings.

With beef, pork, and lamb, a vinegar marinade denatures only the surface of the meat and is not particularly effective at tenderizing it. The only really effective way of tenderizing meat is mechanical. A vinegar solution will penetrate somewhat deeper if the cut has been pricked with a fork, but this also causes a loss of fluids when it is cooked. For flavoring larger cuts of meat such as a beef tenderloin or a leg of lamb, a dry marinade such as a mixture of finely chopped parsley or rosemary, lemon zest, and garlic works best. Liquid oil and vinegar marinades are excellent for flavoring cubed or thinly sliced meats for stews, curries, and kababs.

Because the action of vinegar on certain proteins works counter to what we want, we must be careful not to let its denaturing action go too far. Yet vinegar can also prevent overcooking—or the coagulation of the protein—in emulsified sauces made with eggs. It can save us before we have gone too far. Coagulation is the one problem in an emulsified sauce that cannot be corrected. A sauce can break—that is, the oil can separate out of the emulsion—and be repaired, but chunks of coagulated egg will never become uncoagulated. Harold McGee cites a study in his book *On*

Food and Cooking that demonstrates the principle: In emulsified sauces with a neutral pH, the egg protein curdled at temperatures between 160 degrees and 175 degrees. The addition of vinegar allowed the sauces to be heated up to 195 degrees. Under normal conditions, these sauces are made at temperatures below 160 degrees, the temperature at which butter begins to separate out from an emulsion. But every cook looks away for a moment, gets distracted, or occasionally lets the heat rise too high, and it is helpful to know that vinegar widens the margin of error. A cook whose warm emulsions curdle would do well to get into the habit of adding a teaspoon of compatible vinegar before beginning.

PART 3
The Annotated Oil & Vinegar Pantry

Today we all live such varied lifestyles that no common formula can address all of our culinary and nutritional needs. In the 1950s when the two-parent family was the American norm, everyone ate at home, Mom cooked, and on occasion, the family visited a restaurant together. That common fabric has frayed and people tend to their nutritional needs in all manner of ways, from the familiar and traditional to the strange and bizarre. Some families still eat nearly every meal together, the meals are cooked from scratch from well-stocked cupboards and refrigerators, and Mom is still at the helm. But many people rarely or never cook, relying instead on a plethora of fast-food restaurants and gourmet take-out delicatessens. Others nourish themselves on the prepared foods offered for sale in grocery stores, eating dishes that need no more attention than the opening of a package and the turning of a dial on a microwave oven. Our pantries look very different from those of our mothers and grandmothers.

Even with today's diverse eating styles and the great number of people who never cook, we have more culinary options than we did when Mrs. Cleaver opened her cupboard to prepare dinner for Ward, Wally, and the Beaver. Angelo Pellegrini, in his book *The Unprejudiced Palate,* tells a revealing story—written in the 1940s—of cooking at a college friend's house and requesting olive oil to douse the rabbit he was preparing. None was to be found in the pantry, but there was some in the medicine cabinet, kept there by his friend's mother and used to rub on her scalp. How far we have come. We may not cook as regularly as Mrs. Cleaver did, but our culinary horizons have broadened immensely and deliciously.

In the twenty-plus years since I wrote the first edition of this book, there has been quite a change in home cooking, almost a renaissance. Young people are turning to farming, to hands-on, from-scratch food preparation that embraces not just the making of meals but fermentation, pickling, preserving, and canning. There is reason to be optimistic.

Whether we cook frequently or out of rare desperation, it is a good idea to have a well-planned and well-stocked pantry available when the need or impulse strikes us. Certain items—a selection of dried pastas, for example, fresh farm eggs, butter, and Tabasco sauce—make it simple to put a meal together on short notice. The proper selection of oils and vinegars makes the process even easier and our spur-of-the-moment repertoire more diverse.

When stocking your oil and vinegar pantry, assess your cooking habits realistically and purchase quantities that reflect them. Do not buy olive oil by the gallon or even by the liter if you will use it only three or four times a year. Likewise, do not buy six-ounce bottles of your favorite oil or vinegar if you use it up in a week or even a month. For both oils and vinegars, purchase sizes that you will use within six months. Many oils and vinegars will keep longer than that, of course, but the flavor of most products will begin to deteriorate after a few months on the shelf.

When shopping for olive oils for their flavor, keep in mind that freshness is primary. Olive oil is at its peak of flavor the moment it is pressed. The fresher an oil, the better it should be. This puts California olive oils at the top of the list because they don't have to travel as far to reach our shelves.

With vinegars, strength—i.e., acidity—is crucial, as is the substrate from which it has been made.

You must also store things correctly. Heat and light are enemies of olive oil and most other oils, so keep them in a cool spot away from light. It's a good idea not to buy olive oil in clear bottles unless those bottles are packaged in boxes, as several premium oils are. Vinegars are a bit hardier but do not benefit from exposure to heat or light, so keep them in a cool place, too.

The Well-Stocked Pantry

For the culinary enthusiast, a well-stocked pantry will have a diverse selection of oils and vinegars. In mine, I include the following.

Oils

General cooking: peanut, olive oil, and good extra virgin olive oil

For flavoring: premium extra virgin olive oil, ultra-premium extra virgin olive oil; late-harvest extra virgin olive oil; Meyer lemon olive oil; grapefruit olive oil; lime olive oil; chili oil; toasted sesame oil

Vinegars

General purpose: distilled, apple cider

General cooking: white wine; Champagne; red wine; sherry

Specialty: pear; raspberry; rice; black; homemade cranberry; low-acid berry; good-quality balsamic; aceto balsamico tradizionale

The Not-Quite-Bare Cupboard

For the reluctant cook, the essentials are fewer, hut you never know when an emergency may arise, and if you keep these items on hand, you'll usually be able to handle it with ease and comfort. You might even be inspired to try your hand at a few recipes.

Oils

General cooking: peanut oil or olive oil

For flavoring: 1 small bottle best-quality extra virgin olive oil; 1 small bottle toasted sesame oil; 1 small bottle chili oil (great on pizza!)

Vinegars

For general cooking: apple cider

For flavoring: white wine or Champagne; red wine

A Glossary of Oils & Vinegars

Recommended oils and vinegars are marked with a star

Oils

Almond Oil: A mildly flavored oil high in monounsaturated fats, low in saturated fats, with a high smoke point. Almond oil, like almonds, is, however, expensive, and the oil is not widely used for general cooking.

Apricot Kernel Oil: A refined oil without much flavor; used in high-heat cooking and in skin care products.

Avocado Oil: A delicate, nutty-flavored oil pressed directly from the fruit of the avocado. It has a high smoke point and is rich in monounsaturated fatty acids, but limited production, almost exclusively in California, keeps it relatively expensive.★

Canola (Rapeseed) Oil: The flavorless oil from the rapeseed is praised for its low percentage of saturated fat. It was widely used in Europe, though its popularity declined during the 1940s, probably because it contains erucic acid, which can cause liver damage. New species of the plant have resulted in a recent dramatic increase in production in Europe. The Canadian variety has had most of the acid bred out of the plants, though it is still present in trace amounts. Rapeseed oil is widely used in vegetable oil blends.

Coconut Oil: One of the healthiest saturated fats in the world; excellent for most cooking except for deep frying.★

Corn Oil: The widely used oil of the corn kernel. Its high smoke point, mild taste, and high percentage of polyunsaturated fatty acids makes refined corn oil one of the most popular of the commercial oils.

Cottonseed Oil: A by-product of cotton production, cottonseed oil has been widely used in commercial food production primarily because it is cheap. It is also high in saturated fats and contains residual pesticides in substantial quantities.

Flaxseed Oil: A relatively new oil marketed as a food supplement rather than a cooking oil; high in two essential fatty acids, linoleic acid and alphalinolenic acid. This highly unstable oil must be stored in a cool, dark place and used within a few months of processing.

Grape Seed Oil: A by-product of the wine industry, with a high smoke point.*

Hazelnut Oil: A highly perishable oil full of the rich flavor of the nut. The delicate taste is destroyed by heat, so this oil is best used for dressings and uncooked sauces; it must be refrigerated.*

Linseed Oil: A highly refined oil pressed from flax seeds, it oxidizes rapidly and is generally considered inedible, although it was sold regularly in health food stores until recently because of its reputed health benefits; it has been replaced by unrefined flaxseed oil.

Mustard Oil: A typically inexpensive oil generally found only in specialty shops that sell international products. Widely used only in India, it is also used in some commercial food production in spite of the fact that it contains erucic acid. It has a mild yet distinctive flavor with a flash of heat on the palate.

Olive Oil, Extra Virgin: Designation "extra virgin" certifies that the oil is free of defects and meets certain chemical and aesthetic standards. This category includes premium and ultra-premium olive oils*

Olive Oil, Flavored: The best flavored oils are made with whole citrus crushed with olives, so that their essential oils perfume the oil but do not contaminate it with liquid juice.*

Olive Oil, Lite: "Lite" refers to taste; this is typically an oil with little olive character

Olive Oil: Sometimes labeled "pure," this is typically refined olive oil with little if any olive character; good for high-heat cooking.★

Palm Oil: Inexpensive and tasteless, the oil of both the fruit and the kernel are used throughout the world in commercial food production and general cooking. Environmental issues—destruction of rain forests in Southeast Asia, make this a poor choice.

Peanut Oil: The oil of the peanut, typically refined, is a good choice for high-heat cooking. Roasted and unrefined offers excellent peanut flavor.★

Pumpkin Seed Oil: A dark and richly flavorful oil that is both unstable and hard to find. It has a low smoke point and its taste is destroyed by heat, thus making it appropriate for salads and cold sauces.★

Rice Bran Oil: A refined oil common in Japan but expensive and hard to find in the United States; heralded briefly as the new "healthy" oil, it has a fatty acid profile that makes it inferior to less expensive, better-tasting oils.

Safflower Oil: Light in color and tasteless.

Sesame Oil: Likely the first oil used by humans; typically used in Asian cooking.

Sesame Oil, Toasted: A key flavoring agent in many Asian cuisines, it has a rich, dominant flavor. Best for flavoring, not cooking.★

Soy Oil: A flavorless oil with a fatty acid profile that does not make it particularly attractive for culinary uses. It is often hydrogenated and used in commercial food preparation. Grown from GMO seeds; foams at high temperature.

Squash Seed Oil: Produced by a single company in New York State, from estate grown fruit. Types include roasted pumpkin seed; Butternut squash seed; Delicata squash seed; Acorn squash seed. Nutty flavors; high smoke point.★

Sunflower Oil: A common cooking oil around the world and used extensively in commercial food production.

Walnut Oil: A delicate, fragrant oil pressed from toasted walnuts. For flavoring, not cooking; must be refrigerated.★

Vinegars

Balsamic Vinegar: An aged wine vinegar from Modena, Italy, that has been fortified with caramelized sugar, vanilla, herbs, and other flavorings; developed to satisfy the demand for traditional balsamic vinegar, which is rare and costly. Sometimes called "balsamico industriale."★

Balsamic Vinegar, Traditionl: A rare, expensive vinegar made from the cooked juice of grapes and aged for a minimum of twelve years in a series of wooden casks known as a batteria; must bear the offical seal of the consortium of producers and is sold only in specific 100ml bottles. Increasingly available in the United States; prices start at about $100.★

Black Vinegar: A very low-acid vinegar (2.5 percent) blended with rice, sugar, and spices and frequently aged in wood; limited uses.

Cane Vinegar: Fermented from sugar cane extract and water, this low-acid vinegar is common in the cuisine of the Philippines.

Champagne Vinegar: Made from fermented Champagne varietals, not from actual Champagne; delicate and suave.★

Cider Vinegar: Made from apples and essential for making chutneys; sprinkled on French fries in Canada; good in pies and pie crusts; excellent all-purpose vinegar.★

Distilled (Spirit) Vinegar: Called for in certain pickling recipes; excellent for cleaning; this is the vinegar used in most commercial food products.

Malt Vinegar: Once made from beer and now made from a sugar infusion of cereal starches, its claim to fame is as a condiment for fish and chips, especially in England; good for pickling, and for making ketchup and chutney; the vinegar of choice in Great Britain.*

Pineapple Vinegar: A common and flavorful vinegar used widely in Mexico. Writer Diana Kennedy mentions it in her texts on the foods of Mexico and provides instructions for making it.

Raspberry Vinegar, High-Acid: White wine or red wine vinegar that has been flavored with raspberry syrup. Certain imported brands produce versions that retain a great deal of raspberry flavor after cooking, which makes them excellent for marinades, sauces, and warm vinaigrettes.*

Raspberry Vinegar, Low-Acid: Produced in the same manner as the high-acid versions, the low acid allows the flavors of the fruit to blossom.*

Red Wine Vinegar: Made from red wine; the best have a rich depth of flavor.*

Rice Vinegar, Seasoned: The sweetened version of this Asian vinegar made from rice has limited use. Depending on the brand, the sweetness can be overbearing, and the other flavorings frequently contribute a chemical taste.

Rice Vinegar, Unseasoned: An evocative, subtle sweetness informs the vinegar and it is a natural component of many Asian dishes. Its flavor is common at sushi bars, where it is used to make the pickled ginger that is invariably served as a condiment and as a dressing on the sliced cucumbers known as sunumono, after *su*, the name of the vinegar in Japanese.*

Sherry Vinegar: Produced in Spain from sherry wine, this vinegar is flavorful and distinctive. It is aged in wooden casks and blends well with olive oil, walnut, and hazelnut oils, slightly sweet dishes, and smoked poultry salads.*

Varietal Vinegars: Premium producers in California are making flavorful vinegars that retain the flavor of the original wine. Cabernet Sauvignon,

Pinot Noir, Sauvignon Blanc, and Pinot Noir are among the best of this category.*

Vinegars, Flavored: There are now so many flavored vinegars that it is impossible to catalog them all. California produces a huge array of balsamic vinegars flavored with various fruits; other wine vinegars are flavored with citrus, including the rare yuzu, with herbs, with spices, and more.*

White Balsamic: A sweet wine vinegar with a pale yellow color, it is not truly a balsamic vinegar. Made in both California and Italy. The reason to use it is because you like it.

White Wine Vinegar: Made from white wine, this vinegar can be sharp or mellow, depending on the original substrate. Essential for light vinaigrettes and beurre blanc.*

PART 4
An Oil & Vinegar Cookbook

As with *The Good Cook's Book of Salt & Pepper,* a book about oil and vinegar could include millions of recipes from around the world. Oil, especially, is essential in cooking. We use it to lubricate foods, to facilitate the transfer of heat, and to create a pleasing texture. We use vinegar for its ability to denature protein and for its sparkle on the palate.

We also use specialty oils and artisan vinegars for their unique and pleasing flavors and this was my guideline as I chose what to include and what to ignore. *Does it taste good? Does it taste better with a certain oil or specific vinegar? Are ingredients readily available to most home cooks?* These were the questions I asked myself as I gleaned recipes from my years as a chef and my lifetime as a home cook, as I have cooked actively, almost daily, since I was eight years old.

My focus in this book and in my life is on deliciousness, freshness, and ease of preparation. Health is a consideration, too, but I see the consideration as a foundation, not an approach. When you use good ingredients, grown, raised, or produced as close to home as possible and enjoyed in their true season, health follows naturally, individual illnesses and allergies aside. My market is a general market, not a niche market, and so I rely upon each reader to understand and research whatever limitations they may have. If, for example, you are allergic to vinegar—I've met one person who claims to be—I won't encourage you to try one of my favorite artisan vinegars, no matter how pure.

I've included a few recipes that demonstrate how certain oils and vinegars are used in other cultures but only when these dishes are enjoyed by the general population. Thus, you'll find a recipe for ochazuke, a rice and tea dish from Japan that gets its zip, so to speak, from toasted sesame oil, but not for pig's feet cooked in black vinegar, a traditional Chinese dish given to new mothers to help them regain their vitality.

There are two rules that I consider essential in the kitchen. The first is that it is all about ingredients. Don't expect great results from poor products. The second is to have fun! Enjoy yourself and don't worry if something doesn't turn out. It's just one meal and we all mess up now and then. As I finish this manuscript, I'm trying to figure out why my homemade sauerkraut spoiled instead of completing fermentation.

Snacks, Nibbles & Appetizers
Fettunta, Bruschetta, Crostini, Sandwiches & Pizza
Soups
Eggs
Salads
Pasta, Rice & Other Grains
Flesh
Vegetables
Flavored & Seasoned Oils, Vinegars & Sauces
Dressings, Salsas & Condiments
Desserts
Beverages
Lagniappe

Snacks, Nibbles & Appetizers

A few olives and some good bread with a little bowl of olive oil and a little bowl of vinegar alongside: What could be simpler? Sometimes it is just what the afternoon or evening calls for and it is not a compromise to offer such humble nibbles to guests, especially when you use high-quality ingredients. This is the time to break out the best, the ultra-premium olive oils, your favorite vinegars, the best handcrafted hearth breads.

This book's opening chapter celebrates this delicious simplicity and also explores slightly more complex dishes from around the world that feature either oil, vinegar, or the famous duo.

Three Easy Appetizers, Great Together, Great Solo

Any one of these appetizers makes a lovely start to a meal and, served together side by side with good bread, they are perfect for a cocktail party or, really, any time you simply want to linger with friends and a lovely adult beverage.

Anchovies in Red Wine Vinegar

Serves 3 to 4

1 small tin of anchovies
1 large garlic clove, crushed
⅓ to ½ cup red wine vinegar
Hearth bread, preferably sourdough

Put the anchovies and garlic into a small bowl and add enough vinegar to cover generously.

Set aside for 30 minutes.

Heat the hearth bread and set it in a basket.

Serve right away, with small plates and small forks. Guests tear off a piece of bread, dip it in the vinegar, lift out an anchovy and put it on top of the bread and enjoy.

Warm Olives with Marcona Almonds

Serves 3 to 4

8 ounces mixed olives, not pitted
3 tablespoons extra virgin olive oil
Zest of 1 lemon
Black pepper in a mill
4 ounces Marcona almonds

Put the olives in a small saucepan, add the olive oil and set over a very low flame. Agitate the pan gently until the olives are just warm.

Remove from the heat, add the lemon zest and season with several turns of black pepper. Tip into a small serving bowl, add the almonds and toss once or twice. Serve right away.

Marinated Mozzarella

Serves 3 to 4

8 ounces bocconcini (small mozzarella balls)
Meyer lemon olive oil or blood orange olive oil
Grated lemon zest
Grated orange zest
Flake salt
Black pepper in a mill

Put the bocconcini into a medium bowl, add a good splash of olive oil, along with the lemon and orange zest and toss. Season with a little salt and pepper, tip into a serving bowl, cover and let rest at room temperature for up to 30 minutes before serving with either toothpicks or plenty of napkins.

Variation:

In the summer and fall, add about a cup of quartered cherry tomatoes, a splash of red wine vinegar, and a pinch of red pepper flakes to the mozzarella. Omit the citrus oil and zests, add best-quality extra virgin olive oil, season with salt and pepper, cover and let rest for 15 to 30 minutes.

Bagna Cauda

Serves 10 to 12 as an appetizer

Bagna cauda, which means "hot bath," is or can be a bit of an extravaganza. One way to think about it is as Italian fondue, as there is typically a central pot that holds the sauce over a candle, with bread and vegetables for dipping. The best way to select what vegetables you will serve is to shop at a farmers market or farm stand; if you see it, it's in season nearby. Some versions of bagna cauda call for a splash of cream and in northern Italy, above where olive trees thrive, there is traditionally no olive oil at all, just cream, butter, and the other ingredients.

8 ounces (2 sticks) butter, preferably organic
1 garlic bulb, cloves separated, peeled and minced
2 or 3 anchovy fillets
1 cup extra virgin olive oil
Seasonal vegetables (see Suggestions on next page)
Hearth bread, hot

Put the butter, garlic, and anchovies into a saucepan and set over medium-low heat. When the butter is melted, add the olive oil and heat through.

Meanwhile, arrange the vegetables on a platter.

Set the sauce on a stand over a candle to keep warm and serve right away, with small plates, long forks, and plenty of napkins. Guests spear a piece of vegetable or bread on forks and swirl it in the sauce. Alternately, guests can set bread and vegetables on their plates and drizzle sauce over it; this works best with warm cooked vegetables, not raw, as the sauces will solidify as it cools.

Serving Suggestions:

Spring:

Young lettuce leaves; radishes; snow peas; roasted asparagus; grilled fava pods; steamed artichokes; sautéed cardoons; very small carrots; roasted carrots, in thin diagonal slices; celery; grilled garlic fronds; grilled spring onions; grilled spring garlic; roasted new potatoes.

Summer & Fall:

Cherry tomatoes; heirloom tomato wedges; lemon cucumber wedges; roasted sweet peppers; blanched green beans; radishes; okra; zucchini, raw or grilled; roasted beets; steamed broccoli; Belgian endive; young lettuce leaves.

Winter:

Twice-baked sweet potato wedges; roasted potatoes; roasted Brussels sprouts; roasted cauliflower; braised puntarella; roasted sunchokes; roasted turnips; roasted winter squash wedges; roasted and sliced carrots; roasted and sliced parsnips.

Southern Bath

Makes about 1 cup

I originally made this sauce, inspired by Bagna Cauda, to serve with grilled oysters. It is so very good and can also be used with other grilled seafood, grilled vegetables, and bread. It can also replace Bagna Cauda, should you like a kick of heat with your fresh vegetables and bread.

4 ounces (1 stick) butter, preferably organic
6 to 8 garlic cloves, crushed and minced
½ cup extra virgin olive oil
1 or 2 anchovy fillets
2 tablespoons Tabasco sauce, plus more to taste

But the butter and garlic into a small saucepan set over medium-low heat. When the butter is melted, add the olive oil and anchovies and simmer gently for 2 minutes. Stir in the Tabasco sauce and remove from the heat.

Use right away or cool, cover and store in the refrigerator for 2 to 3 days.

Lebanese Chickpeas with Toasted Bread and Yogurt-Tahini Sauce

Serves 6 to 8

To understand this lovely dish, think nachos, but with entirely different ingredients and flavors. It is adapted from a traditional Lebanese dish common in both private homes and cafés that I came across it in a delightful book, Arabesque: A Taste of Morocco, Turkey, and Lebanon *(Knopf, 2006, $35) by Claudia Roden. I made her version many times and it eventually evolved into my own, with just a couple of variations. In Claudia's recipe, she calls for a Lebanese flatbread called khobz halabi; if you cannot find it, use fresh lavash or pita bread in its place. Before preparing this, be certain to read the note about pine nuts.*

1 ½ cups dried chickpeas
Kosher salt
3 garlic cloves, crushed and minced
3 large (12 inches) or 6 small thin flat-breads, preferably Lebanese
4 cups plain whole milk yogurt
2 ½ tablespoons tahini
Juice of ½ lemon, plus more to taste
½ cup extra virgin olive oil
½ cup pine nuts
Arils of 1 small pomegranate, optional

Put the chickpeas into a medium saucepan, add water to cover them by 1 inch and bring to a boil over high heat. Reduce the heat to low and simmer, covered, until they are very tender, about 1 ½ hours. Add water as needed to keep the level at about an inch above the chickpeas. When the chickpeas have begun to soften, season with salt.

When the chickpeas are done, drain off some of the water but leave enough to just cover them but not come above their level. Stir in the minced garlic, cover and set aside.

Shortly before the chickpeas are done, toast the bread in a 400-degree oven until it just crisp; do not let it brown. Set the toasted bread on a clean work surface and use the heal of your hand to gently break it into small pieces. Transfer the broken bread to a wide shallow serving bowl.

Put the yogurt into a mixing bowl, add the tahini and whisk until very smooth. Sprinkle some salt in a little pile, pour the lemon juice onto it, let it dissolve and then whisk again. Taste and correct for salt and acid.

Pour the olive oil into a sauté pan set over medium-low heat, add the pine nuts and cook, stirring continuously, until the pine nuts are golden brown.

Ladle the chickpeas and some of their liquid over the bread, pour the yogurt sauce over them and then gently pour the hot olive oil and pine nuts on top. Scatter the pomegranates on top, if using.

Serve right away, with mint tea or a shrub, pages 370 to 375, alongside.

NOTE

In recent years, China has flooded the world market with pine nuts and it has become very hard to find Italian or domestic pine nuts. Some people, myself included, have a bad reaction to one of the varieties grown in China. A day or two after eating the pine nuts, people who are sensitive to the pine nut develop a bitter taste in the mouth that can persist for weeks. If you can find pine nuts from Korea, more readily available than Italian ones, use them, as they don't seem to cause the problem.

Fresh Ricotta with Olive Oil, Lemon & Black Pepper

Serves 4 to 8

For this lovely dish to be worth eating, you must use very fresh whole milk ricotta, preferably made of sheep's milk, not the packaged skim milk type found in most American supermarkets. You'll find it at specialty cheese shops and sometimes at farmers markets in regions of the country where sheep are raised.

1 pound whole milk ricotta, preferably from sheep's milk, as fresh as possible
2 to 3 tablespoons best-quality extra virgin olive oil
½ lemon
Kosher salt
Black pepper in a mill
Hearth bread

Put the cheese on a small serving platter or divide it among individual plates. Drizzle with olive oil, squeeze some lemon juice on top, sprinkle a little salt over it and add several generous turns of black pepper.

Serve with hearth-style bread, grilled, toasted, or heated, and enjoy right away.

Feta with Olive Oil, Black Pepper, & Celery

Serves 3 to 4, easily doubled

Good feta cheese and olive oil complement each other beautifully, as you would expect, given that they both hail from the Mediterranean. If you find feta too salty or otherwise overpowering, look for French feta, as it is smoother and milder. Once you get used to its flavor, experiment with feta from Bulgaria and Greece. There is good domestic feta, too, made by small regional producers.

2 to 3 celery stalks, trimmed and cut into very thin diagonal slices
Kosher salt
6 to 8 ounces feta, preferably Bulgarian, freshly drained
3 tablespoons best-quality extra virgin olive oil
Black pepper in a mill
Warm hearth bread, optional

Put the cut celery in a small bowl, season it lightly with salt and set aside.

Crumble the cheese, taking care not to make the pieces too small—you want them to range from the size of a pea to the size of a marble.

Mound the crumbled cheese in the middle of a medium plate (a soup plate works well) and scatter the celery around it.

Drizzle most of the olive oil over the cheese and a little of it over the celery. Grind a generous amount of black pepper over the cheese.

Serve with or without warm bread alongside.

Variations:

- Scatter 1 tablespoon brined green peppercorns, 2 tablespoons fried capers, or 1 tablespoon grated lemon zest over the cheese after adding the olive oil.
- Serve over fresh salad greens.

Whipped Feta

Makes about 2 cups

You can, if you prefer, make this tangy condiment in a food processor, though I find it easier to simply mash the cheese with a sturdy dinner fork and mix in the ingredients by hand. Although I first made it to serve with marinated eggplant and peppers, it is excellent as an appetizer with hot pita bread and sliced roasted beets.

12 ounces feta, crumbled
⅓ cup extra virgin olive oil, plus more as needed
1 to 2 tablespoons red wine vinegar or 2 tablespoons fresh lemon juice
2 to 3 tablespoons chopped fresh herbs, see Note below
2 teaspoons freshly cracked black pepper

Put the feta in a medium mixing bowl and mash it with a fork until it is reduced to a fine crumb. Add the olive oil, mixing thoroughly as you pour it in. Stir in a tablespoon of vinegar or lemon juice, taste, and add additional vinegar or lemon juice until you achieve a proper balance.

NOTE

When selecting herbs, use what is in season, thyme in the spring, basil in the summer and early fall, sage in the winter, and Italian parsley any time at all. If you like dill, use just 1 teaspoon so that it does not overpower other flavors.

Formaggio All'Argentiera

Silversmith's Cheese

Serves 6 to 8

This dish is so very delicious, with an aroma that captures you and makes your appetite blossom. It is tempting to eat too much of it so be careful if you are serving it as an appetizer. If you want to indulge for dinner, this recipe will serve 2 or 3 and all you'll need alongside is a big green salad and a rustic red wine. If you cannot find Caciocavallo, a Sicilian cheese that is increasingly available in the United States, you can use Scamorza, Provolone, or a domestic smoked mozzarella.

2 teaspoons olive oil
2 garlic cloves, crushed
1 ½ pounds smoked Caciocavallo, cut into ½-inch thick rounds
1 tablespoon fresh oregano leaves or 2 teaspoons dried oregano
2 to 3 tablespoons red wine vinegar
½ teaspoon sugar
1 loaf of rustic hearth bread or 1 baguette, hot

Heat the olive oil in a heavy frying pan—cast iron or heavy non-stick is ideal—over medium-low heat, add the garlic and sauté 30 seconds. Use tongs to remove the garlic, set the cheese in the pan in a single layer and cook for 3 to 4 minutes. Use a metal spatula to quickly turn the cheese over and cook until it is on the verge of melting completely, about 2 minutes. Working quickly, sprinkle the oregano, the vinegar, and sugar over the cheese, cook 1 minute more and then transfer the cheese in its pan to the table, setting it on a trivet or thick pot holder. Serve immediately, with the hot bread alongside.

Olive Oil–Poached Quail Eggs on Crostini

Serves 6 to 12

This appetizer is delicious and rather adorable but it is not as labor intensive as it seems before you've made it. The reason I call for each egg to be cracked into a separate dish is that, first, they can be a challenge to crack at the last minute and, second, they cook so quickly that you need them all at the ready so that you don't have to bother cracking them once you've begun cooking. Ten seconds—the time the egg will be in the oil—goes very quickly. If you don't have small glass bowls, use ¼-inch canning jars.

Asian markets typically have quail eggs but they are increasingly available at farmers markets, too.

12 baguette slices, lightly toasted
12 quail eggs
Extra virgin olive oil
Flake salt
Black pepper in a mill
Minced fresh herbs, tapenade, or hot sauce of choice

Set the sliced baguettes—crostini—on a serving platter.

Break the quail eggs into 12 little dishes (yes, 12; you'll thank me once you've done this) and set near the stove.

Pour about 2 inches of olive oil into a very small deep pan and set over medium-high heat. Have a small slotted spoon nearby.

When the temperature of the oil reaches about 360 degrees, quickly slip a quail egg into the oil, standing back as the oil bubbles up. After 10 seconds, use the slotted spoon to tip the egg over, lift it out, shake off excess oil and set it on top of a crostini. Continue until all eggs are cooked.

Top each egg with salt, pepper, and either herbs, tapenade, or a shake of hot sauce.

Serve right away.

About Tapenades, Hummus & Skordalia

The Mediterranean is ringed with delicious olive oil–based condiments and pastes, some that tend to be served as components in more elaborate dishes and others that are typically enjoyed simply, with a bit of flatbread, perhaps, or a few vegetables. Here, I highlight the ones I most enjoy as appetizers.

Tapenade hails from Provence, where olive trees flourish near the sea, and from Italy. It has become quite popular in the United States and is something that people typically buy. But it is best made at home, where it needs no preservatives.

Hummus, native to the Middle East and once rare in the United States, is now everywhere, at farmers markets, specialty stores, supermarkets, and national chain restaurants, everywhere, that is, except in home kitchens. My hope is that anyone reading this book will give homemade hummus a try; it is never better than when it is made in your own kitchen. There are dozens of commercial versions, all contemporary variations on hummus made with chickpeas and sesame tahini. In this chapter, I include my personal favorite, along with a contemporary treatment that highlights the sweet earthy flavor of hazelnuts and hazelnut oil.

Finally, there is skordalia, an ancient Greek condiment originally made with ground almonds seasoned with garlic, vinegar, and olive oil. My favorite version, the one that calls to me from the refrigerator in the middle of the night, is based on potatoes and it is sensational, absolutely irresistible. Some versions of skordalia, especially one made of bread and one based on yellow chick peas—both included here—are sometimes thinned with water, wine, vinegar, or lemon juice and used as a sauce for fried fish.

Basic Tapenade

Makes about 1 cup

This is a good basic tapenade that you can use as a template, varying the olives and other ingredients based on what will be offered with it. For ideas, see the Variations that follow the recipe. Most of the time, I prefer tapenade that has been chopped; if you prefer a smoother texture, pulse the ingredients together in a food processor until you achieve the texture you like.

8 ounces mixed olives, pitted and minced
1 tablespoon salted capers, rinsed and dried
3 garlic cloves, minced
1 tablespoon minced fresh Italian parsley
1 tablespoon minced fresh basil, optional
1 minced anchovy fillet
2 teaspoons grated lemon zest
Black pepper in a mill
2 to 3 tablespoons extra virgin olive oil

In a small bowl, toss together the olives, capers, and garlic. Add the parsley, basil, if using, anchovy, and lemon zest, season generously with black pepper, stir in the olive oil and set aside for 30 minutes before serving. The tapenade will keep in the refrigerator for a day or two, after which time its flavors will deteriorate.

Variations:

- To pair with red wine, use 4 ounces oil-cured black olives and 4 ounces California black olives, omit the basil and replace the lemon zest with orange zest.
- To enjoy with a dry white wine, use all green olives, such as Picholines.

Serving Suggestions:

Tossed with hot pasta such as spaghettini and 2 cups sliced cherry tomatoes; spooned over baked potatoes.

Walnut Tapenade, with Hazelnut Variation

Makes about ¾ cup

Make this tapenade when you have access to a new crop of domestic walnuts. Harvest is typically in October and they start appearing in farmers markets soon thereafter.

½ cup green olives, such as Picholine, pitted and chopped
⅓ cup shelled walnuts, lightly toasted, chopped
1 garlic clove, minced
2 teaspoons best-quality white wine vinegar
Black pepper in a mill
2 to 3 tablespoons unrefined walnut oil or extra virgin olive oil
2 tablespoons chopped fresh Italian parsley
Flake salt, as needed

Put the olives and walnuts into a small bowl, add the garlic and vinegar, and season generously with black pepper. Stir in the walnut oil or olive oil and the parsley. Taste, correct for acid balance and salt. Cover and let rest 30 minutes before serving. This tapenade is best the day it is made.

Variations:

- To make hazelnut oil, use pitted black olives of choice (but not oil cured), lightly toasted and peeled hazelnuts, and hazelnut oil. Add the zest of ½ orange and a little squeeze of orange juice along with the vinegar.
- If you prefer a smoother tapenade, simply make it in a food processor, pulsing until you achieve your desired consistency.

Tuna Tapenade

Makes approximately 2 cups

Maggie Klein of Oliveto, a wonderful restaurant in Oakland, deserves credit for this recipe, as inspiration came from her delightful book, The Feast of the Olive *(Aris Books). Traditional tapenade does not include tuna but the addition here makes for a wonderfully robust condiment.*

I serve this version most often with lightly toasted hearth bread or water crackers, but it is also excellent on sandwiches of thinly sliced potato and sliced hard-cooked egg.

4 or 5 anchovy fillets, packed in oil
1 can (6 ½ ounces) tuna, preferably Italian, drained
3 large garlic cloves, crushed
1 tablespoon chopped Italian parsley
1 cup Kalamata olives, pitted
½ cup extra virgin olive oil
¼ cup finely chopped red onion
¼ cup capers
1 hard-boiled egg, finely grated
Hearth bread or crackers

Place the anchovies, tuna, garlic, parsley, and pitted olives in a food processor or blender. Blend the mixture until it is smooth and, with the motor still running, drizzle in the olive oil. The tapenade should be smooth, similar in consistency to mayonnaise.

Transfer to a bowl or crock, using a rubber spatula to scrape the sides of the work bowl. Cover and refrigerate for about 30 minutes.

To serve, scatter the chopped onion, capers, and grated egg on top, set the bread or crackers alongside and enjoy.

A Good Hummus for Red Wines

Makes about 3 cups

I typically add a generous teaspoon—and sometimes more—of chipotle powder and a shake of ground cayenne to my hummus but there are times when I need to serve an elegant red wine alongside. I don't want heat to turn the wine bitter and so I turn down its volume.

2 ½ cups (from ¾ cup dried beans) cooked chickpeas (see Note on next page)
½ cup cooking liquid from the chickpeas or water
4 to 5 large fresh garlic cloves, crushed
2 teaspoons kosher salt, plus more to taste
2 teaspoons cumin seeds, lightly toasted and ground
2 tablespoons fresh lemon juice, plus more to taste
¾ cup raw sesame tahini
5 tablespoons extra virgin olive oil
Black pepper in a mill

Set aside ½ cup of the chickpeas and put the rest, along with ¼ cup of the cooking liquid or water, the garlic, and the 2 teaspoons of salt into the work bowl of a food processor fitted with a metal blade. Pulse until the ingredients form a smooth puree, adding the remaining cooking liquid or water if needed.

Add the cumin, lemon juice, and tahini and pulse until the tahini is fully incorporated into the mixture.

Transfer the hummus to a mixing bowl, using a rubber spatula to scrape all of it from the work bowl. Fold in 3 tablespoons of the olive oil.

Taste the hummus, paying careful attention to the balance of salt and acid. It should taste bright but not lemony and the flavors should be bold, not flat. If it seems flat, add a generous sprinkling of salt in one corner and squeeze a little lemon juice on top to dissolve the salt. Fold into the hummus, taste again and repeat until the hummus is irresistible.

Transfer the hummus into a serving bowl, cover and refrigerate for at least 30 minutes and as long as a few hours before serving.

While the hummus chills, combine the reserved chickpeas and reserved olive oil in a small bowl and season with salt and pepper. Set aside.

To serve, pour the reserved chickpeas and olive oil over the hummus. Serve right away, with warm pita bread, crackers, crostini, celery sticks, and carrot sticks alongside.

Covered and refrigerated, the hummus will keep for 3 to 4 days.

NOTE

You can use canned chickpeas if you like but they should be drained and rinsed. To use dried chickpeas, simply soak the dried peas overnight, rinse, cover with fresh water by 2 inches, season with salt and cook over medium heat until tender, about 45 minutes. Cool in the cooking liquid and then drain.

Hazelnut & White Bean Hummus

Makes about 3 ½ cups

This hummus is for anyone with a passion for hazelnuts, as white beans form the perfect canvas for the hazelnut's seductive flavors. It makes a lovely winter holiday appetizer, especially with oranges or tangerines served alongside.

1 cup (6 ounces) dried white beans, preferably marrowfats, cooked until tender, cooled in cooking liquid
2 to 3 garlic cloves
Generous pinch of ground cardamom
2 teaspoons kosher salt, plus more to taste
Grated zest of 1 orange
2 tablespoons freshly squeezed orange juice, preferably from a Seville (sour) orange, or 2 tablespoons rice wine vinegar
⅔ cup hazelnut butter
4 tablespoons hazelnut oil
3 tablespoons chopped fresh Italian parsley
¼ cup raw hazelnuts, peeled and chopped
Black pepper in a mill

Put the cooked beans into the work bowl of a food processor fitted with the metal blade, add the garlic, cardamom, and the 2 teaspoons of salt and pulse until smooth. Scrape the sides of the bowl with a rubber spatula, add the orange zest, orange juice or vinegar, and hazelnut butter. Pulse until very smooth.

Scrape into a mixing bowl, fold in 3 tablespoons of the oil and the parsley, taste and correct for salt and acid.

Transfer to a serving bowl, cover and refrigerate for at least 1 hour and as long as 3 hours.

To serve, scatter the hazelnuts over the hummus, drizzle with the remaining hazelnut oil, season with salt and several turns of black pepper and serve right away, with thin crackers.

Skordalia Me Kapari

Makes about 2 cups

This version of skordalia is from the island of Tinos, where caper bushes hang from cliffs and rocks high above the blue sea. In early summer, their fragrant buds are collected and either cured in salt, brined, or dried in the sun. They contribute a unique taste to many island dishes. This version is often thinned with water or broth and served with fish or grilled vegetables.

2 cups cubed two-day-old whole wheat hearth bread, soaked in water until softened
4 garlic cloves, crushed
Kosher salt
⅓ cup extra virgin olive oil
4 tablespoons capers, preferably salt-packed, rinsed and drained
3 to 4 tablespoons freshly squeezed lemon juice or red wine vinegar
½ cup blanched whole almonds, soaked overnight in water and drained
1 medium potato, boiled, peeled, and mashed
Freshly ground white pepper

Squeeze the soaked bread until fairly dry; put it in the work bowl of a food processor fitted with the metal blade. Add the garlic, season with salt and pulse into a smooth paste.

With the motor running, slowly drizzle in the olive oil oil. Add 3 tablespoons of the capers and 3 tablespoons of the lemon juice or vinegar. Add the almonds and pulse a few times, until they are coarsely ground.

Scrape the mixture into a medium bowl and fold in the potato. (Do not be tempted to use the food processor for this; potatoes become gluey in food processors.) Season with white pepper. Taste to correct for salt, if needed, for acid, and for pepper. Cover and refrigerate for at least 2 hours.

To serve, transfer to a bowl, sprinkle the remaining capers on top and serve with flatbread or crackers.

My Favorite Skordalia

Makes about 2 cups

If forced to choose, I might have to pick this skordalia as my favorite thing in the world. Made correctly, it is almost indescribably good. It is not difficult to make but there comes a point when you are adding the olive oil that it becomes a bit counter-intuitive. At this point, you need to keep going to achieve the proper flavor and consistency. If you use less olive oil than the recipe calls for, you'll wonder what the big deal is, as you'll have something resembling garlicky olive oil mashed potatoes. It will be good but not transcendent. Just trust me and keep adding olive oil until the mixture becomes slick and will not absorb another drop. Then you must let it rest a while so that the heat of the garlic calms down.

2 or 3 (about 1 ¼ pounds total) russet potatoes
8 to 10 garlic cloves
1 teaspoon kosher salt, plus more to taste
2 egg yolks
¾ to 1 cup best-quality extra virgin olive oil
Juice of 1 lemon
Black pepper in a mill

Preheat the oven to 400 degrees. Use a fork to pierce the potatoes in several places and bake them until they are tender, about 40 to 60 minutes, depending on their size. Let the potatoes cool slightly, but not completely. Meanwhile, crush the garlic and salt in a mortar or suribachi and grind it until it is nearly liquefied; mix in the egg yolks.

Break each potato in half, put one half at a time in a potato ricer, and press it through into a medium bowl. Remove the skin from the ricer, discard it, and continue until all of the potatoes have been riced. Use a rubber spatula to fold the garlic mixture into the riced potatoes. Mix in the olive oil, a tablespoon or two at a time, until the skordalia is thick and dense and will not absorb any more oil. Taste, season with a little more salt if needed, and add a little of the lemon juice. Taste again, and continue to add lemon juice until the flavors all come together and no one flavor dominates. Transfer the skordalia to a serving bowl, cover, and refrigerate for at least 1 hour before serving with crackers or toasted slices of baguette.

Yellow Split Pea Skordalia with Garlic

Makes about 3 cups

Here is another skordalia, this one from Cyprus, where it is used as a dip for vegetables and spread on barley biscuits, in addition to other traditional uses as a sauce for fish, poultry, meat, vegetables, and even pasta. It can also be made with dried peeled favas, chickpeas, or white shell beans.

2 cups yellow split peas, picked over and rinsed
2 bay leaves
2 teaspoons salt
4 to 6 garlic cloves
½ cup extra virgin olive oil
3 to 4 tablespoons red wine vinegar
3 to 4 tablespoons dry white wine
2 tablespoons dried oregano, crumbled, plus more for garnish
Freshly ground black pepper
Toppings (see Suggestions on next page)

Place the split peas in a large pot, add water to cover by 4 inches and bring to a boil. Reduce the heat to low and simmer, skimming often, for 5 minutes. Add the bay leaves and simmer for 40 minutes more, stirring occasionally and adding a little warm water as needed to keep the peas covered as they cook. Add 1 teaspoon of the salt and simmer for 15 to 20 minutes more, or until the peas are soft and nearly dry. Do not let them scorch.

Puree the peas with an immersion blender, or transfer to a food processor and puree. Let the puree cool completely; it will thicken considerably.

In a large mortar, grind the garlic with the remaining 1 teaspoon salt into a smooth paste. Add 2 cups or so of the puree and continue grinding to incorporate the garlic. Alternately, you can use a blender or a small food processor.

In a large bowl, combine the garlic mixture, the remaining pea puree, the oil, 3 tablespoons each vinegar and wine, the oregano and pepper to taste, stirring vigorously to incorporate. Taste and adjust the seasonings as necessary. Cover and refrigerate for at least 3 hours, or overnight.

If the skordalia seems too thick, add a little vinegar, wine, or water to thin. Spread on a large plate, sprinkle with oregano, and garnish with toppings of your choice.

Topping Suggestions:

- 1 cup chopped fresh cilantro
- 3 tablespoons pitted and chopped kalamata olives
- 1 medium-ripe tomato, peeled, cored, seeded, diced, and drained
- 2 to 3 green garlic bulbs or ramps, thinly sliced
- Several leaves of arugula, thinly sliced
- A few sprigs of purslane or fresh Italian parsley, minced
- Extra virgin olive oil

Pot Stickers with Soy Sauce, Sesame Oil, Vinegar & Chili Sauce

Makes about 2 dozen

Ahh, pot stickers: Asian comfort food at its best! What I love most about them is the combination of flavors in the condiments—the salty savor of soy sauce, the bright tang of vinegar, the earthy toast of sesame oil, and the delicious heat of chili sauce—that makes the succulent dumplings soar. Pot stickers are not difficult to make at home, especially when you use commercial wrappers, available in most Asian markets.

1 cup shredded Napa cabbage
Kosher salt
¾ pound freshly ground pastured pork, about 25 percent fat
3 scallions, trimmed and very finely minced
1 tablespoon grated fresh ginger
1 teaspoon ground white pepper
1 tablespoon soy sauce, plus more for the table
1 tablespoon rice wine vinegar or black vinegar, plus more for the table
1 tablespoon toasted sesame oil, plus more for the table
Asian chili sauce, such as Chili Garlic Sauce or Sriracha
Hot chili oil, optional
1 package Gyoza wrappers (see Note on next page)
Peanut oil, for frying

Put the cabbage into a bowl, sprinkle fairly heavily with salt and use your fingers to toss and turn the cabbage. Set aside for at least 30 minutes and up to 1 hour. Tip the cabbage into a strainer or colander, rinse under running water and squeeze out as much moisture as possible. Transfer to a small bowl and set aside.

Put the pork, scallions, ginger, white pepper, soy sauce, vinegar, and sesame oil into a bowl and use your fingers to mix it thoroughly. Mix in the cabbage. Cover and refrigerate for at least 30 minutes and as long as 2 hours.

To fill the dumplings, open the package of wrappers and top it with a slightly damp tea towel. Set a small bowl of water near a clean work surface. Remove the filling from the refrigerator. Line a baking sheet or other flat tray with wax paper.

Set a wrapper on your work surface and add a generous amount of filling, about 2 teaspoons or so. Dip your finger in the bowl of water and run it around the inner edge of the wrapper. Fold the wrapper over and press it so that it sticks to itself. Set the filled dumpling on the wax paper and continue until you have made all of them. (Alternately, you can use a pot stick press, which will seal them for you, though I've not found it necessary.)

Set a serving platter in the oven and preheat the oven to 200 degrees.

Pour a little peanut oil into a large sauté pan set over medium heat and when it is hot, add several dumplings. Fry for 2 to 3 minutes, turn and fry 2 to 3 minutes more. Carefully add about ½ cup of water to the pan, cover and cook for 2 minutes. Uncover, cook until the water is evaporated and then transfer the dumplings to the platter in the oven. Continue until all the dumplings have been cooked. Adjust the heat as necessary so that the dumplings don't burn and add a bit of oil whenever the pan seems too dry.

To serve, pour soy sauce, vinegar, sesame oil, and hot chili oil, if using, into small individual bowls. Add a dollop of chili sauce to the vinegar and enjoy right away.

NOTE

Although wonton wrappers are easier to find than gyoza wrappers, it is worth the effort to find gyozas, as they are thinner and more traditional. They are also round instead of square. Gyoza No Kawa, a Japanese brand, and Dynasty, a well-distributed Chinese brand, work beautifully.

Ahi Tuna Poke

Serves 6 to 8

Poke (poe'-kay) is Hawaii's soul food. At its simplest—and best—it is very fresh raw fish seasoned with a bit of salt, a bit of seaweed, and a bit of inamono (ground kukui nut, also known as candlenut). That said, it has become so popular that there are now dozens of versions, several cookbooks, and and an international poke festival and recipe competition. You'll find contemporary poke made with cooked tuna, raw and cooked salmon, fried marlin, octopus, squid, shrimp, crab, limpets, scallops, surf clams, raw and cooked lobster, seared beef, raw beef liver, purple sweet potatoes, all manner of fruits and vegetables, and even tofu. It may be served on top of a salad or folded into one, mixed with mayonnaise and served as a sandwich, tossed with tomatoes and served as salsa, tossed with noodles, or folded into scrambled eggs.

The best of the best, though, is the simplest and most traditional, like this one.

2 pounds sashimi-grade ahi tuna, trimmed of any dark flesh and cut into 1-inch cubes
½ cup ogo (brownish-red seaweed), cut in 1-inch pieces, if available
3 tablespoons soy sauce, more or less to taste
2 teaspoons toasted sesame oil
Hawaiian alaea salt or flake salt
1 tablespoon inamono (ground kukui nut, also known as candlenut)

Put the tuna in a medium bowl, add the ogo, if using, soy sauce, and sesame oil and toss gently. Cover and chill for at least one hour.

To serve, transfer the poke to a serving bowl or plate. Sprinkle lightly with salt and inamono and serve Immediately.

Variations:

- Cut 2 trimmed green onions into very thin diagonal slices and toss with the tuna when ogo is not available.
- Add 1 or 2 teaspoons crushed red pepper flakes to the tuna before adding the other ingredients.
- Cut 2 firm-ripe avocados into 1-inch cubes, toss with a bit of lime juice and season with salt. Serve the poke on top.

Anticuchos

Marinated & Grilled Beef Heart from Peru & Bolivia

Serves 16 or more as an appetizer

When I wrote the first edition of this book, Barbara Karoff was a colleague at Aris Books in Berkeley. I loved her book South American Cooking *(Aris Books) and include a version of this recipe in the book as a demonstration of the way vinegar can transform an inexpensive cut of meat. These skewers of tangy beef heart are popular street food in both Peru and Bolivia. A single beef heart is enormous and will make dozens of these little appetizers so you may want to freeze a portion.*

1 beef heart, crushed and minced
7 garlic cloves, crushed and minced
3 serranos, seeded and minced
3 tablespoons ground cumin
2 tablespoon dried oregano, crumbled
Kosher salt
Black pepper in a mill
1 ½ cups red wine vinegar, plus more as needed
½ cup dried hontaka chili peppers or other dried hot chili peppers, seeded
32 bamboo skewers, soaked in water for at least 30 minutes
Kosher salt
Black pepper in a mill
1 teaspoon ground annatto or achiote paste
1 tablespoon safflower oil, pumpkinseed oil, or mild olive oil

Set the heart on a clean work surface, trim it of veins, arteries, and excess fat and cut it into 1-inch cubes. Put the cubes into a large glass bowl and set aside.

Next, make the marinade. To do so, put the garlic, serranos, cumin, and oregano in a medium bowl, season generously with salt and several turns of black pepper and stir until evenly combined. Sprinkle the mixture over the meat and toss thoroughly until the meat is evenly coated. Pour the vinegar over it, adding more if needed to cover the meat completely. Cover and refrigerate for at least 12 hours and as long as 24 hours; turn the meat now then.

Shortly before grilling, prepare a fire in an outdoor grill (or preheat a stove top grill).

Remove the marinating meat from the refrigerator and thread it onto skewers. Pour the marinade in a saucepan, set over medium heat and simmer gently until reduced by half.

Meanwhile, remove the stems from the dried chilies, shake out the seeds and put the chilies into a bowl. Cover with warm water for 30 minutes, drain and transfer to the work bowl of a food processor fitted with the metal blade. Add the ground annatto or achiote and the oil and pulse to form a thick paste. Add ¾ cup of the reduced marinate, pulse several times, taste and correct for salt, if needed. Pour into a bowl.

Grill the skewers of meat for 2 minutes, turn, brush with sauce and grill 2 minutes more. Transfer to a serving platter, brush all over with a little more sauce and serve right away, with the remaining sauce alongside for dipping.

Fettunta, Bruschetta, Crostini, Sandwiches & Pizza

Over the last two decades, bread in America has gotten so much better, inspired, to a large degree, by early pioneers in the San Francisco Bay Area, where Berkeley-based Acme Bread Company and Della Fattoria, located in Petaluma, changed everyone's expectations by introducing us to the singular pleasure of true hearth breads. Soon, there were others, Artisan Bakers in Sonoma, Downtown Creamery and Bakery in Healdsburg, Raymond's Bakery in Cazadero, and so many who deserve to be included here but aren't. The bread revolution caught fire in the 1990s and there is now outstanding hearth bread in nearly every major metropolitan area of the United States.

Certain classic examples of the use of olive oil and vinegar on bread did not make it into this chapter, primarily for practical reasons. New Orleans extraordinary muffaletta gets much of its signature flavor from the tangy olive salad that tops the layers of meats and cheese and oozes into the bread itself. But the bread, a special loaf created specifically for the sandwich, is essential. My advice is to give it a try in New Orleans or somewhere, such as Rustic, the restaurant at Francis Ford Coppola Winery in Geyserville, California, that uses the signature bread, flown in from Nola.

The Vietnamese bahn mi, a category of sandwiches rather than a single sandwich, warrants a shout-out, too, as lightly pickled vegetables are essential to it. But, it, too, requires special bread, a certain type of soft white French roll, the insides of which are pulled out to make room for the ingredients. My favorite has always been barbecued pork with slightly sweet mayonnaise, pork paté, pickled radishes and carrots, thinly sliced perfectly, on the diagonal—jalapeños, and a fluffy mound of fresh cilantro but I've enjoyed each one I've ever had. To find the best, seek out a true

Vietnamese bakery—there are a couple of fabulous ones in Biloxi, Mississippi, and several in Manhattan's Chinatown and San Francisco's Clement St.—and eat your way through the list of sandwiches.

Simple Fettunta
Fettunta Embellished with Crab, Radishes & Avocado
Basic Bruschetta, with Year Round & Seasonal Variations
Crostini
Croutons
Baguette with Chévre, Prosciutto, Black Pepper &
Meyer Lemon Olive Oil
Portobello & Caciocavallo Sandwiches
Pacific Pan Bagnat
Grilled Pizzas, Neat & with Toppings

Fried Sage Leaves

Olive oil

24 medium to large sage leaves

Pour just enough olive oil into a small heavy sauté pan to cover the bottom of the pan with a thin film. Set over medium-high heat. When the pan is hot, add the sage leaves and cook for about 20 seconds, during which time the leaves with shrink up and become crunchy. Turn and cook about 10 seconds longer.

Transfer to absorbent paper to drain and cool.

Crostini

Crostini are little bruschetta, typically made of thin slices of a good baguette and prepared slightly differently. Sometimes you see them called croutons, which is not incorrect but can be confusing if you don't know what is called for, slices or cubes. Cut a baguette into ¼-inch slices, brush both sides of the bread with olive oil, arrange in a single layer on a baking sheet, and set in a 400-degree oven for 5 to 7 minutes, until just golden brown. Remove from the oven and let cool before adding toppings.

You can use the exact same toppings as for bruschetta but there are other options, too. Serve them alongside or slather them with tapenade, skordalia, or hummus, or example, or tuck several into a green salad.

Simple Fettunta

Serves 4

The first time I had fettunta is exactly how everyone should enjoy it for the first time. I was at Frantoio, an olive mill and restaurant in Northern California, where an early harvest of DaVero olives was being crushed and pressed. The owner of the press came in with a plate of grilled bread. Its toasty and garlicky aromas mingled with the scent of the brand new oil spilling, that very minute, into the world. One by one, he quickly put the bread into the stream of oil that was pouring out of the spout and handed each of us a piece, sprinkling each one with a little salt. It was so pure, so fresh, so delicious, so true.

Olive oil is never better than at the moment of its birth and fettunta is never better than when it captures that newest oil.

That said, all you need is good bread, good garlic, the best olive oil you can find, and some good flake salt to indulge in one of the world's finest and most humble dishes.

To make fettunta with Olio Nuovo, as the year's newest oil is called, you'll need to prepare this in December, possibly in November, and in January.

8 slices good crusty bread, such as sourdough hearth bread or other hearth bread of choice
3 or 4 garlic cloves, cut in half
Very best, very fresh extra virgin olive oil
Flake salt

Toast the bread until golden brown on both sides and rub one side with garlic. Pour olive oil over the bread and don't be skimpy about it! Season with salt and enjoy right away, using bread crusts or more bread to sop up the olive oil that remains on the platter.

Photo provided by Ridgely C. Evers

Fettunta Embellished with Crab, Radishes, & Avocado

Serves 6

Stephen Singer of Baker Lane Vineyards near where I live in Sebastopol, California, imported premium Tuscan olive oils for years, until he sold his company. One year, he brought some Olio Nuovo from San Giusto in Tuscany to my radio show and talked about how much he loves it with fettunta. He left the bottle with me and after making simple fettunta, I decided to make an embellished version as a first course for Christmas dinner. It was every bit as good as I expected it would be.

2 firm-ripe avocados, peeled and cut into ¼-inch dice
6 radishes, cut into ¼-inch dice
2 tablespoons minced fresh Italian parsley or cilantro
Best-quality extra virgin olive oil, preferably Olio Nuovo
1 or 2 Meyer lemons
Kosher salt
Black pepper in a mill
Meat from 1 Dungeness crab or other crab meat of choice
6 large slices sourdough hearth bread

Put the diced avocado into a medium bowl, add the radishes and parsley or cilantro and toss very gently with two forks. Season with a generous splash of olive oil, a squeeze of lemon juice, several pinches of kosher salt and several generous turns of black pepper. Taste and correct for acid and salt.

Put the crab meat in a bowl, add a generous splash of olive oil and a squeeze of lemon juice and toss. Season with salt and pepper, taste and correct for acid and salt.

Toast or grill the bread until it is deep golden brown. Set the toast on individual serving plates and drizzle a generous amount of olive oil on each slice. Add a little mound of avocado salad and a little mound of crab alongside, season the bread with salt and serve immediately.

Basic Bruschetta, with Year Round & Seasonal Variations

Serves 4 to 6

Bruschetta is very easy to make. It is simply good hearth bread, grilled or toasted until golden brown, rubbed with garlic, drizzled with olive oil, and seasoned with salt. How you do the toasting is up to you. It can be done traditionally, in a wood-burning oven or an outdoor grill, or it can be accomplished on a stove top grill or ridge grill pan. It can even be toasted in a conventional toaster or toaster oven. Once you've made it a time or two, it's easy to vary the toppings seasonally or with whatever catches your fancy at the moment. And bruschetta needn't be an appetizer; with a big green salad alongside, it can make an excellent simple dinner on a hot or busy night. Following this basic recipe are my favorite variations.

1 loaf hearth bread of choice
4 large garlic cloves, cut in half lengthwise but not peeled
Best-quality extra virgin olive oil
Flake salt
Black pepper in a mill

Prepare a fire, if you plan to grill the bread or toast it in a wood-burning oven.

Cut the bread into medium-thick slices (⅜- to ½-inch), and grill it or toast it until golden brown on both sides. Transfer to a clean work surface, rub each piece with a cut clove of garlic, pressing the clove into the bread as you rub, and drizzle with olive oil. Sprinkle with a little coarse salt and black pepper and serve right away.

Variations:

Year Round

- Spread a spoonful of creme fraiche on top of each piece of bread before seasoning with salt and pepper.
- Arrange sliced mozzarella fresca and fresh cured anchovies on a platter and serve alongside the bruschetta.
- Top each piece of bruschetta with a smear of tapenade.
- Serve Anchovies in Red Wine Vinegar (page 75) with the bruschetta.
- Preheat the oven to 400 degrees. Prepare the bread as directed in the main recipe and then cover each piece with thin slices of caciacavallo or smoked mozzarella. Set on a sheet pan in the oven until the cheese is just melted, about 2 to 3 minutes. Sprinkle with a little dried oregano and a bit of red wine vinegar and serve.
- Toss 8 ounces or so of Oregon baby shrimp with a small minced shallot, the zest of a lemon, 2 tablespoons of extra virgin olive oil, and a generous squeeze of lemon juice. Add some snipped chives or chopped Italian parsley, season with salt and pepper and spoon on top of brushchetta. Top each one with a tiny, thin lemon wedge.

Spring

- After rubbing the bread with garlic, cover it with fresh sheep's milk ricotta. Drizzle with olive oil, season with salt and pepper and enjoy immediately.
- Shell a pound or so of young fresh favas, blanch them for 90 seconds in simmering water, peel them and put them into a small bowl. Season with a little salt and serve alongside the bruschetta.

- Prepare egg salad by combining 3 diced hard-cooked eggs with 2 tablespoons mayonnaise and 1 tablespoon Dijon mustard. Season with salt and pepper and serve in a bowl alongside the toasted bread, with a smaller bowl of capers, green peppercorns, or crisp crumbled bacon alongside. Spoon some of the egg salad on the bread after drizzling it with olive oil and sprinkle with a bit of the capers, peppercorns, or bacon.
- Preheat the oven to 400 degrees. Set 3 asparagus spears, trimmed to fit, on top of each piece of bread after it has been rubbed with garlic. Top with a slice of Italian fontina, set on a sheet pan and bake for 2 to 3 minutes, until the cheese is just melted. Top with a turn of black pepper before serving.
- Cut 2 or 3 cleaned leeks (white and pale green parts only) into very thin slices, sauté in olive oil or butter until very tender, season with salt and remove from the heat. Spread over the bruschetta before seasoning with salt and pepper.

Summer & Fall

- Cut 2 or 3 ripe heirloom heirloom tomatoes into small dice, add 1 or 2 minced garlic cloves, some finely shredded basil and season with salt and pepper. Spoon on top of the bruschetta.
- Cut 2 cups of cherry tomatoes into quarters, add 1 or 2 minced cloves of garlic, a tablespoon of snipped chives and 2 teaspoons of red wine vinegar and toss gently. Spoon on top of the bruschetta and grate some cheese—Parmigiano-Reggiano, Vella Dry Jack, or similar cheese—on top and enjoy right away.
- Cut 1 avocado into small dice, toss with quartered cherry tomatoes, a minced serrano, and some chopped cilantro. Spoon over the bruschetta.

- Grate 2 or 3 small zucchini on the large blade of a box grater. Add 1 or 2 minced garlic cloves, a squeeze of lemon juice, and a bit of salt and pepper. Top the bruschetta with the mixture just before serving.
- Chop about ¾ cup shelled walnuts, preferably from the year's new crop, and lightly toast them. Toss with ¼ cup grated cheese, such as dry Jack or Parmigiano-Reggiano, 2 tablespoons chopped fresh Italian parsley, and 1 tablespoon chopped fresh sage. Spread over the bread before adding the olive oil, salt, and pepper.

Winter

- Mash 2 or 3 cups cooked white beans into a course puree, season with salt and pepper and add some minced fresh sage. Spread over bruschetta before drizzling with olive oil, and top with one or two fried sage leaves (recipe follows).
- Sauté winter greens in a little olive oil, add a pressed clove or two of garlic and the grated zest of 1 lemon. Serve on top of or alongside the bruschetta.
- Top bruschetta with cooked black eyed peas seasoned with salt and pepper and crumbled bacon.
- Sauté wild mushrooms in butter or olive oil, minced shallots, and a good splash of white wine until they are limp and tender. Season with salt and pepper, add some minced fresh Italian parsley, snipped chives or fresh thyme leaves and spoon over bruschetta just before serving.

Croutons

Makes 3 cups

Croutons are probably most familiar to us in Caesar salad, for which I typically use the version with garlic. You can use them in other salads, in soups, and in stuffing for poultry. When you find yourself with good bread that may go to waste, either make croutons or cut the bread into crouton size and freeze it to use for croutons at another time. This is a simple, foolproof method for making great croutons with a minimum of fuss. The quantities can easily be adjusted, and aromatics and spices can be added to accommodate specific recipes.

½ cup extra virgin olive oil
3 cups ¾-inch cubes of fresh or day-old sourdough bread
Kosher salt

Preheat the oven to 250 degrees.

Put the olive oil in a 1-quart Mason jar, add the bread, secure the lid and shake until the bread has absorbed all the oil and the cubes are evenly coated. Tip out the bread onto a baking sheet, spread it in an even layer, season lightly with salt, set on the middle rack of the oven and cook until dry and golden brown, from 12 to 20 minutes, depending on the type and age of bread. Cool, use immediately, or store in an air-tight container.

Variations:

- Pepper Croutons: After the croutons have absorbed the oil, add several generous turns of black pepper, close the jar and shake it again and continue as directed in the main recipe.
- Garlic Croutons: Press 3 or 4 cloves of garlic into the oil and shake well before adding the bread cubes.
- Cheese Croutons: After shaking the croutons with the oil, add ½ cup freshly grated Parmesan cheese to the jar and shake again to distribute the cheese evenly.

Baguette with Chévre, Prosciutto, Black Pepper & Meyer Lemon Olive Oil

Serves 3 to 4

The sandwich is both refreshing and satisfying. It is also a perfect way to showcase Meyer lemon olive oil.

½ cucumber, peeled, seeded, and minced
Kosher salt
8 ounces fresh chévre, such as Laura Chenel chabis
1 very fresh baguette, cut in half lengthwise
6 to 8 very thin slices of prosciutto
Black pepper in a mill
Extra virgin olive oil, preferably Meyer lemon olive oil

Put the cucumber into a small bowl, toss with a little salt, let rest for about 30 minutes and the tip into a strainer and press out the liquid that has formed.

Put the chévre into a small bowl, add the minced cucumber, taste, season with salt and mix with a fork until well blended.

Spread the cheese over the cut side of the bottom half of the baguette and layer the prosciutto on top. Season with several turns of black pepper.

Drizzle or brush the cut side of the top piece of the baguette with olive oil and set it, cut side down, on top of the prosciutto.

Press the sandwich together, cut into 3 or 4 sections and enjoy.

Portobello & Caciocavallo Sandwiches

Serves 2 to 4

This is a by-request sandwich, one I made for a now-forgotten event where I needed about 50 box lunches for vegetarians. Everything can be prepared in advance and then assembled at the last minute. The sandwich is best when the mushrooms are kept warm so that they melt the cheese a bit.

1 tablespoon balsamic vinegar
2 garlic cloves, crushed
Kosher salt
Black pepper in a mill
3 tablespoons extra virgin olive oil
1 large (8 to 10 ounces) portobello mushroom, stem removed
Olive mayonnaise, page 327
4 thin slices Caciacavallo or smoked mozzarella
2 sourdough rolls, cut open

Combine the vinegar and garlic in a medium bowl, season with salt and pepper and stir in the olive oil. Add the whole mushroom and turn it in the marinade to coat it. Let it rest for at least 1 hour or refrigerate it, covered, overnight.

Heat a stove top grill or ridged grill pan. When the grill is hot, set the mushroom on it, cap side down, and cook for about 7 minutes, giving it a 90-degree turn halfway through cooking to mark it. Turn the mushroom over and cook, cap side up, rotating the mushroom once, until it is completely tender, about 10 to 15 minutes, depending on the size of the mushroom and heat of the grill. Transfer to a work surface and let rest.

Toast the bread while the mushroom rests.

With your knife at a sharp angle, cut the mushroom into ¼-inch diagonal slices. Spread mayonnaise over the cut surfaces of the rolls and arrange sliced mushrooms on the bottom pieces. Season with salt and pepper, top with 2 pieces of cheese and close the sandwiches. Cut in half and serve immediately.

To drink:

Pinot Noir from Russian River Valley

Pacific Pan Bagnat

Serves 4

Pan bagnat is a classic sandwich from the south of France, where it is made with canned tuna and sold almost everywhere. The best one I've had was in the old town of Nyons, where I found a booth in the town square that offered them. We devoured them with greedy passion as olive oil, vinegar, and other juices dripped down our arms. What a memorable meal! I frequently make a version using Pacific King salmon, especially in those years when it is in abundance. When it is not available, I use the best canned tuna I can find.

2 ounces anchovy fillets, drained
2 tablespoons red wine vinegar
6 garlic cloves, minced
⅓ cup best-quality extra virgin olive oil
1 ½ cups cooked wild Pacific King salmon, broken into chunks (not too small)
2 tablespoons capers, rinsed, drained, and patted dry
2 teaspoons brined peppercorns
3 tablespoons pitted black olives, sliced
1 sourdough baguette
1 small red onion, peeled and very thinly sliced
2 to 3 hard-cooked farm eggs, peeled and sliced
Kosher salt
Black pepper in a mill

Put the anchovies into a small bowl, cover with the vinegar and set aside.

Put the garlic into a small bowl, add the olive oil and set aside.

Put the salmon into a medium bowl, add the capers, peppercorns, and black olives and toss together quickly. Do not overmix; the salmon should be distinctly chunky.

Slice the baguette in half lengthwise and open on a clean work surface.

Use a pastry brush to coat the cut surfaces of the bread with the olive oil and garlic, using all of it.

Spoon the salmon mixture onto the bottom half of the bread, covering the entire surface of the baguette, spreading it evenly and gently pressing it into the bread.

Scatter the onions on top of the salmon and season lightly with salt. Arrange the eggs on top, overlapping them slightly, and again season with salt and pepper.

Spoon the anchovies and vinegar over the cut side of the top half of the baguette, pressing it into bread.

Invert the top piece onto the sandwich and cut it into four pieces. Wrap each piece tightly in parchment or wax paper and then in plastic wrap. Set the sandwiches on a baking sheet or flat platter, top with a heavy cutting board and refrigerate at least 2 hours and as long as overnight.

Remove from the refrigerator 30 minutes before serving.

Variation:

For a traditional pan bagnat, replace the salmon with an equal amount of best-quality canned tuna, drained.

To drink:

A chilled dry rosé from either the South of France or California is a perfect quaffer with this sandwich.

Grilled Pizzas, Neat & with Toppings

Serves 4 to 6

Cooking pizza on a grill has become very popular and for good reason: It is delicious. It is also a fun way to entertain. You can make all the dough in advance and set up an area with ingredients so that guests can cook and assemble their own. Teenagers love it and so do adults. Be sure to use a good olive oil, as there is no tomato sauce to mask its taste.

Four 8- to 10-inch rounds of pizza dough (see recipe, this page)
Extra virgin olive oil
Flake salt
Crushed red pepper flakes

Prepare the pizza dough.

Build a fire in an outdoor grill.

Cut the dough in half and cut both pieces in half again. Use your hands to slowly stretch both pieces into roundish disks; do not worry about being precise. Grill the stretched doughs over direct heat until the dough becomes firm and is lightly toasted, about 1 to 2 minutes. Turn the dough over and cook until the other side is lightly toasted and the crusts are cooked through and golden brown. Transfer to a work surface.

Cut the pizzas into pieces, set on a platter, drizzle with olive oil, sprinkle with salt and red pepper flakes and serve immediately.

Topping Suggestions:

Add after turning:

- Olive oil, thinly sliced mozzarella fresca, halved cherry tomatoes, flake salt, black pepper
- Olive oil, grated Scamorza or similar cheese, thinly sliced soppressata
- Olive oil, thin slices of prosciutto, black pepper; top with young arugula after removing from the grill
- Olive oil, sautéed wild mushrooms, and a farm egg; leave on the grill until egg white is set; flake salt and pepper

Add after removing from grill:

- Tapenade of choice
- Creme fraiche, minced herbs, olive oil, flake salt, black pepper

Relatively Fast Pizza Dough

Makes four 8- to 10-inch shells

Some recipes for pizza dough require 6 to 8 hours for rising, a slow process that results in outstanding flavors and textures. Yet those recipes require more advance planning than this one, which gives excellent results in less than half the time. You can decide in the afternoon that you want homemade pizza for dinner. This recipe can easily be doubled, though you should not increase the quantity of yeast.

2 teaspoons active dry yeast
1 ⅓ cups warm water
4 ½ to 5 cups all-purpose flour
1 teaspoon salt
6 teaspoons extra virgin olive oil

Combine the yeast and water in a large mixing bowl, and set aside for 10 minutes. Use a whisk to stir in 1 cup flour, the salt, and the olive oil. Add more flour, ½ cup at a time, until you have 1 cup remaining. As the dough thickens, switch from a whisk to a wooden spoon.

Turn the dough out onto a heavily floured surface and knead it until it is smooth and velvety, about 7 minutes, working in as much of the remaining flour as the dough will take. Brush a large, clean bowl lightly with olive oil, set the dough in the bowl, and cover it with a damp towel. Let the dough rise for 3 hours, until it has more than doubled in size. Gently turn the dough onto a lightly floured work surface and let it rest for 5 minutes.

Cut the dough into 3 or 4 equal pieces. Use the heel of your hand to press the dough into a flat circle and then use both hands to pick it up. Hold the dough perpendicular to your work surface and move your hands around its outer edges, shaking gently as you do. If it doesn't stretch easily, put one hand on either side of the disk and pull gently until the dough is about ¼ inch thick, or slightly thinner. The edges will be thicker. Using your hand or a floured rolling pin, flatten it into a 12-inch circle about ⅜ inch thick. Top the dough and bake as directed in specific recipes.

Variation:

When you're first working with dough, you might be nervous during the stretching part. Instead of using your hands, sprinkle your work surface with flour, flatten the dough into a disk, and use a floured rolling pin to stretch it into a circle. As you become more comfortable, try stretching by hand until you get the hang of it.

Soups

Soup, soup, beautiful soup, who doesn't love a well-made soup? In this chapter, I feature my favorite soups that rely on oil or vinegar to shape their essential character, so that were it to be omitted, the soup would be entirely different and likely diminished.

One important category of soups is not included here and that is contemporary gazpachos, which almost always include a good vinegar and excellent olive oil. I tell their story in *The Good Cook's Book of Tomatoes* and here feature just two, one that honors the original gazpacho, enjoyed in Spain long before the love apple made its way across the Atlantic, and a refreshing fruit gazpacho.

Many other soups benefit from a swirl of olive oil, a shake of toasted sesame oil, or a splash of vinegar, added at the table, as a condiment. If you agree, the best way to do this is to simply keep cruets of each on your dining table.

Garlic Soup with Fresh Herbs & Garlic Croutons

Serves 4 to 6

This soup is best in late spring, when there is a new crop of garlic that has not yet been cured. This garlic is plump and juicy and makes a delightful, delicate soup; look for young garlic at farmers markets.

2 tablespoons olive oil
2 cups young garlic cloves, peeled
Kosher salt
6 cups homemade chicken stock
1 ¼ cups fresh herbs, loosely packed (a mixture of Italian parsley, thyme, oregano, chives, sage, and summer savory)
½ cup heavy cream
½ cup freshly grated Asiago cheese
Black pepper in a mill
Garlic croutons, page 124
Aïoli, page 332 to 333

Put the olive oil in a large saucepan set over medium-low heat, add the garlic, season with salt and stir gently for 2 minutes. Pour in the stock and 1 cup of the herbs, bring to a boil, reduce the heat and skim off any foam that forms on the surface. Reduce the heat to low and simmer gently until the garlic is tender, about 20 minutes.

Remove from the heat, cool slightly and puree with an immersion blender until very smooth. (For a more refined soup, strain through a fine sieve into a clean saucepan.) Return the soup to low heat, add the cream and the cheese and stir gently until the cheese is just melted; do not let the soup reach a boil.

Ladle into soup plates and top with croutons, some of the remaining herbs, and a big spoonful of aïoli, and serve right away.

Ajo Blanco

The Original Gazpacho

Serves 6 to 8

Gazpacho, typically thought of today as a chilled tomato soup with lots of vegetables, began as something quite different. It was a peasant dish, developed to use bread crumbs, bits of bread, and stale bread. It was thickened with crushed almonds and seasoned with vinegar and olive oil. At some point it became common to top the soup with sliced green grapes, a tradition that continues today, though I don't consider them essential.

- 5 to 6 ounces, approximately, sturdy hearth bread, a few days old, in pieces
- 5 or 6 garlic cloves
- Hot water
- 1 cup unpasteurized raw almonds, blanched and peeled
- 4 tablespoons sherry vinegar
- 1 teaspoon hot Spanish paprika
- Kosher salt
- Black pepper in a mill
- 6 tablespoons boldly flavored extra virgin olive oil, plus more for drizzling
- ½ cup sliced green grapes, see Note below
- ⅓ cup toasted and salted Marcona almonds

Put the bread into a deep bowl and pour water to cover it. Set aside for at least 30 minutes and as long as a couple of hours. Put the garlic into a small bowl, cover it with hot water and set it aside for the same amount of time.

When the bread is very soft, squeeze out as much water as possible and put the wet bread into the work bowl of a food processor fitted with its metal blade. Drain the garlic and add it to the bread, along with the almonds and sherry. Add 1 cup of water and pulse several times, until the mixture is smooth and even. Add the paprika, season very generously with salt and add several turns of black pepper. Pulse several more times and then slowly drizzle in the olive oil, with the machine operating.

Taste the soup and adjust for salt, adding as much as needed to make the flavors blossom. Adjust for acid balance, too, adding a bit more vinegar if not tart enough and a bit more olive oil if too tart.

Pour the soup into a bowl or other container and chill thoroughly. For a more refined soup, strain it before chilling it.

To serve, pour into small cups or little bowls and add a swirl of olive oil to each portion. Top with a few grape slices and a few almonds and enjoy right away.

NOTE

Grapes have a brief season in late summer and early fall. When they are not in season where you live, use pomegranates if they are available, as they should be from late September through December. At other times, simply serve the soup without fruit.

Fall Fruit Gazpacho

Serves 4 to 8

I love this soup on those scorching fall days when it is nearly too hot to eat. Served ice cold, it is refreshing, cooling, and elegantly evocative of childhood afternoons spent eating as much watermelon as my mother would let me have. For the best results, use melons grown close to where you live and make this only when they are in season.

3 cups yellow or watermelon, seeded and minced
1 cup minced orange musk melon, Crane, cantaloupe, or orange Honeydew
1 cup dry white wine, still or sparkling
1 serrano chili pepper, minced
4 cups mixed melon cubes (¼ inch)
Juice of ½ lime
2 tablespoons unseasoned rice vinegar or pineapple vinegar
4 or 5 peppermint leaves, cut into a very thin julienne
1 tablespoon chopped cilantro leaves
Small sprigs of mint and cilantro for garnish
¼ cup pomegranate seeds, optional

Put the minced melons, wine, and serrano into large bowl, cover and set aside for 30 minutes. Set a food mill or large strainer over a deep bowl, pass the mixture through it and discard what is left behind.

Stir the cubed melon, lime juice, vinegar, peppermint, and cilantro, stir, cover and chill for at least 2 hours and as long as overnight.

To serve, ladle into chilled bowls or soup plates. Garnish with mint, cilantro, and pomegranate arils, if using. Serve right away.

Avocado Soup
with Radishes & Cilantro Cream

Serves 4 to 6

Avocados have a mildly nutty flavor that is enhanced by using either walnut oil or avocado oil. You can make the soup and the cilantro cream a day in advance, but it is best to prepare the radishes just an hour or two before serving, so that they remain pleasantly crisp. This refreshing soup is ideal on a hot summer night.

2 tablespoons avocado oil or walnut oil
1 medium yellow onion, cut into small dice
4 garlic cloves, peeled and minced
½-inch piece of fresh ginger, grated
3 serranos, stemmed, seeded, and minced
Kosher salt
4 cups homemade chicken stock
3 medium-ripe avocados
2 limes, plus more as needed
½ cup creme fraiche
¼ cup chopped fresh cilantro leaves
1 teaspoon ground coriander
1 bunch radishes, trimmed
Black pepper in a mill

Pour 2 tablespoons of the oil into a large saucepan set over medium-low heat, add the onion and sauté until soft and fragrant, about 7 to 10 minutes. Add the garlic, ginger, and half the serranos, sauté 2 minutes more and season with salt. Add the stock, simmer for 10 minutes, remove from the heat, cover and let cool to room temperature.

Meanwhile, cut the avocados in half, remove the pits, scoop out the flesh, put it into a bowl and add the juice of 1 lime. Season with salt and toss gently. When the stock has cooled to room temperature, whisk in the avocado and then strain into a large bowl, using a sturdy wooden spoon to press the avocado and all juices through the strainer into the bowl. Taste, correct for salt and pepper, cover and refrigerate for at least three hours and as long as overnight.

To make the cilantro cream, put the creme fraiche into a bowl, add the remaining serrano and remaining tablespoon of oil, the juice of ½ lime, the cilantro, and the coriander. Stir and season to taste with salt. Cover and refrigerate until ready to use.

Shortly before serving, cut the radishes into small julienne, toss with the juice of ½ lime and season with salt.

To serve, taste the soup and correct for salt and acid. Ladle into soup plates, add a generous dollop of cilantro cream to each serving, top with radishes, grind black pepper on top and serve right away.

The Simplest White Bean Soup

Serves 6

There are more complex versions of this traditional Tuscan soup, some that include meat, one in which the soup is poured over thick slices of olive oil–drenched bread. I first made this version to show off a fabulous olive oil I carried home from a monastery in the hill country east of Siena, Italy. The deep green oil sparkles in little pools on the white canvas of the soup, offering a feast for the eye as well as the palate. For best results, use the very best beans and the very best olive oil you can find.

1 pound white beans, such as marrowfats or cannellini
1 onion, white or yellow, cut into small dice
8 large garlic cloves, peeled
Kosher salt
6 ounces (1 ½) cups freshly grated Parmigiano-Reggiano
Black pepper in a mill
Best-quality extra virgin olive oil

Rinse the beans under cool water and pick through them to remove any small rocks or other varieties of bean.

Put them into a clay bean pot or large saucepan, set over medium heat and slowly bring to a boil. (If using a bean pot, follow the manufacturer's instructions.) Reduce the heat, skim off any foam that rises to the surface and cook until the beans have begun to soften. Add the onion and garlic, season with salt and continue to cook until the beans are very tender; add water as needed so that the beans do not dry out or scorch.

Remove from the heat, let cool slightly and puree with an immersion blender until very smooth. Return to low heat, stir in the cheese, taste, correct for salt and season very generously with black pepper.

Ladle into soup plates, drizzle with olive oil and serve right away.

This soup will keep well, properly refrigerated, for several days.

Variation:

If you have true aceto balsamico tradizionale, this is a perfect dish to highlight it. Immediately before serving the soup, use an eyedropper to add 5 or 6 small droplets on each portion. Serve right away.

Chickpea Soup with Sautéed Celery, Feta & Black Olive Tapenade

Serves 6 to 8

This soup has the same flavors as a favorite salad—garbanzos, celery, feta, and olives—but in an entirely different context. If you're craving intense flavors, this is perfect. If you'd like bread alongside, use pita, warmed until soft and tender but not crisp.

1 pound dried chickpeas, cooked until tender, or three 15-ounce cans garbanzo beans
4 tablespoons olive oil
1 small yellow onion, minced
1 small celery rib, minced
6 garlic cloves, minced
Kosher salt
Black pepper in a mill
4 cups chicken or vegetable stock
4 medium celery ribs, cut into thin diagonal slices
4 tablespoons black olive tapenade, page 91
2 to 3 ounces feta cheese, crumbled

Cook the chickpeas or rinsed canned ones, if using. Set aside briefly.

Put 2 tablespoons of the olive oil into a medium soup pot set over medium-low heat, add the onion and celery and sauté until soft and fragrant, about 12 minutes. Add the garlic, sauté 2 minutes more and season with salt and pepper.

Add the beans, the stock, and enough water to completely cover the beans and simmer gently for 15 minutes.

Meanwhile, pour the remaining olive oil into a small sauté pan, add the celery and sauté until it just loses its crunch. Season with salt and pepper and remove from the heat.

Remove the soup from the heat, cool briefly and puree with an immersion blender, adding water as needed for the proper consistency. Taste and correct for salt. Reheat if necessary.

Ladle into soup plates and add a generous spoonful of tapenade. Scatter sautéed celery and feta cheese on top and serve immediately.

Roasted Fennel Soup with Hazelnut Gremolata

Serves 4 to 8

I developed this soup to pair with a California-style Chardonnay, a wine that is among the hardest to pair successfully, despite its popularity. The wine was dry but with overtones of sweetness and an aroma of hazelnuts and so I added two vegetables that are naturally sweet—fennel and parsnips—and both hazelnuts and hazelnut oil. It was a beautiful match.

1 pound parsnips, trimmed, peeled, and cut in large chunks
¾ pound fennel bulbs (preferably 1 large bulb), trimmed and quartered
5 or 6 garlic cloves, peeled
Olive oil
Kosher salt
Dry white wine
Hazelnut Gremolata (recipe follows)
1 yellow onion, cut into small dice
1 large (about ¾ pound) potato, such as German Butterball, peeled and thinly sliced
4 cups homemade chicken stock or vegetable broth
6 ounces grated Asiago or similar cheese
White pepper in a mill
Unrefined hazelnut oil

Preheat the oven to 350 degrees.

Put the parsnips and fennel into an oven-proof dish, tuck the garlic cloves here and there, drizzle with olive oil, toss and season with salt. Pour in about ¼ inch of wine. Cover, set in the oven and cook until the vegetables are very tender, about 40 minutes.

Remove from the oven and let cool slightly.

Meanwhile, make the gremolata and set it aside.

Pour a little olive oil into a medium saucepan set over medium-low heat, add the onion and sauté until very soft and fragrant, about 20 minutes. Add the potatoes, cook 2 minutes more and season with salt. Add the stock or broth and simmer gently until the potatoes are just tender, about 15 minutes.

Add the parsnips, fennel and garlic, along with the pan juices to the stock mixture and simmer together gently for about 10 minutes.

Remove from the heat and cool slightly. Use an immersion blender to puree the soup and return it to very low heat. Stir in the cheese, taste, correct for salt and season with several turns of pepper.

Ladle into soup plates, top with a spoonful of gremolata and a drizzle of hazelnut oil and serve right away.

Hazelnut Gremolata

Makes about 6 tablespoons

3 tablespoons hazelnuts, lightly toasted and chopped
Grated zest of 1 orange
2 tablespoons fresh snipped chives
Kosher salt or other flake salt
White pepper in a mill

Put the hazelnuts into a small bowl, add the orange zest and chives and toss gently. Season lightly with salt and a few turns of pepper, toss again, cover and set aside until ready to use.

Gremolata is best used the day it is made.

Roasted Carrot Soup with Toasted Coconut

Serves 4 to 6

When I wrote the first edition of this book, I called for coconut cream as well as coconut milk, as it was hard to find really good carrots. Now they are a staple at farmers markets throughout the country and I no longer find that the sweetness of the coconut cream is necessary. If, however, the finished soup tastes a tad flat, adding a pinch of sugar should perk it right up.

1 pound organic carrots, preferably Nantes variety, trimmed and peeled
3 shallots, trimmed and peeled
Olive oil
Kosher salt
Black pepper in a mill
2 tablespoons coconut oil or mild olive oil
2 garlic cloves, minced
1 tablespoon freshly grated ginger
2 teaspoons ground cumin
1 teaspoon coriander seed, crushed
¾ teaspoon ground cardamom
3 cups homemade chicken stock or vegetable stock
One 14-ounce can coconut milk
1 tablespoon lime juice
2 tablespoons chopped fresh cilantro leaves
2 tablespoons shredded coconut, lightly toasted

Preheat the oven to 350 degrees.

Put the carrots and shallots into a roasting pan or on a baking sheet, drizzle with a little olive oil and toss to coat them thoroughly. Season with salt and pepper. Set on the middle rack of the oven and roast until tender when pierced with a fork. This will take about 45 minutes, a little less if the carrots are small, a bit longer if they are particularly big. Turn the vegetables now and then so that they don't burn. Set aside to cool. When easy to handle, cut the shallots into small dice and cut the carrots into thin slices.

Put the coconut oil or olive oil into a large saucepan or soup pot set over medium heat, add the shallots, garlic, and ginger and sauté for 90 seconds.

Add the cumin, coriander, and cardamom and season with salt. Stir in the carrots, add the stock and simmer gently over low heat for 15 minutes.

Stir in the coconut milk and lime juice, heat through and remove from the heat. Puree thoroughly with an immersion blender.

Season the soup very generously with black pepper and correct for salt.

Ladle into soup plates, garnish with cilantro leaves and toasted coconut and serve right away.

To drink:

This soup is ideal with a dry or slightly off-dry gewurztraminer or riesling.

To drink:

If you love Chardonnay, this soup is a perfect companion. A lighter-style Pinot Noir also flatters this soup.

Roasted Red Pepper Soup with Toasted Coriander Cream

Serves 4 to 6

Roasted peppers provide one of the more delicious flavors of all vegetables. The transformation they go through between the raw and roasted states amazes me. This soup takes advantage of that rich flavor, which is enhanced by the addition of the balsamic vinegar.

3 tablespoons olive oil
1 medium yellow onion, diced
8 garlic cloves, minced
Kosher salt
Black pepper in a mill
2 teaspoons toasted coriander seed, crushed
1 teaspoon ground cumin
½ teaspoon ground cardamom
6 large sweet red peppers, roasted, cooled, peeled, seeded, and chopped
¼ cup Rainwater Madeira
4 cups homemade chicken stock
3 to 4 tablespoons balsamic vinegar
3 tablespoons creme fraiche
Juice of 1 lime
2 tablespoons chopped fresh cilantro

Pour the olive oil into a large saucepan set over medium-low heat, add the onion and sauté until very soft and fragrant, about 20 minutes. Add the garlic and sauté 2 minutes more.

Season with salt, add several turns of black pepper and stir in the coriander, cumin, and cardamom. Add the peppers, stir, increase the heat and pour in the Madeira. Simmer for 2 minutes, pour in the chicken stock, bring to a boil, reduce the heat and simmer very gently for 15 minutes.

Remove from the heat and let cool slightly.

While the soup cools, put the creme fraiche into a small bowl, add the lime juice and parsley, season with salt and pepper, stir and set aside.

Use an immersion blender to puree the soup, return it to the heat and stir in 3 tablespoons of balsamic vinegar. Taste, correct for salt and pepper and add the remaining tablespoon of vinegar for balance, if needed. The soup should be rich and slightly sweet from the peppers, with just an edge of tartness. If it tastes a bit flat, add a pinch of sugar and a pinch of salt. Taste again and adjust as needed.

To serve, ladle into soup plates, add a generous swirl of creme fraiche, grind pepper on top and serve right away.

Variation:

The soup is also delicious chilled. Simply cover it and refrigerate it overnight, taste, correct the seasoning, ladle into soup plates, top with a swirl of creme fraiche and serve.

Golden Beet Borscht

Serves 4

Delicate and subtle, this soup is an evocative starter to any meal and particularly delightful when the menu has Mediterranean or specifically Greek overtones. The yogurt mixture that crowns the golden liquid is a variation of traditional tzatzíki, a Greek yogurt and cucumber salad to which I have added chives.

3 tablespoons olive oil, plus more as needed
1 yellow onion, diced
1 small carrot, diced
1 medium russet potato, diced
Kosher salt
Black pepper in a mill
1 teaspoon minced fresh ginger
1 teaspoon ground cumin
3 cups chicken or beef stock
1 pound golden beets, roasted until tender, peeled and diced
⅓ cup apple cider vinegar or sherry vinegar
1 small cucumber, peeled, seeded, and minced
3 garlic cloves, minced
3 tablespoons snipped chives
8 ounces plain whole milk yogurt
1 teaspoon whole cumin seeds, lightly toasted
Whole chives, for garnish

Pour the olive oil into a heavy saucepan set over medium-low heat, add the onion and sauté until it is soft and fragrant, about 15 minutes. Add the carrot and potatoes, season with salt and cook for 5 minutes. Add several turns of black pepper, along with the ginger and cumin.

Pour in the stock and simmer for about 15 minutes, until the potatoes are almost tender. Add the beets and vinegar and simmer 15 minutes more.

Meanwhile, put the minced cucumber into a colander or strainer, toss with salt and let drain for 20 minutes. Squeeze out excess liquid and transfer to a small bowl. Add the garlic, snipped chives, and yogurt, taste and season as needed with salt and pepper. Set aside.

Remove the soup from the heat and let cool slightly. Puree with an immersion blender and, for a more suave soup, pass it through a fine sieve. Reheat as needed.

To serve, ladle into soup plates and top with a generous dollop of the yogurt. Sprinkle with a bit of cumin seed, garnish with whole chives and serve right away.

Garden Minestrone

Serves 8 to 10

You should vary the ingredients in this soup depending on the season. You can make it in the spring, when the first peas ripen. Try it again when the zucchini are still tiny, about as big as your little finger, and the first Blue Lake green beans beckon. The marvelous thing about this soup, really, is that it is good any time you make it, and rich and nourishing without being heavy.

1 cup olive oil
1 yellow onion, in small dice
3 carrots, in small dice
2 leeks, trimmed with just 2 inches of green remaining, very thinly sliced
1 stalk celery, in small dice
Kosher salt
1 ½ pounds fresh Roma tomatoes, peeled and sliced or neo 28-ounce can sliced tomatoes
1 pound small new red potatoes, in medium dice
2 quarts beef stock
¼ pound pancetta, in small dice
1 head garlic, cloves separated, peeled, and minced
3 tablespoons Italian parsley, finely chopped
1 tablespoon fresh oregano
1 pound baby zucchini or 4 small to medium zucchini
2 cups cooked cannellini or other white beans
6 ounces small dried pasta, such as ditalini, tripolini, farfallini, or small shells
Black pepper in a mill
6 ounces grated aged Asiago or similar cheese

Heat the olive oil in a large soup pot set over very low heat. Add the onion, carrots, leeks, and celery and sauté until the vegetables are very soft, about 25 minutes. Season with salt.

Add the tomatoes, potatoes, and the beef stock and simmer until the potatoes are almost tender, about 12 to 15 minutes.

Meanwhile, sauté the pancetta in a little olive oil until it begins to lose its raw color. Add the minced garlic, sauté for another 2 minutes, add the parsley and oregano, remove from the heat, and add to the soup mixture, along with the zucchini, cannellini beans, and pasta. Simmer until the pasta is tender, about 7 to 10 minutes, depending on the pasta's size.

Remove the soup from the heat and let it rest until ready to serve. Correct for salt and pepper, heat through if necessary and ladle into soup bowls. Add grated cheese to each portion and serve right away.

Variation:

In the summer when basil is in season, stir a little chopped fresh basil into the soup and top with a generous dollop of pesto, page 336, instead of the cheese.

Crab Soup with Olive Oil & Garlic

Serves 4 to 6

This is a very simple recipe, perfect when you have an abundance of fresh crab and have already eaten your fill of it neat. Once you have the crab, you can make it in minutes and it is suitable for both the most humble weeknight dinner and the fanciest dinner party.

½ cup extra virgin olive oil, plus more for drizzling
3 garlic cloves, very thinly sliced
1 teaspoon red pepper flakes
1 tablespoon tomato paste
½ cup dry white wine
Meat from 2 Dungeness crab
1 ½ cups shellfish stock (see Note below)
1 tablespoon minced fresh oregano
1 tablespoon minced fresh Italian parsley
Kosher salt
Black pepper in a mill
Hot crusty sourdough bread

Heat the ½ cup olive oil in a heavy, 8-cup saucepan over medium-high heat. Add the garlic and fry, tossing frequently, until it turns golden brown. Be careful not to burn it. Stir in the pepper flakes, tomato paste, wine, and shellfish broth and simmer for 5 minutes. Add the crab, cover, and cook for 2 minutes more. Add the oregano and parsley, and season to taste with salt and pepper. Ladle into individual shallow soup bowls and serve with hot bread alongside.

NOTE

To make shellfish stock, reserve the shells from the legs, claws, and body of the crab. Put the shells into a pot and cover with 3 cups fish fumet or light chicken stock or broth. Cover and simmer for 30 minutes. Strain, return the stock to a clean saucepan, and reduce to 1 ½ cups.

Hot & Sour Soup, My Way

Serves 4 to 6

Hot and Sour Soup is a staple in Chinese-American restaurants and I've eaten countless versions, most often leaving behind a little pile of firm tofu, as I have no taste for it. When making it at home, I often use left-over shredded pork in its place. In this version, there are subtle layers of heat from peppercorns; if you want more heat, add a splash of hot chili oil.

2 tablespoons cornstarch
2 tablespoons coconut oil
3 leeks, thoroughly washed, white and pale green parts only, very thinly sliced
3 tablespoons grated fresh ginger
3 garlic cloves, minced
Kosher salt
4 cups fresh specialty mushroom (see Note) or 12 dried Chinese black mushrooms, refreshed in hot water for 30 minutes and drained
4 cups homemade chicken stock
3 tablespoon rice vinegar
2 teaspoons freshly cracked black pepper
1 teaspoon freshly cracked white pepper
3 tablespoons Chinese black vinegar
2 tablespoons soy sauce, plus more to taste
1 pound cooked and shredded pork shoulder or 1 pound dried tofu, cut into medium julienne
1 egg, beaten
½ cup cilantro leaves, chopped
2 teaspoons toasted sesame oil
Hot chili oil, page 304

Put the cornstarch into a medium bowl, add ¼ cup water, stir well and set aside.

Put the coconut oil into a soup pot or large saucepan set over medium-low heat, add the leeks, toss and sauté very gently until they are fully wilted and begin to soften. Add the ginger and garlic, sauté 2 minutes more and season with salt. Add the mushroom, stir and cook for 2 minutes.

Add the chicken stock and rice vinegar. Simmer gently for about 5 minutes, skimming off any impurities that rise to the surface. Stir in the peppers, black vinegar and soy sauce, taste and correct for acid and salt balance. Add the pork or tofu, simmer until heated through, about 3 to 4 minutes.

Remove from the heat.

Add a small ladle of the stock to the cornstarch mixture and stir until smooth. Add another ladle and stir again. Pour this slurry into the soup, return to low heat and simmer gently for a few minutes, until the soup thickens. Carefully add the beaten egg, pouring very slowly in large concentric circles. When the egg loses its raw look, stir gently once or twice.

To serve, ladle into soup bowls, top with cilantro and a dash of sesame oil. Serve right away, with the hot chili oil alongside.

NOTE

Although not traditional, I like to make this soup with either black trumpets or Hen of the Woods (maitake) mushrooms, as they are abundant where I live.

Eggs

Have you ever watched hens busy at the business of being hens? It is fascinating to see them as they forage for bugs, nestle down into the dirt for a dust bath, which keeps them free of mites, and reinforce their pecking order. The best shows are put on by happy chickens with lots of room and the very best include a wide range of breeds, some that look like they just fell from another planet.

At night, hens put themselves to bed, as they have extremely poor night vision. If there is a rooster in the flock, he typically gets things started, taking his position on the right of the highest perch. The hen who is highest in the pecking order sits next to him and on and on it goes, by what I guess can be called social standing, the lowliest of the hens sitting on the bottom perch at the far left, as far away as possible from the rooster and the reigning female. Chickens, as they run along foraging, may seem to be moving at random but they actually have a highly organized society.

Once you have seen such flocks and tasted their delicious eggs, it becomes impossible to be satisfied with commercial supermarket eggs, laid by hens confined in small cages stacked on top of one another and subjected to 24-hour light and without any ability to do the many things hens naturally do. I can't eat these eggs and I can't recommend them. Find an alternative source and a whole world of deliciousness opens up to you, including olive oil–poached eggs over greens and eggs scrambled slowly in extra virgin olive oil, just two of the delicious dishes you'll find in this chapter.

The Best Eggs in the World

Serves 2 to 3, easily doubled

This dish came to me by way of Ridgely Evers of DaVero, who described it to me and suggested I head home immediately to make it. I did, for breakfast the next morning. On the DaVero website, Ridgely and his wife Colleen McGlynn give credit for the dish to Ray Tang, most recently of the Presidio Social Club in San Francisco, a mutual friend and fabulous chef, one of the finest I know. This is a lovely breakfast dish, it's good for dinner on a Sunday evening and maybe best late at night, when you're winding down after a celebration.

7 large farm eggs
Kosher salt
Extra virgin olive oil
2 tablespoons DaVero Sparklers, optional
Black pepper in a mill

Gently break the eggs into a bowl, season with salt, use a fork to break each yolk and gently mix the eggs a bit.

Set a medium sturdy non-stick sauté pan over low heat and add about an 1/8 inch of oil to the pan. Let it warm for a couple of minutes, add the sparklers, if using, and the eggs.

Do nothing for about 2 minutes and then begin to push and stir the eggs very gently, using a wooden spoon or wooden spatula. Work slowly, being careful not to manipulate the eggs too much.

The eggs will come together in gentle curds almost all at once. When they are soft scrambled, use a slotted spoon to divide them among individual bowls. Season with salt and pepper and enjoy right away.

Vinegar Eggs with Bacon

Serves 2

Here is an easy way to turn vinegar eggs into a full meal, perfect any time of day.

6 thick rashers bacon, cut into ½-inch crosswise strips
2 large handfuls of frisee, rinsed, dried, and torn into bite-sized pieces
Kosher salt
Black pepper in a mill
6 tablespoons butter
4 large farm eggs
4 thick slices hearth bread, preferably sourdough, lightly toasted
6 tablespoons best-quality red wine vinegar, such as B. R. Cohn Cabernet Vinegar

Cook the bacon in a medium frying pan until it is almost but not quite crisp.

While the bacon cooks, put the frisee into a bowl, season it with salt and pepper and set it aside.

Warm 2 plates in a slow (200 degrees) oven.

Melt all but 2 tablespoons of the butter in a medium frying pan set over medium-low heat. When the butter is foamy, slip the eggs, one at a time, into the pan, cover and cook the eggs slowly, until the whites are firm but the yolks runny, about 2 to 3 minutes.

Set the bread on the plates, add frisee alongside and slip the eggs on top.

Quickly return the pan to high heat, add the vinegar and swirl to deglaze the pan and reduce the vinegar to 2 tablespoons. Add the remaining butter and swirl the pan gently until it is melted; do not let it boil. Remove from the heat, taste the sauce and season with salt and pepper. Pour the sauce over the eggs.

Scatter bacon and a bit of its drippings over everything and serve right away.

Eggs Poached in Olive Oil with Hot Sauce

Serves 2 to 4

Are these eggs fried or poached? I supposed, technically, they are deep-fried but I use the same little saucepan that I use for poaching eggs in water and I use enough moderately priced olive oil to completely submerge the eggs, one at a time, and so I think of them as oil-poached. Whatever you call them, they are both beautiful and delicious. Sometimes I top them with homemade hot sauce or a hot sauce from a favorite farmers market vendor and sometimes I use Tabasco Green Pepper Sauce, which I love for both its tart vinegar flavor and bright green fire.

4 farm eggs, at room temperature
Extra virgin olive oil
Flake salt
Black pepper in a mill
Vinegar-based hot sauce of choice
4 slices hearth bread, lightly toasted

Pour about 2 ½ inches of olive oil into a very small deep saucepan and set over medium-high heat.

While the oil heats, break an egg into a small bowl and set small serving bowls near the stove. Have the condiments and toast ready.

When the oil's temperature reaches about 360 degrees—use a candy thermometer to measure—tip one egg into the hot oil and immediately break another egg into the bowl. Cook the egg for 30 seconds, use a large slotted spoon to tip it over in the oil and then immediately lift it out of the oil and set it in a serving dish.

Continue until all eggs have been cooked.

Season with salt, pepper, and hot sauce and serve right away, with toast alongside.

Enjoy while the oil cools completely. You can save the oil to use to cook eggs another time or two. Simply strain the cooled oil into a glass jar and store in a cool, dark cupboard.

Variations:

- Serve on top of fresh greens, with a simple vinaigrette.
- Serve on top of roasted asparagus.

Wilted Lettuce with Egg Mimosa

Serves 3 to 4

Egg mimosa is a term that refers to hard-cooked eggs that are grated or pressed through a sieve, so that they become light and fluffy. Here, it enlivens a traditional dish I've enjoyed since childhood, when my grandmother made it for her fifth husband, a stern Austrian man whom I knew as Uncle Ed.

6 cups red-leaf lettuce, cut into ⅓-inch crosswise strips
Kosher salt
3 slices bacon, diced
1 tablespoon sugar
⅓ cup medium-acid red wine vinegar
2 hard-cooked eggs, shelled and grated with a small blade
Black pepper in a mill

Put the lettuce in a wide, shallow bowl, sprinkle it lightly with salt, toss gently and set aside.

Cook the bacon in a small sauté pan until it is just crisp, add the sugar and red wine vinegar, and heat until the mixture is hot and bubbling. Pour the dressing over the lettuce, toss quickly and season with several turns of pepper. Taste and correct for salt.

Scatter the egg on top, season with a little more salt and several turns of black pepper and serve right away.

Kermit's Vinegar Eggs

Serves 1

Kermit Lynch, a wine merchant in Berkeley, California, and the author of Adventures on the Wine Route *(Farrar, Straus and Giroux, 2013) included this recipe in one of his monthly newsletters and I immediately wrote him a letter–a real letter, by snail mail–asking his permission to include it in the first edition of this book. He responded with an enthusiastic yes!*

I love everything about it, from the spirit in which it is written to the ingredients and the underlying passion for good living that it reveals. It is also delicious, one of my all-time favorite dishes.

"This is not breakfast!" Kermit emphasizes.

1 bottle good of Beaujolais
2 farm eggs
Butter, preferably grass-fed
Kosher salt
Black pepper in a mill
2 tablespoons red wine vinegar
Good hearth bread

First you pour yourself a glass of cool Beaujolais. Then you fry fresh eggs slowly in butter, covered, until the whites are firm but the yolks remain runny. Add salt and pepper and then slide the eggs out onto a warm platter. Deglaze the pan with the vinegar and reduce it by half. Thicken the sauce with a slice of butter and pour it over your eggs. You will want bread or toast for sopping up the sauce.

You will also want another glass of Beaujolais.

Roasted Asparagus with Poached Eggs & Warm Shallot Vinaigrette

Serves 3 to 4

If you serve this delicious dish as the first course of a larger meal, you'll want to allow a single egg per person. If you serve it as a main course at breakfast, lunch, or dinner, allow 2 eggs per person. For variations, consult the end of the recipe.

16 to 20 fat asparagus stalks
Olive oil
Kosher salt
2 shallots, minced
2 garlic cloves, minced
4 tablespoons Champagne or white wine vinegar
3 to 8 large farm eggs
Black pepper in a mill
6 tablespoons extra virgin olive oil
1 lemon, cut in wedges

Preheat the oven to 450 degrees.

Snap off the tough stalks of the asparagus, set it on a baking sheet and drizzle with a little olive oil. Turn the asparagus in the olive oil so that each stalk is lightly and evenly coated. Season lightly with salt and set aside.

Pour a little olive oil into a small sauté pan, add the shallots and set over medium-low heat. Sauté until soft and fragrant, about 7 minutes. Add the garlic and sauté 2 minutes more. Season with salt, add 2 tablespoons of the vinegar and remove from the heat.

Put the asparagus into the preheated oven and cook until tender, from 7 to 12 minutes.

Fill a large wide saucepan half full with water (about 4 inches deep), add the remaining vinegar and bring to a boil over high heat. Reduce the heat so that the water simmers.

When the asparagus is cooked, arrange it on three to four warmed plates.

Working quickly, break an egg into a bowl and carefully slide it into the simmering water. Quickly add 3 more eggs, one at a time. Cook for

90 seconds; if you prefer the yolks slightly firmer, cook 30 seconds more. Use a slotted spoon to lift out an egg, shake off the water and set alongside the asparagus.

Continue until all of the eggs have been cooked; season the eggs lightly with salt.

Return the pan with the shallots to a medium flame, season with several turns of black pepper, add the olive oil and heat through. Taste and correct for salt.

Spoon the warm vinaigrette over each portion, scatter with chives, garnish with lemon wedges and serve immediately.

Variations:

- With Green Peppercorns: Drain 2 teaspoons of green peppercorns and add to the shallot and garlic mixture along with the vinegar.
- With Smoked Salmon: Drape 1 or 2 slices of smoked salmon over each portion of asparagus before adding the poached eggs.
- With Bacon: Sauté 3 or 4 slices of bacon until crisp, transfer the bacon to absorbent paper and pour off all but 2 tablespoons of bacon fat. Sauté the shallots and garlic in the bacon fat. Crumble the bacon and scatter it over each portion after adding the chives.

Truita de Patata with Allioli

Tortilla Espagñola, Spanish Omelet

Serves 6 to 8

This is the classic omelet of Spain, though it is nothing like what we think of as an omelet; it is closer to a frittata. If you find yourself in Spain longing for the type of omelet served in bistros and diners, ask for a tortilla francesa. *This one, however, is what you'll find in tapas bars and homes throughout Spain; kids take it in their lunch boxes and it is also common picnic fare. It is traditionally served with allioli.*

½ cup olive oil
2 large yellow onions, trimmed and thinly sliced
2 pounds potatoes, peeled and very thinly sliced
Kosher salt
Black pepper in a mill
6 large eggs, beaten
Allioli, page 332 to 333

Heat 3 tablespoons of the olive oil in a sauté pan, add the onion, and sauté very slowly, until it is very soft, fragrant, and beginning to color, about 20 to 25 minutes. Add the garlic and sauté 2 minutes more. Season with salt and pepper and transfer the mixture to a bowl.

Pour 3 more tablespoons of the olive oil into the sauté pan and fry the potatoes, tossing frequently, until they are golden brown and tender, about 20 minutes. Season with salt and pepper and remove from the heat.

In a large bowl, beat the eggs with a whisk as you would for an omelet; fold in the onion mixture and the potatoes.

Heat the remaining olive oil in a clean sauté pan—use a non-stick pan, if you like—and set the pan over medium heat. When the pan is hot but not smoking, pour in the egg mixture, reduce the heat to medium low, and cook without stirring until the bottom is golden brown, about 10 minutes. Loosen the edges of the tortilla with a rubber spatula. Set a plate that is slightly larger than the pan on top of the pan and turn both over together, so that the tortilla drops onto the plate. If the pan seems very dry or if egg has stuck to it, add another tablespoon of olive oil and heat it through before sliding the tortilla back in, cooked side up. Cook until the eggs are completely set and the bottom is golden brown, about 3 to 4 minutes more.

Transfer to a serving plate, let rest 5 minutes, cut into wedges, and serve warm, with allioli alongside.

Salads

Our Garrick's a salad; for in him we see
Oil, vinegar, sugar, and saltiness agree!
—Oliver Goldsmith, *Retaliation*

Mention oil and vinegar and people think salads. "Another book about vinaigrettes?" I've been asked? No, I explain, adding that there is still so much more to say about salads than simply their dressings. A well-chosen olive oil can transform an ingredient or two into an exquisite meal, just as the right vinegar can make a simple potato salad soar. That's what I hope these recipes do at your table, as they do at mine.

The recipes in this chapter, some new and many from the first edition of this book, touch on specialty oils and vinegars and the delicious ways they can shape all manner of salads, from a bowl of just-picked lettuces to grains, legumes, root vegetables, fruit, seafood, poultry, and meat. Our pantries have expanded since I wrote the first edition of this book and all manner of ingredients are much more readily at hand than they were then.

Enjoy the salads that I share here, please, but use them to inspire your own, too.

Sweet Onion Salad
Saucy Melon Salad
Pear & Hazelnut Salad
Avocado, Pear & Macadamia Nut Salad
Kale Salad with Avocado & Avocado Oil Dressing
Watercress Salad with Avocado, Blue Cheese & Walnuts
Wilted Spinach Salad with Bacon, Blueberries & Blueberry Vinaigrette
Warm Moroccan Beet Salad with Wilted Beet Greens
Warm Asian Pear, Brie & Wine Grape Salad
Asian-Inspired Chicken Salad with Toasted Sesame Ginger Dressing
English Pea, Brie & Smoked Duck Crackling Salad
Honeyed Pasta & Shrimp Salad
Sesame Shrimp Pasta Salad with Corn, Peas & Cilantro
Mary's Potato Salad
Summer Panzanella
Wild Rice Salad
White Bean Salad
Italian Bean & Sausage Salad

How to Dress a Green Salad

The best way to dress a green salad is with your hands, freshly washed and dried, of course. If composing the dressing in the bowl, sprinkle the greens with some salt, add a spendthrift's quantity of good oil, and gently turn the leaves to coat them thoroughly. Sprinkle a miser's bit of acid and turn the leaves again. Add a few turns of pepper if you like and enjoy the salad right away.

If using a dressing you have made separately, put some—about 2 teaspoons per serving—in the bottom of a generously sized salad bowl, put the leaves on top and sprinkle with a little salt. Turn the leaves to distribute the salt and pick up the dressing. Continue, very gently, until the leaves are fully coated. Add some black pepper if you like and enjoy right away.

The Simplest Green Salad, with Variations

Serves 2, easily doubled

I prefer salad at the end of a meal, not beforehand, as I love to end on a bright, refreshing note. Generally, I prefer it to dessert, an admission that I understand undercuts my credibility with dessert lovers everywhere. I have no defense, except that I was born this way. This is the salad I make almost every night, varying it as inclination and ingredients at hand dictate. I make it at the table, immediately before serving it.

3 generous handfuls of very fresh leafy salad greens
Kosher salt
Extra virgin olive oil
White wine vinegar, red wine vinegar, or ½ lemon
Black pepper in a mill

Put the greens in a wooden salad bowl, sprinkle lightly with salt and toss gently.

Drizzle with olive oil, using just enough—2 to 3 tablespoons—to coat the leaves. Toss gently.

Add a very modest amount of acid, sprinkling it over the greens and tossing all the while. Taste and if the salad is not quite bright enough, add a little more acid. There should be an appealing balance between oil and acid, so that neither stands out unpleasantly. Grind black pepper over the top and serve immediately.

Variations:

- Crumble 3 or 4 tablespoons of good blue cheese or feta cheese over the salad before adding the black pepper.
- Use walnut oil in place of olive oil, use orange juice in place of lemon juice or vinegar, and add a handful of fresh mint leaves just before serving.
- Use hazelnut oil in place of olive oil, use fresh pomegranate juice in place of lemon juice or vinegar, and scatter 3 or 4 tablespoons of pomegranate arils over the salad just before serving.
- Use a vegetable peeler to make curls of Parmigiano-Reggiano or Dry Jack and scatter over the dressed greens.
- Add a tablespoon of minced fresh herbs—choose your favorites—to the greens before dressing.
- Lightly toast 2 tablespoons pine nuts, cool and toss over the salad just before serving.
- Use lime juice and add half an avocado, cut into very thin slices, to the salad before adding the black pepper.
- Toss several radishes, cut into very thin rounds, with the lettuce.

Butter Lettuce Salad with Fresh Artichoke Hearts & Tarragon

Serves 4

Butter lettuce is the most delicate of all salad greens, and it is a perfect canvas for other flavors, including the herbs in this dish, the earthy artichoke hearts, and the fragrant brown butter, with its aromas of hazelnuts.

4 jumbo artichokes, boiled in salted water until tender, drained, and cooled
2 tablespoons brown butter, hot (see Note on next page)
4 teaspoons minced fresh tarragon
2 teaspoons minced fresh Italian parsley
2 teaspoons fresh snipped chives
2 teaspoons minced fresh chervil
1 head butter lettuce, leaves separated, core removed and discarded
Kosher salt
3 tablespoons hazelnut oil, late-harvest extra virgin olive oil, or a blend of the two
1 tablespoon Champagne wine vinegar, plus more to taste
1 avocado, peeled and thinly sliced
Black pepper in a mill
4 small tarragon sprigs

Remove all of the artichoke leaves and set them aside for another use. Remove and discard the choke and trim the heart. Put the brown butter in a small pan, add 2 teaspoons of the tarragon, set aside and keep warm.

In a small bowl, toss together the remaining 2 teaspoons fresh tarragon, the parsley, the chives, and the chervil.

Put the butter lettuce in a large bowl, sprinkle lightly with salt, and toss gently. Drizzle the oil over the greens and turn very gently, until the leaves are evenly coated. Sprinkle with vinegar, turn again, add the avocado and the herb mixture and toss gently.

Divide the greens among four individual plates and add an artichoke heart, setting it alongside the salad. Spoon browned butter over each artichoke heart, garnish with a tarragon sprig and enjoy right away.

NOTE

Brown butter is simply clarified butter heated until it takes on a golden glow and gives off an aroma similar to hazelnuts.

Simple Cucumber Salad for Erica

Serves 3 to 4

"Someone gave me seven cucumbers," my sweet niece Erica told me a while back, "and I don't know what to do with them other than just eat them." I gathered up a few favorite recipes for her, including this one, which offers a perfect way to use rice vinegar.

4 or 5 lemon cucumbers
¼ cup rice wine vinegar
¼ cup sugar
Juice of 1 lime
½ teaspoon red pepper flakes

If the lemon cucumbers have unblemished skins, wash them thoroughly, dry them, and cut them in half. Cut each cucumber half into ⅛-inch-thick slices. Put them in a shallow serving bowl. In a small bowl, mix together the vinegar, sugar, lime juice, and red pepper flakes and stir until the sugar is dissolved. Pour the dressing over the cucumbers and let sit for 30 minutes before serving.

Sunomono with Wakame & Rice Noodles

Serves 4 to 6

Japanese cucumber salads are among the most delicate and refreshing salads imaginable.

2 cucumbers, preferably Japanese or Armenian, washed and very thinly sliced
Kosher salt
Small handful of wakame, optional
2 ounces mung bean (cellophane) noodles
½ cup unseasoned rice vinegar
1 tablespoon sugar
1 teaspoon soy sauce
Toasted sesame oil
Pinch of crushed red pepper flakes
3 scallions, trimmed and cut into thin diagonal slices
1 teaspoon lightly toasted sesame seeds

Put the cucumbers into a medium bowl, sprinkle with salt, toss and set aside.

Put the wakame, if using, and the noodles into a medium bowl, cover with hot water and let rest until the noodles turn clear and tender. Tip into a strainer and press out as much moisture as possible. Tear the wakame into pieces and put both the seaweed and noodles into a serving bowl. Set aside.

Put the vinegar, sugar, and soy sauce into a small bowl, add the red pepper flakes, stir and taste; correct for acid, sugar, and salt balance. Set aside.

Tip the cucumbers into a strainer, press off any liquid that has formed, rinse and press again.

Add the cucumbers to the bowl with the noodles and seaweed, pour the dressing over everything, cover and refrigerate for 15 to 30 minutes.

To serve, scatter the scallions and sesame seeds on top and enjoy right away.

Simple Tomato Salad

Serves 1 hearty eater and is easily doubled or tripled

This recipe is given in quantities for one person because I typically prepare it for myself at lunch. Eating tomatoes right out of the garden, still warm from the sun, is one of my favorite solitary pastimes. It is big enough to share with another if it is part of a meal and it is also easily doubled.

3 ripe medium tomatoes, trimmed and cut into ¼-inch rounds
3 cloves garlic, crushed and minced
Kosher salt
2 tablespoons extra virgin olive oil
1 anchovy fillet, marinated in vinegar (see page 75)
1 to 2 teaspoons red wine vinegar
Black pepper in a mill

Arrange the tomatoes on a plate, scatter the garlic over them and season with salt.

Drizzle olive oil over the tomatoes.

Chop the anchovy, put it in a small bowl, add the vinegar, stir and then scatter it over the tomatoes. Season with several turns of black pepper and enjoy within 30 minutes.

Cherry Tomato Salad for a Picnic

Serves 3 to 4

Packing salads and other foods in Mason jars to take on a picnic is my preferred method of transportation, as the jars work for serving, for keeping leftovers, and can be used over and over again. They rarely leak. This salad is best at the height of tomato season, from early summer to late fall.

1 pint ripe cherry tomatoes, preferably a mix of colors, quartered
3 garlic cloves, minced
1 tablespoon minced red onion
Flake salt
1 tablespoon red wine vinegar
3 to 4 tablespoons best-quality extra virgin olive oil
Black pepper in a mill
3 tablespoons minced fresh herbs (basil, Italian parsley, thyme, oregano, mint, summer savory)

Put the quartered tomatoes into a medium bowl, add the garlic and onions, season with salt, add the vinegar and toss gently. Add the olive oil, taste, and correct for salt and acid balance. Add the herbs and toss.

Serve right away or pack into a Mason jar and enjoy at your picnic destination.

Sicilian Orange Salad

Serves 4 to 6

Oranges have long been an essential part of the Sicilian diet. This recipe has evolved considerably from the simple combination of oranges, olive oil, salt, and pepper described to me by my friend A. J. His father, Antonio, mm in his nineties, enjoys it regularly. The clear; simple tastes in this dish make it an ideal opener for more complex main courses.

6 medium oranges, preferably Cara Cara or blood oranges, or a mix of the two
Kosher salt
3 to 4 tablespoons best-quality extra virgin olive oil
1 teaspoon Champagne vinegar
Black pepper in a mill
10 to 12 curls pecorino cheese, about 1 inch long, made with a vegetable peeler, optional

Using a sharp paring knife, peel the oranges, removing the white, spongy pith completely, and slice them into ¼ inch thick rounds.

Arrange the oranges on a serving platter in concentric circles, overlapping the oranges just slightly. Season with salt, drizzle with olive oil, and sprinkle on the vinegar.

Season with several turns of black pepper, scatter the curls of cheese on top, if using, and enjoy right away.

Sweet Onion Salad

Serves 4 to 6

Sweet onions are best enjoyed simply, on sandwiches or in salads, so that their subtle flavors are not eclipsed by cooking or by a lot of other ingredients. This salad can be served solo as a simple side salad or with other salads as part of a spring or summer meal.

1 large or 2 to 3 small sweet onions, peeled and very thinly sliced
2 teaspoons sugar
Kosher salt
Black pepper in a mill
⅓ cup low-acid raspberry vinegar

Arrange the onions in a small, wide dish. Sprinkle the sugar over them and season with salt and pepper. Pour the vinegar over and set aside for up to 1 hour before serving.

Saucy Melon Salad

Serves 6

Small farmers now grow a wonderful selection of heirloom muskmelons and I recommend making this salad in late August and through September, when the melon harvest is at its peak.

3 small muskmelons, 1 green, 1 white, 1 orange
3 tablespoons Southern Comfort liquor
1 large head butter lettuce or red-leaf lettuce, cleaned and dried
Vanilla Vinaigrette, page 325
Kosher salt
Black pepper in a mill
¼ cup lightly toasted and coarsely chopped macadamia nuts, pecans, or walnuts
6 sprigs fresh mint

Cut the melons in half, scoop out and discard the seeds, and cut half of each melon into wedges about ⅓ inch thick. Peel the wedges, set them in a wide bowl and set aside.

Use a melon scoop to make round balls from the remaining melon, add them to the bowl with the wedges, sprinkle Southern Comfort over them, cover and refrigerate for 30 minutes.

Chill six salad plates.

Put the lettuce into a large bowl, sprinkle lightly with salt, turn and divide among the chilled plates. Add the melon and spoon dressing over each portion.

Season with salt and a few turns of black pepper, scatter nuts on top, add a mint sprig and serve right away.

Pear & Hazelnut Salad

Serves 4

The elements in this pretty salad resonate intriguingly well with one another. The nuttiness of the hazelnut oil and hazelnuts echoes the nutlike flavor of the avocado, and the hint of pear in the vinegar resonates with the fresh fruit itself. A strikingly delicious and harmonious relationship is played out on the palate.

1 head butter lettuce, thin outer leaves and core removed
Kosher salt
1 pear, peeled, cored, and cut lengthwise into ⅛-inch-thick slices
1 avocado, peeled and cut lengthwise into ⅛-inch-thick slices
1 cup smoked chicken, smoked trout, or smoked salmon, cut or torn into small pieces
Hazelnut Vinaigrette, page 324
Black pepper in a mill
¼ cup hazelnuts, lightly toasted, skinned, and chopped
Borage flowers, optional
Whole chives, for garnish

Put the lettuce into a bowl, sprinkle with salt, toss and divide among individual plates. Add the pear and avocado, followed by the chicken, trout or salmon.

Drizzle with vinaigrette, season with a few turns of black pepper and scatter hazelnuts and borage flowers, if using, on top. Garnish with a few chives and serve right away.

Avocado, Pear & Macadamia Nut Salad

Serves 2, easily doubled

If you happen to have good macadamia nut oil—brought back from Hawai'i, perhaps, or received as a gift—this is fall or winter salad is the perfect time to use it.

1 small shallot, minced
2 tablespoons Champagne vinegar or rice wine vinegar
Kosher salt
Black pepper in a mill
1 firm-ripe avocado
1 firm-ripe pear, preferably Anjou or Comice
1 lime
Handful of small arugula or young salad greens
4 to 6 tablespoons avocado oil, macadamia nut oil, or olive oil
½ cup whole macadamia nuts, lightly toasted and chopped

Put the minced shallot in a small bowl, add the vinegar and season with salt and pepper. Set aside while you prepare the avocado and pear.

Cut the avocado in half lengthwise, remove the pit and use a paring knife to cut very thin lengthwise slices. Use a large spoon to scoop the slices out of the skin. Fan half an avocado on individual serving plates and squeeze a little lime juice over it.

Peel the pear, cut it in half lengthwise, cut out the seed core and cut into thin lengthwise slices. Arrange on the plate with the avocado and squeeze a little lime juice over it.

Mound greens in the middle of the plate and season with a little salt.

Stir the oil into the shallot and vinegar mixture, adding as much as is necessary for a proper balance of acid and oil. Spoon dressing over the avocado, pear and greens, season lightly with salt and pepper and scatter macadamia nuts on top.

Serve right away.

Kale Salad with Avocado & Avocado Oil Dressing

Makes 3 to 4 servings

The secret to raw kale salad, I believe, is three-fold: Slice the kale into thin crosswise slices, massage them or pound them with salt and then let them rest before adding other ingredients.

1 bunch Lacinato kale, rinsed, dried, and large central stems removed
Kosher salt
3 garlic cloves, pressed
Red pepper flakes
6 tablespoons avocado oil or best-quality extra virgin olive oil
Juice of 1 lemon
1 firm-ripe avocado, cubed
Black pepper in a mill

Stack several leaves, roll them tightly lengthwise and cut into ⅛-inch-wide crosswise slices. Continue until all the leaves have been cut. Put the leaves into a deep bowl, use your fingers to separate and fluff them and season with several generous pinches of salt. Massage the leaves for several minutes or use a wooden pestle to gently pound them until they begin to relax.

Add half the garlic, a pinch of red pepper flakes, half the oil and half the lemon juice, toss and set aside for about 30 minutes.

Meanwhile, put the avocado into a bowl, season lightly with salt and add the remaining garlic, olive oil, and lemon juice. Taste, correct for salt and season with several turns of black pepper. Cover and set aside.

To finish the salad, toss the kale, taste a piece and adjust the seasoning, if needed. Divide it among individual plates or bowls and top with some of the avocado-tomato mixture. Serve right or pack it into a quart Mason jar, refrigerate for a day or two and enjoy on a picnic.

Variations:

- Add 2 cups of small quartered cherry tomatoes to the avocado.
- Add 4 ounces feta cheese broken into chunks to the salad when you add the avocado.

Watercress Salad with Avocado, Blue Cheese & Walnuts

Serves 3 to 4

It is easiest to separate an avocado from its peel after you have cut it in half lengthwise. Remove the pit, make lengthwise cuts in the flesh, and then carefully scoop out the slices. For watercress, try to find naturally grown, not hydroponic, which can be quite tough. This salad can also be made with pea shoots or almost any microgreen.

2 large bunches watercress, large stems discarded
Kosher salt
4 tablespoons walnut oil
1 to 2 tablespoons sherry vinegar or Champagne vinegar
1 firm-ripe avocado, cut into thin lengthwise slices
4 ounces Pt. Reyes Original Blue, broken into small pieces
Black pepper in a mill
⅓ cup walnut pieces, toasted

Put the watercress in a large salad bowl, season lightly with salt, and toss. Add the olive oil, toss again, add the vinegar or lemon juice, and toss one more time. Add the avocado, blue cheese, and several turns of black pepper, toss gently, and divide among individual plates. Top each portion with some of the walnuts and serve immediately.

Wilted Spinach Salad with Bacon, Blueberries & Blueberry Vinaigrette

Serves 4 to 6

Although there are a few brands of blueberry vinegar in the marketplace, it is very easy to make your own, especially if you live in an area where blueberries are abundant, as I do. Just refer to page 306 to make your own.

Spinach, as we all understand, is very good for human health but what a lot of people don't know is that the spinach must be cooked for its full range of nutrients to be available to us. Make sure the dressing is nice and hot, so that it wilts the spinach.

5 ounces best-quality bacon, chopped
2 shallots, minced
3 tablespoons blueberry vinegar (4.5 percent acidity) or other low-acid red wine vinegar
½ teaspoon ground cloves
½ teaspoon ground allspice
1 pound baby spinach leaves, rinsed and dried
Kosher salt
4 tablespoons hazelnut oil
1 small red onion, cut into very thin rings
3 tablespoons peanut oil
1 cup fresh blueberries
3 hard-cooked farm eggs, cut in lengthwise slices, 6 per egg, or chopped coarsely

Fry the bacon until it is just crisp. Use a slotted spoon to transfer the bacon to absorbent paper to drain. Add the shallots to the bacon drippings, sauté until soft, add the vinegar and spices and remove from the heat and set aside.

Put the spinach into a large bowl, season with salt and drizzle with hazelnut oil. Using your hands, gently turn the leaves until they are evenly coated with oil. Add the onion, toss and set aside.

Return the pan with the dressing to medium heat, add the peanut oil, taste and correct for salt. Season generously with black pepper. When the dressing is very hot, pour it over the spinach. Add the blueberries and use tongs to turn the salad as the spinach wilts.

Working quickly, divide among individual plates. Top with egg wedges or chopped eggs, season with salt, scatter the bacon over everything and serve right away.

Warm Moroccan Beet Salad with Wilted Beet Greens

Serves 3 to 4

If you love Moroccan food, as I do, you might want to keep a tube of harissa on hand. DEA is a good brand, perfect when you don't have time or the ingredients to make your own and need just a bit, as is called for in this salad.

4 medium or 8 small golden beets, with their greens
Olive oil
1 garlic clove, pressed
1 teaspoon ground cumin
2 wedges preserved lemons, commercial or homemade, minced
1 to 2 teaspoons harissa paste, commercial or homemade
3 tablespoons extra virgin olive oil
1 tablespoon freshly squeezed lemon juice, plus more to taste
Kosher salt
3 to 4 tablespoons chopped fresh cilantro leaves

Preheat the oven to 375 degrees.

Cut the greens from the beet roots, wash the roots and set on a tea towel to dry. Rinse the greens but do not dry them.

Set the beets in a baking dish, drizzle with a little olive oil and turn in the oil to coat them evenly. Set on the middle rack of the oven and cook until the beets are fully tender when perceived with a fork or bamboo skewer. Remove from the oven, let cool and remove the skins, using your fingers or a sharp pairing knife. Cut the beets into wedges and set aside.

Put the garlic into a small bowl, add the cumin, preserved lemons, and harissa paste and stir well. Add the extra virgin olive oil and the lemon juice and stir. Taste and correct for salt and acid balance. Set aside.

Put a medium sauté pan over medium heat, add a splash of extra virgin olive oil and the beet greens. Cover the pan and cook for about 2 minutes, until the leaves begin to wilt. Uncover, turn the leaves, season with salt and cook until just tender, about 5 minutes. Remove from the heat.

Divide the greens among individual plates and top with the beet wedges. Spoon dressing on top, add cilantro leaves and enjoy right away.

Warm Asian Pear, Brie & Wine Grape Salad

Serves 6 to 8

Where I live in Northern California, there are many pomegranate trees, planted for their appearance and allowed to grow quite tall. Many go unharvested and I love to walk along tree-lined streets and gather those I can reach. The same is true with Asian pears; many hang from trees, yours for the picking.

1 cup red wine grapes of choice, stemmed
Sugar
Kosher salt
1 pomegranate
1 lemon
1 Asian pear
1 young head frisee (curly endive)
1 small head radicchio
8 ounces Brie or other ripened cheese, very thinly sliced
2 tablespoons olive oil
1 shallot, minced
2 tablespoons verjus (see Note), sherry vinegar, Vinaigre de Banyuls or cabernet sauvignon vinegar, plus more to taste
4 tablespoons walnut oil
Black pepper in a mill
½ cup freshly shelled walnuts, lightly toasted and coarsely chopped

Put the grapes in a bowl and use a fork to crush them, being sure to break up each grape. Add a pinch of sugar and a pinch of salt and set aside.

Cut the pomegranate in half through its equator, remove the arils and discard the skin and membranes. Set the arils aside.

Fill a medium bowl with water and squeeze in the juice of half the lemon.

Peel the pear, cut it in lengthwise quarters, remove the seed core and cut each quarter into very thin lengthwise slices. Put the sliced pear into the acidified water.

Remove the frisee from its stalk and if the leaves are large tear them into smaller pieces. Put the leaves into a medium mixing bowl.

Remove the core of the radicchio and use a sharp knife to cut the leaves into thin crosswise slices.

Add the radicchio to the frisee and toss gently to fluff the leaves and combine them.

Sprinkle the frisee and radicchio lightly with salt and toss again. Set aside.

Put the olive oil in a small sauté pan, set over medium heat, add the shallot and sauté until soft and fragrant, about 7 minutes.

Season with salt.

Set a strainer over a small bowl and strain the grapes, pressing out as much juice as possible. Add the juice to the pan with the shallots and warm through. Add the verjus or vinegar and the walnut oil, heat through and immediately remove from the heat. Taste the mixture and correct for salt and balance, adding a bit more verjus, vinegar, or the juice of the remaining half lemon if it is not quite tart enough.

Drain the Asian pears and dry them on a tea towel.

Add the pears to the frisee and radicchio, spoon half of the warm dressing over the mixture and toss gently. Divide among individual plates. Arrange the sliced Brie over each portion and scatter pomegranate arils on top. If the dressing has cooled, quickly warm it and spoon it over the salads, drizzling it over the cheese so that the cheese begins to melt. Sprinkle with a little salt and several generous turns of black pepper, scatter the walnuts on top and serve immediately.

NOTE

Verjus is the tart juice of unripe grapes. There are several brands on the market.

Honeyed Pasta & Shrimp Salad with Cherry Tomatoes

Serves 6 to 8

My daughter Nicolle deserves credit for this recipe. Rummaging through the refrigerator one summer afternoon, she came upon a container of Honey Pepper Vinaigrette and proceeded to create this sweet and summery salad, at its best when cherry tomatoes are freshly picked from the garden.

Kosher salt
1 pound small pasta, such as tripolini, small shells, or farfallini
Honey Pepper Vinaigrette (see Note)
4 cups ripe cherry tomatoes, quartered
8 garlic cloves, crushed and minced
4 very small red onions, torpedo if available, very thinly sliced
8 ounces bay shrimp
A handful of chopped fresh herbs, such as mint, cilantro, oregano, and Italian parsley
Black pepper in a mill

Fill a large pot two-thirds full with water, add a generous tablespoon of salt and bring to a boil over high heat. When the water reaches a rolling boil, add the pasta and stir until the water returns to a boil. Lower the heat so that the water does not boil over and cook until just done. Tip into a colander, rinse under cool water and drain thoroughly.

Meanwhile, make the dressing and set it aside. Put the tomatoes, garlic, onions, shrimp, and herbs into a large serving bowl. Add half the dressing and toss gently. Taste and correct as needed for salt and pepper. Enjoy right away.

NOTE

To make the Honey Pepper Vinaigrette, whisk together ¼ cup sherry vinegar, ¼ cup honey (warmed), 2 tablespoons freshly ground black pepper, 1 teaspoon salt, 1 shallot (minced), 3 cloves garlic (minced), ¼ cup finely chopped mint, and 1 cup olive oil.

Asian-Inspired Chicken Salad with Sesame Ginger Dressing

Serves 4 as a main course

This dish is for my daughter Gina, who loves Chinese chicken salad, a dish that has always left me rather cold. Why? I eventually wondered and set out to make a version I would enjoy. That lead me in short order to chicken thighs cooked on the bone instead of boneless skinless breast meat, dry rice noodles fried in a little peanut oil instead of commercial chow mein noodles, fresh citrus instead of canned Mandarin oranges, cashews instead of almonds and homemade instead of bottle dressing.

Sesame Ginger Dressings (recipe follows)
3 to 4 cooked chicken thighs (see Note on next page)
½ Napa cabbage, shredded, cooked
4 or 5 scallions, trimmed and cut into very thin rounds
¼ cup very fresh mint leaves
½ cup very fresh cilantro leaves
1 small carrot, peeled and cut into thin julienne
½ small jicama, peeled and cut into thin julienne
1 blood orange or Cara Cara orange, peeled, membranes removed
1 small jalapeño, cut into very thin diagonal slices
¾ cup crisp noodles (fried dry rice noodles, chow mein noodles, etc.)
Kosher salt
½ cup roasted cashews

Make the dressing and set it aside.

Pull the chicken off the bone and cut it into lengthwise slices. Set it aside.

Put the cabbage into a large bowl, add the scallions, mint, cilantro, carrot, jicama, orange, and jalapeño. Season lightly with salt, add a tablespoon or two of dressing, toss and divide among individual plates or bowls. Add the crisp noodles and toss again.

Divide the chicken among the portions, scatter cashews on top and spoon dressing everything. Serve right away.

NOTE

I usually cook chicken thighs for this salad in my toaster oven, seasoning them all over with salt and pepper and then setting them on the little rack with the oven preheated to 375 degrees on the baking setting for 20 to 25 minutes, depending on the size of the thighs. The skin turns out beautifully crisp and you can, if you like, cut it into thin julienne and use it in place of the noodles.

Sesame Ginger Dressing

2 tablespoons Chinese black vinegar or rice vinegar
1 tablespoons soy sauce, plus more to taste
1 tablespoon minced fresh ginger
2 teaspoons honey or sugar, plus more to taste
1 teaspoon chili garlic sauce or other Asian or Asian-style hot sauce, plus more to taste
2 tablespoons toasted sesame oil
4 tablespoons peanut oil, preferably roasted
2 teaspoons lightly toasted sesame seeds

Put all the ingredients into a small Mason jar, close tightly with its lid and shake. Taste and correct for salt by adding more soy sauce as needed, for sweetness and for acid.

English Pea, Brie & Smoked Duck Crackling Salad with Warm Shallot Vinaigrette

Serves 4 as a hearty luncheon salad, 8 as a starter

This is a devastatingly delicious salad, the sort of combination of flavors that makes you want to eat forever, regardless of common sense or consequences. Smoked duck cracklings are delicious by themselves, and the warm vinaigrette makes the Brie melt into everything else, and, oh, happy day, it's simply divine.

1 cup duck crackling, recipe follows
4 cups very fresh salad greens of choice
Flake salt
Best-quality extra virgin olive oil
Black pepper in a mill
One 4-inch round of Brie or similar cheese
1 cup freshly shelled peas or fresh favas, blanched and freshened in ice water
Warm Shallot Vinaigrette (page 170)

Make the cracklings and set them aside.

Put the salad greens into a large bowl, season with salt and toss gently. Add a small drizzle of olive and use your hands to turn the leaves until they are evenly coated with oil. Add several turns of black pepper, toss and divide among individual plates.

Cut the Brie in half vertically. Using a very thin sharp knife, cut the Brie into thin slices and set them on top of the greens. Scatter the cracklings and peas or favas on top and set aside.

Make the dressing, drizzle it over the salads and serve right away.

Smoked Duck Cracklings

Cut the skin of 1 duck, preferably smoked, into strips measuring ½ inch by 1 ½ inches. Place the strips in a heavy skillet with ½ cup water and set over very low heat. When the fat has been rendered out of the duck skin, increase the heat to medium. The water will evaporate and the pieces of skin will be golden and crispy. Use a slotted spoon to transfer the cracklings to a piece of absorbent paper to drain.

Duck cracklings can be made in advance and stored in the refrigerator, but they should be warmed in a 200-degree oven for about 10 minutes before serving.

Sesame Shrimp Pasta Salad with Corn, Peas & Cilantro

Serves 8 to 10

I began making this lovely summer salad when unrefined corn oil was readily available. Alas, the oil, which was delicious but unstable and prone to going rancid fairly quickly, has disappeared from the market place and so I used roasted peanut oil instead. The salad is a perfect addition to a summer buffet.

Kosher salt
1 pound small pasta, such as orzo, melone, rosamarina, or similar shape
4 tablespoons unseasoned rice vinegar
2 tablespoons freshly squeezed lime juice
1 tablespoon sugar
2 garlic cloves, pressed
1 small serrano, minced
½ cup peanut oil, preferably roasted
3 tablespoons toasted sesame oil
2 cups fresh corn kernes (from 2 to 3 ears of corn, quickly cooked)
1 cup blanched fresh English peas, blanched, or blanched and peeled fresh favas
1 pound Bay shrimp, drained
⅔ cup Sesame Mayonnaise, page 329
Black pepper in a mill
4 tablespoons chopped cilantro leaves
Sprigs of cilantro

Fill a large pot two-thirds full with water, add a generous tablespoon of salt and bring to a boil over high heat. When the water reaches a rolling boil, add the pasta and stir until the water returns to a boil. Lower the heat so that the water does not boil over and cook until just done. Tip into a colander, rinse under cool water and drain thoroughly.

Meanwhile, put the vinegar and lime juice into a small bowl, add the sugar and stir until it dissolves. Add the garlic and serrano and whisk in the oils. Taste and correct for salt, sugar, and acid balance. Set aside.

When the pasta is completely drained, tip it into a bowl, add the corn and peas, toss and pour the dressing over it. Cover and set aside.

Put the shrimp into a bowl, add the sesame mayonnaise and mix gently; taste, correct for salt and season with a few turns of black pepper.

Transfer the pasta salad to a serving platter, mound the shrimp in the center, scatter cilantro leaves on top and serve right away.

Mary's Potato Salad

Serves 4 to 6

Long before it became trendy to put salads into Mason jars, my dear friend Mary Duryee brought me a quart jar full of the most delicious potato salad. I live in a charming cottage on her large ranch in west Sebastopol and have often enjoyed her fabulous cooking. She is the best home cook I know. When I told her, years later, how much I'd loved her potato salad, she laughed and said she had no idea what she made. Like the best cooks, she simply cooks, without looking at recipes. I've found my way back to the flavors in that salad many times but have yet to ask her what she thinks of my version.

2 to 3 large russet potatoes, scrubbed and cut into medium cubes or thick half-rounds
Kosher salt
8 ounces Blue Lake green beans, trimmed and cut into thirds
2 cups quartered cherry tomatoes
1 red onion, cut into small dice
Chopped fresh herbs
⅓ cup red wine vinegar, plus more to taste
Black pepper in a mill
⅔ cup mild olive oil
3 hard-cooked eggs, peeled and cut into wedges, optional

Cook the potatoes in rapidly boiling salted water until tender but not falling apart. Use a slotted spoon to transfer the potatoes to a colander or strainer to drain and cool. Meanwhile, cook the green beans in the same water until tender, 4 to 5 minutes. Drain thoroughly.

Put the cooled potatoes and the green beans into a large bowl. Add the tomatoes, onion, and chopped herbs and toss well. Season with salt, add the vinegar and several turns of black pepper and toss. Add the olive oil and toss again.

Taste, correct for salt and acid, fold in the eggs, if using, and let rest for 30 minutes before serving.

Enjoy right away or pack into Mason jars and enjoy on a picnic.

Summer Panzanella

Serves 4

When you have leftover hearth bread that is too stale for other uses, make bread salad, a casual and lusty dish that easily adapts to the seasons. This version is for the summer months, when basil is plentiful and it is hard to keep up with cherry tomatoes. If you grow your own basil, add some basil flowers just before serving.

4 cups (about ½ loaf) torn hearth bread, a day or two old
½ cup extra virgin olive oil
3 tablespoons red wine vinegar
Kosher salt
Black pepper in a mill
1 cup quartered cherry tomatoes
1 cup olives of choice, pitted and diced
1 small red onion, diced
4 garlic cloves, minced
3 tablespoons Italian parsley, minced
3 tablespoon fresh shredded basil leaves
Best-quality extra virgin olive oil, for drizzling

Put the bread into a large bowl, add the olive oil and vinegar, season with salt and peper, toss, cover and set aside for about 30 minutes.

Add the tomatoes, olives, onion, garlic, parsley, and basil to the bread and toss gently and thoroughly.

Transfer to a serving platter or bowl, drizzle with olive oil, season with a bit more salt and pepper and serve right away.

Wild Rice Salad

Serves 6 to 8

When I wrote the first edition of the is book, delicious smoked duck was produced in Petaluma, not far from where I live in Sonoma County. The smoked duck was particularly good, with a lovely velvety texture and it became the inspiration for this dish. The company closed a number of years ago and I can no longer get that particular style of smoked duck, so I use what I can find, including readily available smoked turkey. As I have stated elsewhere in this book, I use balsamic vinegar quite sparingly. This salad and its dressing, fragrant with vanilla, is an example of one of its best uses, as its flavors complement those of the rice, poultry, and walnuts.

1 cup (6 ounces) uncooked wild rice
Kosher salt
Vanilla Vinaigrette, pg. 325
1 shallot, minced
1 cup shelled walnuts, lightly toasted and chopped
3 tablespoons chopped fresh Italian parsley
1 tablespoon snipped chives
2 cups smoked duck, smoked chicken, or smoked turkey, in medium julienne

Put the wild rice in a heavy saucepan, add 3 cups of water and a very generous pinch of salt. Bring to a boil over high heat, lower and simmer, covered, until the rice is tender, about 30 minutes. Leave covered, remove from the heat and let rest 10 minutes. Fluff with a fork and tip out into a wide shallow bowl.

Add a third of the vinaigrette and toss gently. Add the shallot, walnuts, parsley, and chives and toss again. Add half the poultry, toss and drizzle with all but a tablespoon of the remaining dressing. Divide among individual plates, top with some of the remaining poultry and a drizzle of vinegar and enjoy right away.

White Bean Salad

Serves 4

When you use good beans—grown for taste and fairly fresh—bean salads are wonderful. My favorite ones are made with white beans, which have an earthy flavor and voluptuous texture. If you find yourself in a pinch, you can make a good salad using canned cannellini beans but be sure to rinse them first.

1 cup dried marrowfats or cannellini beans, cooked until tender and drained
Kosher salt
3 tablespoons best-quality red wine vinegar, plus more to taste
6 to 8 tablespoons best-quality extra virgin olive oil, plus more to taste
1 small red onion, cut into small dice
Several garlic cloves, minced
2 roasted red peppers, cut into small julienne
¼ cup chopped Italian parsley
2 tablespoons chopped fresh mint
Black pepper in a mill

Put the cooked beans into a wide shallow bowl, season with salt, add the vinegar and oil, toss and set aside for 30 minutes.

Add the onion, garlic, roasted peppers, and parsley, toss, taste and correct for salt. Season with several turns of black pepper, transfer to a bowl or platter and serve right away.

Variation

Add a small can of drained tuna along with the other ingredients and top the salad with fresh bread crumbs that have been lightly toasted.

Italian Bean & Sausage Salad

Serves 8 to 10

This is another recipe I developed for my daughter Nicolle. "Include more recipes for beans," she always tells me. They are good for a student's budget and will keep well for several days. Beans also take to a vinaigrette like a fish to water, as they say. This hearty salad is another ideal picnic dish; just be sure to keep it properly chilled.

1 pound dried shell beans (see Note), cooked until tender, drained and cooled
Kosher salt
1 cup beef stock
1 pound best-quality Italian sausages
3 large sweet peppers, preferably a mix of colors, roasted, peeled, seeded, and cut into medium julienne
1 small red onion, diced
Several garlic cloves, minced
⅓ cup red wine vinegar
½ teaspoon fennel seed or fennel pollen
Generous pinch of crushed red pepper flakes
⅔ cup extra virgin olive oil, plus more to taste
3 tablespoons chopped Italian parsley
1 teaspoon chopped fresh oregano
1 teaspoon fresh thyme leaves
Black pepper in a mill

Put the drained and cooled beans into a wide shallow bowl, season with salt and add the stock.

Fry or broil the sausages until cooked through, let cool slightly and cut into ⅓-inch-wide diagonal slices. Add to the beans, along with the peppers, onion, garlic, vinegar, fennel seed or pollen, and red pepper flakes. Toss gently, taste and season with salt.

Add the olive oil, stir, cover and let rest for a few minutes. Taste and correct for salt and acid balance. Toss in the herbs, add season turns of black pepper, stir and serve right away.

NOTE

You can use a single bean in this salad or a mix of beans. I like to use three varieties, one white, one black and one of another color. I cook each one separately so they are all evenly tender and retain their colors. This can be done the night before serving the salad. Be sure to cool them separately, too.

Pasta, Rice & Other Grains

Steamed rice with toasted sesame oil and rice vinegar; spaghettini with extra virgin olive oil and minced garlic; farro or creamy polenta with Meyer lemon olive oil: These simple dishes need no recipe and will, on a busy night when you need to go shopping but don't feel like it, save you. Even more complex pasta and rice dishes don't always need recipes, not once you've learned your way around good ingredients and keep your pantry well stocked with them. You can even dress up humble grains like lentils with a good oil and suave vinegar.

The best pasta is made in Italy, with the exception of Mammarella brand, a New York-based pasta and sauce company owned by Francis Coppola. The pasta is excellent with an interesting assortment of uncommon shapes in addition to the familiar ones. The company also has the best crushed red pepper flakes I have found anywhere.

Three Very Simple Pastas

If you keep your pantry well stocked, it is easy to make a quick pasta dinner, after a night of school sports, holiday shopping, meetings, or too much work. These three pastas can be ready in the amount of time it takes to boil water and cook the pasta. You should even have time to put together a simple green salad or vegetable side dish and a quick fruit dessert.

Spaghettini with Olive Oil, Garlic & Red Pepper Flakes

Serves 2, easily doubled

Simple, fast and easy to prepare, and delicious: That's this pasta. Add a big green salad alongside and it's dinner on a busy night or any time you don't feel like something more elaborate.

Kosher salt
4 to 6 ounces dried spaghettini or other long thin pasta
3 tablespoons extra virgin olive oil, plus more to taste
1 to 2 garlic cloves, minced
Generous pinch of crushed red pepper flakes
Black pepper in a mill
Flake salt

Fill a large saucepan half full with water, season generously with salt and bring to a boil over high heat. Add the pasta and stir until it returns to a rolling boil. Cook according to package directions until just done; stir it now and then as it cooks.

Meanwhile, pour the olive oil into a small pan, add the garlic and red pepper flakes and warm over very low heat.

Drain the pasta, tip it back into the pot or into a bowl and pour the warmed olive oil over it. Divide between two pasta bowls, season with black pepper and salt and enjoy right away.

Spaghetti with Olive Oil, Nutmeg & Black Pepper

Serves 1, easily increased

Kosher salt
2 to 3 ounces spaghetti or other long thin pasta
Best-quality extra virgin olive oil
Whole nutmeg, preferably in a grinder
Black pepper in a mill

Fill a saucepan half full with water, season generously with salt and bring to a boil over high heat. Add the pasta and stir until it returns to a rolling boil. Cook according to package directions until just done; stir it now and then as it cooks.

Drain the pasta, tip it into a pasta bowl and drizzle olive oil over it. Grind a generous amount of nutmeg on top (if you don't have a nutmeg grinder, use the small blade of a grater), followed by several generous turns of black pepper. Sprinkle a little salt on top and enjoy right away.

Pasta with Tapenade & Cherry Tomatoes

Serves 3 to 4

When you need to keep up with all the cherry tomatoes in your garden, this quick pasta dish is ideal. If you have basil, too, toss in some basil flowers at the last minute.

Kosher salt
8 to 12 ounces bucatini, spaghettini, or other long thin pasta
½ to ⅔ cup tapenade of choice, commercial or homemade
2 cups quartered cherry tomatoes
2 garlic cloves, pressed
2 tablespoons chopped fresh Italian parsley or a mix of parsley, basil, and thyme
Black pepper in a mill
Best-quaility extra virgin olive oil

Fill a large saucepan half full with water, season generously with salt and bring to a boil over high heat. Add the pasta and stir until it returns to a rolling boil. Cook according to package directions until just done; stir it now and then as it cooks.

While the pasta cooks, put the tomatoes in a bowl, add the garlic and herbs, season with salt and several turns of black pepper and set aside.

Drain the pasta and tip it into a large bowl. Add the tapenade and use two forks to lift and turn the pasta several times so to distribute the tapenade. Add the tomatoes and toss gently.

Divide among individual plates, drizzle some olive oil over each portion, season with a little salt and pepper and serve right away.

Pasta for a Cold Night with Friends

Serves 3 to 4

This is the sort of recipe that you should be able to make with a moment's notice, when a friend stops by unexpectedly or you don't feel like going to the store, which was exactly the position I found myself in the other night, when my friend Evelyn arrived with her new puppy. A well-stocked pantry and an herb garden with plenty of parsley are all you need. You will be astonished at how good this simple combination of ingredients can be.

Kosher salt
10 ounces mparrettati, bucatini, or other long round pasta
2 tablespoons extra virgin olive oil
5 or 6 garlic cloves, minced
½ teaspoon red pepper flakes
Best-quality extra virgin olive oil, such as DaVero Olio Nuovo
1 cup chopped fresh Italian parsley
Black pepper in a mill
Chunk of Parmigiano-Reggiano, Pecorino, Toscano, or Dry Jack cheese

Fill a large pot two-thirds full with water, add a generous tablespoon or two of salt, and bring to a boil over high heat. When the water has come to a rolling boil, add the pasta and cook, stirring occasionally, until it is al dente, about 12 minutes. Drain thoroughly.

Meanwhile, heat the olive oil in a small sauté pan set over medium-low heat, add the garlic, and sauté until it is fragrant and just barely turning golden brown. Do not let it burn. Remove from the heat and stir in the pepper flakes.

Put the cooked and drained pasta into a warmed wide serving bowl, add the garlic mixture, and drizzle generously with the Olio Nuovo or other premium olive oil. Add the parsley and toss gently but thoroughly. Grate cheese over the pasta, toss again, and season with salt and several turns of black pepper. Cover the pasta with a cloth napkin or tea towel to keep it hot.

Serve immediately, with the remaining cheese and a grater alongside.

Roasted Peppers, Tomatoes & Onions with Mozzarella & Pappardelle

Serves 4

The vegetables can be prepared a day or two in advance so that all you have to do to fix dinner is cook the pasta. Make this in late summer and early fall, when there is an abundance of sweet peppers and good tomatoes.

3 to 4 tomatoes, cored and halved
1 onion, cut in lengthwise wedges
Olive oil
4 to 5 sweet peppers, roasted, peeled, seeded, and cut into ¼-inch julienne
2 to 3 hot peppers, roasted, peeled, seeded, and cut into very thin julienne, optional
2 tablespoons brined capers, drained
8 to 10 ounces dried pappardelle or other wide pasta
Kosher salt
4 ounces mozzarella fresca
3 tablespoons extra virgin olive oil

Preheat the oven to 325 degrees.

Put the tomatoes and onion in a baking dish, drizzle with a little olive oil and cook until very tender, about 20 to 25 minutes.

Remove from the oven and cool slightly. Use your fingers to remove the tomato skins.

Put the sweet peppers, hot peppers, if using, tomatoes, and onions into a wide shallow bowl, add the capers and toss gently. Let sit at least 30 minutes.

To serve, fill a large pot two-thirds full with water and bring to a boil over high heat. Add a tablespoon of kosher salt and the pasta and stir until the water returns to boil. Cook according to package directions until just done.

Meanwhile, cut the mozzarella into ¼-inch-thick slices and toss it with the vegetables.

Drain the pasta, toss it with the vegetables and cheese and correct the seasoning. Serve immediately.

Variation:

Add 2 or 3 grilled zucchini, cut into medium julienne.

Sunshine Pasta

Serves 4

If you have a summer garden, you likely have too much zucchini. Even a single vine puts out more than most families can keep up with. A good solution to this situation is to use the blossoms before they turn into fruit. There are many recipes for stuffed zucchini blossoms, deep-fried zucchini blossoms, and zucchini blossom strips in salad. I add this one to the mix, doing my part to keep us safe from too much zucchini.

2 dozen medium (about 2- to 3-inches) zucchini flowers, rinsed and dried on a tea towel
2 tablespoons butter
2 shallots, minced
2 garlic cloves, minced
4 ounces prosciutto, cut in thin strips
Kosher salt
1 pound dried linguine
2 tablespoon extra virgin olive oil
4 ounces (1 cup) aged Asiago, Dry Jack, or Parmigiano-Reggiano, grated
Black pepper in a mill
Kosher salt
2 tablespoons snipped chives
Small zucchini blossoms, for garnish, optional

Bring a large pot of salted water to a boil. Cut the zucchini flowers in half lengthwise, remove the stalk and stamen, and cut the flower petals into medium julienne. Cover with a tea towel and set aside.

Melt the butter in a medium sauté pan, add the shallots, and sauté over medium-low heat until soft and fragrant, about 5 minutes. Add the garlic and sauté 2 minutes more.

Meanwhile, cook the linguine in the boiling water according to package directions. Drain thoroughly but do not rinse. When the linguine is almost done, add the prosciutto and zucchini blossoms to the shallot mixture, toss quickly, and sauté for 2 minutes, until the flowers are just wilted. Remove from the heat and cover to keep warm.

Place the pasta in a large bowl, add the zucchini flowers, all of the pan drippings, and the olive oil. Toss together quickly, add the cheese, and toss again. Season with a generous amount of black pepper, salt to taste, add the chives, toss thoroughly, garnish with zucchini blossoms (if using) and serve immediately.

Spaghettini with Walnut & Parsley Sauce

Serves 4 to 6

If you keep your pantry well stocked, this is the sort of dish you can make without a trip to the store, especially if you have walnuts in the freezer and parsley in the garden.

1 tablespoon kosher salt, plus more to taste
1 pound dried spaghettini
3 cups Italian parsley leaves
6 garlic cloves, minced
1 cup walnut pieces, toasted
Zest of 2 lemons, minced
Juice of 2 lemons
2 teaspoons Dijon mustard
Black pepper in a mill
½ cup extra virgin olive oil, plus more to taste
1 tablespoon capers

Fill a large pot two-thirds full with water, add the 1 tablespoon kosher salt, and bring to a boil over high heat. When the water boils, cook the pasta according to package directions until it is al dente. Drain the pasta but do not rinse it, and reserve about ¼ cup of the cooking water.

Meanwhile, put the parsley into the work bowl of a food processor, along with the garlic, walnuts, lemon zest, lemon juice, and Dijon mustard. Pulse several times, scraping the sides of the work bowl with a rubber spatula if necessary, until the mixture is uniformly minced. Transfer to a medium bowl, season with salt and black pepper, stir in the olive oil and capers, taste, and correct the seasoning. If the sauce seems a little tart, add 2 or 3 tablespoons more of olive oil.

Put the cooked pasta in a wide shallot bowl, pour the sauce over it, and add 2 tablespoons of the cooking water. Toss until the pasta is evenly coated with the sauce; if it seems too thick, add more cooking water and toss again. Serve immediately.

Spaghettini with Artichokes

Serves 4

If you have leftover artichokes, this is an excellent way to use them.

Kosher salt
12 ounces spaghettini or linguini
3 boiled artichokes, page 278
4 garlic cloves, peeled and crushed
2 to 3 anchovy fillets, optional
2 teaspoons green peppercorns in brine, drained
Juice of 2 lemons
⅓ cup extra virgin olive oil, plus more as needed
¾ cup pitted green olives, such as picholine or lucques, minced
1 teaspoon minced fresh tarragon, optional
¼ cup minced fresh Italian parsley
Black pepper in a mill
¾ cup toasted bread crumbs

Fill a large pot two-thirds full with water, add 2 tablespoons kosher salt, and bring to a boil over high heat. Add the pasta, stir several times, and cook until it is just done (check package directions for exact times, and begin tasting at least 90 seconds before you expect it to be cooked al dente). Drain the pasta but do not rinse it. Put it in a wide shallow bowl.

Meanwhile pull the leaves off the artichokes and discard the tough, dark outer leaves. Stack 3 to 4 of the tender leaves and make 2 crosswise slices to julienne the edible portion. Continue until all leaves have been cut. Put the julienned artichokes into a small bowl.

Use a sharp paring knife or a teaspoon to remove the choke from each artichoke heart. Cut each heart into 3 crosswise slices; dice the sliced heart and add it to the julienned leaves.

Put the crushed garlic and anchovies in a mortar or suribachi and use a pestle to grind them to a paste. Add the green peppercorns, crush gently, and stir in the lemon juice.

Pour the olive oil into a large sauté pan, stir in the garlic mixture, add the artichokes and the olives, and set over very low heat. Stir or toss until just heated through, stir in tarragon, and remove from the heat. Add the artichoke mixture to the pasta and toss gently and thoroughly. Sprinkle with the Italian parsley, add several turns of black pepper, and the bread crumbs. Toss again and serve immediately.

Grilled Radicchio with Anchovies, Capers, Garlic & Pasta

Serves 4 to 6

The bitterness of chicories subsides considerably as it cooks; what does remain is excellent with rich ingredients such as anchovies and tart ingredients such as capers; garlic, of course, is good with almost everything.

1 pound radicchio
Olive oil
Kosher salt
Black pepper in a mill
1 pound spaghettini
4 to 5 garlic cloves, minced
1 tablespoon capers, drained
6 to 8 anchovy fillets, drained
2 to 3 tablespoons red wine vinegar
Piece of dry Jack or Parmigiano-Reggiano

Prepare a fire in a charcoal grill.

Cut each head of radicchio in half, put the cut radicchio into a large bowl, and cover with cold water.

When the coals are covered with a thick layer of white ash—about 45 minutes after starting them—set a clean grill rack on top of them. Remove the radicchio from the water and let it drain on a tea towel. Pour a little olive oil in a bowl and use a pastry brush to coat the cut side of the radicchio with a little of the olive. Grill away from the hottest part of the coals, turning once, until the radicchio is limp but not blackened.

Transfer the cooked radicchio to a work surface, season with salt and pepper, and cover with a tea towel.

Fill a large pot two-thirds full with water, add 2 tablespoons kosher salt, and bring to a boil over high heat. Add the pasta, stir, and cook according to package directions until the pasta is just done. Stir now and then during cooking.

While the pasta cooks, use a sharp knife to shred the radicchio, cutting it into thin ribbons. Put the radicchio into a wide shallow serving bowl. Pour a little olive oil into a small sauté pan, set over medium-low heat, and add the garlic. Sauté 30 seconds, add the capers, and sauté 1 minute more, until the capers "bloom." Pour this mixture over the radicchio, add the anchovies and vinegar, and toss thoroughly. Taste and correct for salt and acid.

Drain the pasta but do not rinse it. Put the pasta in the bowl with the radicchio mixture, toss, and serve, with the cheese and a grater alongside.

Summer Pasta al Pesto

Serves 4 to 6

Although almost everyone makes pesto using a blender or a food processor, it tastes better and has a more pleasing texture when it is ground by hand. I worry that we are losing our taste for the real thing, as the ubiquity of pureed pesto has nearly completely eclipsed the handmade version. If you had an Italian mother or nonna, *you understand the difference. The best tool I've found for making pesto is a suribachi, a Japanese mortar and pestle with a large scored porcelain bowl that is very efficient for crushing and grinding. Suribachis are not expensive; I paid $17 for mine. They are available in specialty cookware stores, Asian markets, and online.*

3 cups fresh small basil leaves, loosely packed
6 garlic cloves, peeled and crushed
1 teaspoon kosher salt
¼ cup fresh Italian parsley, leaves only
2 ounces (½ cup) Parmigiano-Reggiano, grated
1 ounce (¼ cup) aged imported Asiago, grated
½ cup best-quality extra virgin olive oil

Do not wash the basil; brush off any dust or dirt. Remove and discard all stems and tough central veins.

Place the garlic and salt in the mortar and use a wooden pestle to grind in a circular motion, pounding gently now and then to break up the garlic. When it has been reduce to nearly a paste, begin adding a few basil leaves at a time, grinding in a circular motion after each addition until the leaves are completely broken up and reduced to a fine texture. Continue until all of the basil and all of the parsley have been incorporated into the paste.

Mix in the cheese. If necessary, use a rubber spatula to scrape the pesto from the sides of the mortar. Slowly drizzle in the olive oil, mixing continuously to incorporate it into the pesto. Add salt to taste. Cover the pesto with a plate.

Serving Suggestions:

- Cook 1 pound spaghettini or linguine until just done. Stir 2 tablespoons of the cooking water into the pesto. Drain the pasta, put it into a wide shallow bowl and top with half the pesto. Use two forks to toss the pasta and pesto together. Serve immediately, with the remaining pesto on the side.
- Toss cooked fresh green beans with pesto, allowing about 3 tablespoons for each pound of beans.
- For a lusciously rich pesto, fold 2 tablespoons room temperature butter into the pesto just before serving it.
- To make pesto pizza, cook the pizza shell in the oven or on a grill. Transfer the pizza to a work surface, spread pesto on top, cut into wedges and serve.
- Garnish summer soups with a spoonful of freshly made pesto.
- Serve pesto with grilled zucchini.
- Serve pesto over creamy polenta or firm polenta that has been sliced and grilled.

Gemelli with Cauliflower & Tapenade

Serves 4 to 6

If you have tapenade on hand, this makes a fabulous and fast healthy winter meal. Although I usually make this using black olive tapenade, it is also excellent with tapenades made of green olives or a mix of both.

Kosher salt
1 pound gemelli
1 cup tapenade, commercial or homemade, at room temperature
3 tablespoons extra virgin olive oil
Black pepper in a mill
½ cup (from about 1 small bunch) fresh minced Italian parsley leaves
3 cups cauliflower florets in small pieces, blanched until just tender, hot

Cook the pasta in plenty of boiling salted water.

When the pasta is just tender, drain it but do not shake off excess water and do not rinse it. Put it in a wide shallow bowl, add the tapenade and olive oil and toss gently but thoroughly. Add several turns of black pepper along with the parsley and cauliflower, toss quickly and serve.

Creamy Polenta with Olio Nuovo

Serves 4 to 6

Polenta and olive oil are happy companions and when both the ground corn and the olive oil are top quality, make a satisfying meal or course. There are, of course, nearly countless ways to enjoy polenta and its many cousins world wide. I wrote about many of them in my book Polenta *(Broadway Books, 1997), which I hope to revise and reissue sometime soon. For now, this one of the simplest ways to enjoy it and to highlight a really great olive oil.*

2 teaspoons kosher salt, plus more to taste
1 cup coarse-ground polenta, preferably organic
2 tablespoons butter
2 to 3 ounces Parmigiano-Reggiano or similar cheese, grated
Black pepper in a mill
Olio Nuovo or other best-quality extra virgin olive oil

Pour 3 cups of water into a heavy saucepan, add the salt and bring to a boil over high heat. When the water reaches a rolling boil, use a whisk to stir it in the same direction, creating a vortex. Slowly pour the polenta into the vortex, stirring all the while. When all the polenta has been stirred into the water, reduce the heat and continue to stir until the polenta thickens.

Switch from a whisk to a long-handled wooden spoon and continue to stir. When the polenta is quite thick, stir in a cup of water and continue to cook, stirring now and then, until the grains of corn are tender. Add up to 2 more cups of water, a half cup at a time, to maintain a creamy texture.

When fully tender, add the butter and stir, taste and correct for salt. Season with several turns of black pepper.

Remove from the heat, cover and let rest 5 to 10 minutes.

To serve, ladle into bowls or soup plates and add a generous swirl of olive oil to each portion. Enjoy right away as a first course or side dish.

Farro with Olive Oil, Lemon & Parsley

Serves 4 to 6

Farro, known as emmer in the United States, is once again becoming popular, including with farmers. It is a delicious grain, with a toothsome texture and warm, earthy flavor. Use it to make seasonal salads or serve it as a side dish with almost any meat or poultry, include stews and braises.

1 cup farro, rinsed
Kosher salt
Juice of 1 to 2 lemons
Best-quality extra virgin olive oil
Handful of Italian parsley, chopped
Black pepper in a mill

Put the farro into a heavy saucepan, cover with water by at least 2 inches, add a generous tablespoon of salt and bring to a boil over high heat. Skim off any foam that rises to the surface, reduce the heat and simmer gently until the farro is tender but not mushy, from 25 to 40 minutes, depending on the type and age of the farro.

When done, strain off extra liquid and tip into a wide shallow bowl. Add the lemon juice, cover and set aside to cool.

Drizzle with olive oil, fold in the parsley, season with pepper, taste and correct for salt.

Serve warm or at room temperature.

Ochazuke

Serves 2

Ochazuke is a classic Japanese rice and tea dish, traditionally served as a snack or near the end of a meal. It is the sort of thing that doesn't really require a recipe; like jook, a rice porridge popular throughout Asia, ochazuke can be topped with a variety of foods, from leftover salmon and pork to fish roe and toasted sesame seeds. Quantities and ingredients are flexible; it is the concept itself that is important to get right. If you can't quite get your mind around the idea of pouring tea onto rice, think of an American parallel: pouring milk onto cereal. That's the approximate ratio of liquid to solid that you want to achieve in this dish.

2 teaspoons hochicha (toasted green tea) or genmaicha (green tea with toasted rice)
Boiling water
2 to 2 ½ cups cooked sushi rice or Italian risotto rice, hot
1 small carrot, grated
½ cup diced (¼-inch) marinated tofu
Small handful of wakame (seaweed)
2 to 3 scallions, trimmed and thinly sliced
½ to 1 teaspoon powdered wasabi
1 teaspoon umeboshi paste (pickled plum paste)
2 heaping teaspoons red miso
Toasted sesame oil

Put the hochicha or genmaicha in a small teapot, add a generous splash of water and pour it off.

Divide the hot rice between two large bowls and scatter carrots, tofu, seaweed, and scallions and over it.

Divide the wasabi, umeboshi paste, and miso between the two servings, placing it on top of the rice. Shake a few drops of sesame oil over the rice.

Fill the teapot with the hochicha or genmaiche with about 3 ½ to 4 cups boiling water and steep for about 90 seconds. Pour tea over the rice, pouring in concentric circles so that all of the rice is moistened and the tea pools in the bowl.

Use chops sticks to stir the mixture thoroughly so that the umeboshi and miso mix with the tea.

Enjoy right away.

Basic Lentils, with Variations

Makes about 2 cups

Lentils typically don't get a fair shake. When they are well prepared, they are quite good, but more often than not they taste like something we should eat but don't necessarily want to. This is likely due to their decades as a darling of the health food set, which seemed to favor thick lentil soups and heavy lentil loaves.

¾ cup brown or green lentils, rinsed
1 small yellow onion, cut in half
4 garlic cloves
1 carrot, cut in chunks
1 celery stalk, cut in chunks
1 leek, cleaned and trimmed
3 Italian parsley sprigs
1 bay leaf
Kosher salt
Black pepper in a mill

Place the lentils in a medium soup pot, add the onion, garlic, carrot, celery, leek, parsley sprigs, bay leaf, and enough water to cover the lentils plus 1 inch. Add 2 teaspoons salt, bring to a boil over high heat, reduce the heat to medium low, and use a wide spoon to skim off any foam that forms. Simmer until the lentils are tender but not mushy (they should not fall apart), about 30 minutes for brown lentils, 45 minutes for green lentils.

Remove from the heat, strain the lentils and reserve the cooking liquid, and place them in a medium bowl. Using tongs, remove and discard the onion, garlic, carrot, celery, leek, parsley, and bay leaf. Stir ½ cup of the cooking liquid back into the lentils and reserve the remaining liquid for making soup.

Serve neat, as a side dish, or use one of the following suggestions.

Serving Suggestions:

- Over steamed rice, drizzled with Meyer lemon olive oil (Davero or O), and garnished with minced preserved lemons.
- Topped with chard sautéed in olive oil, garlic, and lemon.
- Tossed with 2 to 3 tablespoons red wine vinegar, 3 thinly sliced scallions, and ¼ cup crumbled feta cheese, and served over a bed of wilted red cabbage.
- Top each portion with a poached egg and several shakes of your favorite vinegar-based hot sauce.

Flesh

Here you'll find a collection of dishes with unique flavor profiles contributed by a wide range of oils and vinegars, some in sauces and other condiments, others as marinades and braising liquids. The sauces themselves can be used in other dishes as well as these.

Try to use grass-fed and pastured meats as much as possible, as they taste better, have much healthier nutritional profiles, and are the best choices environmentally, too. When it comes to seafood, it is a good idea to check the annual Seafood Watch guides produced by the Monterey Bay Aquarium, which you can find at seafoodwatch.org. Based on a number of considerations, they recommend best uses, substitutes, and fish and shellfish to avoid, all based on up-to-the-minute science.

Poached Trout for Mary Frances

Serves 4 as a main course, 8 as an appetizer

As I was working on the first edition of this book, I had the wonderful opportunity to host writer M. F. K. Fisher and a couple of mutual friends for lunch in my home. It was one of her last excursions before Parkinson's disease kept her bedridden. I began our meal with white bean soup, the one on page 143, as I knew she and I were both fans of a particular Italian olive oil, which I used to finish the soup. Next came this dish, which I could tell she truly enjoyed. I also served dessert and it is so typical of me that I have forgotten what it was. I like to think it was a perfect pear for each of us.

You can prepare the trout and the mayonnaise the day before serving so that there is very little work to do at the last minute.

Court Bouillon (recipe follows)
Herb Mayonnaise, page 239
4 dressed rainbow trout
3 small or 2 medium fennel bulbs, trimmed
¼ cup extra virgin olive oil
1 tablespoon Champagne vinegar
1 lemon, cut in half
1 tablespoon chopped fresh herbs, such as Italian parsley, thyme, oregano, and chives
Kosher salt
Black pepper in a mill
Sprigs of fresh herbs for garnish

Prepare the court bouillon and while it simmers, make the mayonnaise and set it aside.

When the court bouillon is ready, set it over medium-low heat, add 1 or 2 trout (do not crowd them) and simmer very gently for 7 to 8 minutes. Transfer the poached trout to a clean baking sheet or other tray. Poach the remaining trout.

While still warm, skin and bone the fish and set the fillets in a flat dish, using parchment or wax paper between fillets. Chill for 30 minutes.

Using a very sharp, very thin knife or a mandoline, cut the fennel into the thinnest possible crosswise slices. Put the shaved fennel into a bowl, add the olive oil, vinegar, and juice of ½ lemon. Add the herbs, season with salt and pepper, toss, taste and correct for salt, pepper and acid.

Cut the remaining half lemon into wedges

To serve, mound the fennel on individual plates and drape a trout fillet or two half on and half off the fennel. Top the trout with a generous spoonful of herb mayonnaise, a few herb sprigs, and a lemon wedge and serve right away.

Court Bouillon

½ bottle dry white wine
½ cup apple cider vinegar
½ lemon, cut in wedges
1 large carrot, cut in wedges
1 yellow onion, cut in wedges
1 leek, cleaned, trimmed, and cut into 2-inch lenghts
2 Italian parsley sprigs
2 thyme sprigs
1 bay leaf
2 tablespoons kosher salt

Use a fish poacher or a deep pan large enough to hold a whole trout to make the court bouillon. Pour in the wine and vinegar, add the lemon, carrot, onion, leek, parsley, thyme, bay leaf, and salt. Add 4 cups of water and set over medium heat so that the temperature rises a bit slowly. Simmer for 30 minutes, remove from heat and set aside until ready to use. Discard after using.

Petrale Sole with Beurre Blanc & Sautéed Celery

Serves 2 to 3

This dish is an amalgam of a couple of classic preparations, including sole meuniére, which includes capers. I originally designed it to pair with a specific wine but I like it so much that I make it frquently. It is one of my grandson Lucas's favorite dishes.

Beurre Blanc, page 318
¼ cup all-purpose flour
Kosher salt
Black pepper in a mill
1 ½ to 2 pounds Petrale sole or similar fish
4 tablespoons butter
4 to 5 celery stalks, cut in thin diagonal slices
Juice of ½ lemon
1 tablespoon capers
2 tablespoons fresh snipped chives

Make the beurre blanc and keep it hot over not-quite-simmering water.

Working quickly, put the flour on a plate, season it with salt and pepper and press the fish fillets into it, coating them all over. Pat off excess flour and set the fish aside.

Put a tablespoon of butter into a sauté pan set over medium heat and when it is melted, add the celery and sauté, turning a time or two, until it just loses its raw crunch, about 3 to 4 minutes. Season with salt and pepper, transfer to a bowl or plate and keep hot.

Warm 2 or 3 dinner plates.

Return the pan to the heat, add the remaining butter and when it is melted, add the fish and sauté until golden brown, about 1 ½ to 2 minutes per side. Squeeze the lemon juice over the fish, add the capers (so they are in the pan and not on the fish) agitate the pan a bit for about 1 minute and remove from the heat; let rest for a couple of minutes.

Divide the fish among the plates, spoon beurre blanc over it, add the celery alongside, scatter with capers and sprinkle chives over everything. Serve right away.

To drink:

A dry Sauvignon Blanc, Vermentino, or Albariño work beautifully with this does. A dry sparkling wine, especially a blanc de blanc, is a good match, too.

Planked Wild King Salmon with Buerre Rouge

Serves 4 to 6

Slow-cooked salmon is succulent and delicious, with a texture like velvet. In this recipe, there's an added layer of flavor from the wood on which it is cooked.

1 food-grade cedar plank, soaked per manufacturer's instructions
2 pounds wild king salmon filet, scaled and boned
Kosher salt
Black pepper in a mill
Beurre Rouge, page 318
Herb sprigs, for garnish

Put the cedar plank in an oven, turn the thermostat to 250 degrees, and heat for 15 minutes.

Season the salmon all over with salt and pepper.

Set the salmon on the hot cedar plank and bake for 20 minutes; very thick filets may need to cook for 25 minutes. The salmon should be tender, not firm, when pressed gently with a thumb or finger.

Make the sauce while the salmon cooks.

Using thick pot holders, remove the plank and fish from the oven, set on a solid work surface and let rest for 5 minutes. Spoon sauce over the salmon, garnish with herb sprigs and serve on the plank, being certain to protect the table from its heat.

Remove from the oven, drape a piece of aluminum foil loosely over the chicken and let rest 15 to 30 minutes.

While the chicken cooks, make the wild rice salad.

To serve, mound the salad on a large platter. Carve the chicken into pieces, arrange it on top of the wild rice and drizzle with the remaining vinaigrette. Season with salt and pepper and serve right away.

Stir-Fried Chicken with Black Vinegar & Toasted Sesame Oil

Serves 2 to 3

Sometimes we just need dinner, an easy, delicious and healthy meal that isn't too complicated. This is one I return to again and again, for the simple reason that I love it. I vary it based on what I have on hand but always include vinegar and toasted sesame oil.

1 pound pastured chicken thighs, boned (save the bones for making stock)
Kosher salt
Black pepper in a mill
2 tablespoons peanut oil
3 scallions, cut into 1 ½-inch diagonal slices
1 tablespoon minced cilantro roots
4 garlic cloves, minced
1 to 2 serrano chilies, stemmed, seeded, and minced
½ teaspoon freshly ground black pepper
1 tablespoon soy sauce or fish sauce (nam pla or nuoc mam)
½ cup chicken stock or broth
1 tablespoon black vinegar or rice wine vinegar
1 tablespoon fresh lime juice
1 teaspoon sugar
2 tablespoons minced cilantro leaves
Toasted sesame oil
1 lime, cut in wedges
3 ½ cups (from 1 cup raw) steamed jasmine rice, hot

Cut the chicken thighs into slices about ¾ inches wide by 1 ½ inches long. Season with salt and pepper and set aside for about 10 minutes.

Heat the oil in a wok set over medium-high heat and tip the wok to distribute the oil evenly over its surface. Add the chicken and scallions and sauté, tossing and stirring constantly, until the chicken turns from pink to white, about 1 minute. Add the cilantro roots, garlic, chile, pepper, and fish sauce and sauté, stirring constantly, until the chicken is cooked through, about 3 minutes.

Use a slotted spoon to transfer the chicken to a serving dish; keep it warm.

Return the wok to the heat, add the stock or broth, vinegar, lime juice, and sugar to the pan and simmer until the juices are reduced by half. Return the chicken and any of its juices to the pan, toss to coat it in sauce, add the cilantro and return to the serving dish.

Sprinkle with toasted sesame oil, garnish with lime wedges and serve immediately, with rice alongside.

To drink:

Ice cold pilsner or sour beer.

Gravenstein Chicken with Apple Cider Vinegar Sauce

Serves 4

This recipe is both simple and delicious when you use good chicken, which is abundant in Sonoma County. I use chicken thighs instead of breasts because I prefer both the flavor and the texture of dark meat. You should not attempt to use either boneless or skinless chicken in this dish; the skin protects the texture of the meat and contributes flavor during cooking, and meat cooked on the bone—poultry, seafood, red meat—is always better than meat removed from the bone before cooking.

4 chicken leg-thighs or 8 chicken thighs, preferably local and organic
Kosher salt
Black pepper in a mill
3 tablespoons clarified butter
3 cups filtered apple juice, preferably organic
½ cup apple cider vinegar, preferably organic
1 teaspoon whole black peppercorns
1 teaspoon whole white peppercorns
2 tablespoons butter, chilled, optional
2 tablespoons minced cilantro or Italian parsley

Rinse the chicken under cool running water, dry with a tea towel and set on a clean work surface. Season the chicken all over with salt and pepper.

Preheat the oven to 425 degrees.

Melt the clarified butter in a heavy oven-proof frying set over high heat. When it is melted, add the chicken, skin-side down, and sauté until golden brown, about 3 to 4 minutes. Turn and sauté 3 to 4 minutes more. Transfer the chicken to the hot oven and cook until it reaches an internal temperature of about 155 to 160 degrees, about 20 to 35 minutes, depending on the size of the pieces.

Meanwhile, pour 2 cups of the apple juice into a medium saucepan, add the white and black peppercorns and simmer until set over medium heat until the juice is reduced to about ⅓ cup, just enough to coat the bottom of the pan. Add the remaining apple juice and the vinegar and reduce by 2/3, so that you have about ¾ cup sauce. Strain, discard the peppers and return the sauce to a clean pan.

During the last 10 minutes of cooking, brush the chicken several times with the sauce.

Remove the chicken from the oven, transfer to a warm plate and cover loosely with a sheet of aluminum foil.

If the pan that held the chicken has collected a lot of fat, spoon it off, leaving juices behind. Set the pan over a medium-high flame and pour in the reserved sauce. Stir to pick up pan drippings. Taste, season with salt and pepper and remove from the heat. For a richer sauce, swirl in the butter, a tablespoon at a time.

Set the chicken on individual plates, spoon sauce over each portion, garnish with cilantro or parsley and serve.

Braised Lamb Chops & Carrots in Red Wine and Vinegar

Serves 4 to 6

For this recipe, I've borrowed a technique from Greek home cooking, substituting red wine and vinegar for lemon juice and adding carrots and cloves. These ingredients join with the melt-in-your-mouth lamb to create a rich yet refreshing stew that is absolutely beautiful with the wine alongside. I like to serve it over pappardelle, the wide pasta that is available in most local markets these days.

⅓ cup olive oil
2 ½ pounds shoulder lamb chops (5 to 6 chops), trimmed of most fat
1 cup warm water
½ cup dry white wine
4 to 5 garlic cloves, slivered
1 teaspoon dried oregano, crumbled
2 whole cloves
2 tablespoons best-quality red wine vinegar, 6 percent acidity
3 tablespoons dry red wine
1 teaspoon salt
Black pepper in a mill
4 medium carrots, preferably organic, peeled and cut into 2-inch diagonal pieces
2 tablespoons minced fresh Italian parsley
Sprigs of fresh parsley and oregano, for garnish

In a large, deep skillet with a lid, heat the oil over medium-high heat and sauté the lamb in batches, turning, until it is evenly browned. Add the water, wine, garlic, dried oregano, and clove, reduce the heat to low, cover and simmer for 30 minutes.

Add the vinegar and wine, season to taste with the salt and pepper, turn the lamb and cook for 30 minutes more. Turn the lamb again, add the carrots and simmer for 20 to 30 minutes more, or until the carrots are tender and the meat is very tender. Taste and adjust the seasonings. Transfer to a serving platter, garnish with the herb sprigs and serve.

Grilled Leg of Lamb with Olio Nuovo

Serves 6 to 8

Preparing a leg of lamb is simple; you do not need any special skills, especially if you ask your butcher to butterfly it for you. New olive oil—Olio Nuovo—is available from several California producers in December, shortly after the year's olive harvest is complete. The oil is not stable and flavors drop off fairly quickly; if you make this when Olio Nuovo is not available, use the freshest ultra-premium olive oil you can find.

10 to 12 large fresh garlic cloves, peeled and crushed
2 tablespoons kosher salt, plus more to taste
1 teaspoon crushed coriander seed
Black pepper in a mill
2 tablespoons olive oil
1 leg of lamb, preferably American, boned and butterflied
Best-quality extra virgin olive oil, Olio Nuovo, if available

Put the crushed garlic into a suribache or large mortar, add about half the salt and use a wooden pestle to grind into a paste. Mix in the coriander, several generous turns of black pepper, and the olive oil.

Set the lamb on a clean work surface. Sprinkle the remaining salt over the lamb and then rub the paste over it. Set in a large baking dish or other container, cover and refrigerate at least two hours and as long as overnight.

To cook the lamb, prepare a fire in a charcoal grill. When the coals are evenly covered with ash, set the lamb on a clean grill rack and cook, turning now and then, until the temperature in the thickest part of the muscle reaches about 120 degrees. Time will vary based on the heat of the coals, but it should take about 25 to 30 minutes; begin to test after 20 minutes. Transfer to a platter, cover loosely with a sheet of foil and let rest for 15 to 20 minutes.

Use a very sharp knife to cut the lamb into thin slices.

Arrange the sliced lamb on a platter, grouping rare, medium rare, and well done cuts. Season lightly with salt and pepper and drizzle olive oil over the top.

Serve immediately, with more olive oil alongside.

To drink:

This dish wants a really good red wine alongside but it shouldn't be hugely tannic and it shouldn't be a fruit bomb. A Dry Creek Valley Zinfandel, a Carneros Pinot Noir, or an Italian varietal such as Carignano or Primotivo are all perfect. A Rhone blend makes a nice match, too.

Chorizo with Farm Eggs & Tortillas

Serves 4 to 6

Chorizo, a category of spicy pork sausage traditional in Mexico, Spain, and Argentina, is one of the most delicious sausages in the world. Its tangy flavor, the taste that sets it apart from other types of spicy sausage, is vinegar, a hefty dose of it.

Spanish chorizo is typically dried; in Mexico and Argentina, fresh sausage is more common. There are regional variations, too, in Mexico. My favorite is chorizo verde, green chorizo, traditional in Toluca. Spanish chorizo is widely available in the United States and you'll find Mexican chorizo if you live in an area with a large Hispanic population. Some independent butcher shops make their own and offer it in bulk, which is what you want for this recipe. If you buy link chorizo, make sure the casings are not plastic, which are indicative of an inferior product and not one I recommend. You can also make it yourself, which is not at all difficult.

1 pound Mexican chorizo, preferably bulk or homemade (recipe follows)
6 large farm eggs, beaten
Kosher salt
Black pepper in a mill
⅓ cup chopped fresh cilantro leaves
Mexican hot sauce of choice
12 corn tortillas, hot but soft

Put the sausage (if links, remove casings) into a large, heavy sauté pan set over medium heat and use a fork to break up the meat until it loses its raw look and releases its excess fat. Drain off all but 2 tablespoons of fat and return the pan to high heat.

Stir the chorizo one more time and pour in the eggs into the pan. Season with salt and pepper and cook without disturbing them using they are almost set, about 1 ½ minutes. Gently turn the eggs and chorizo but do not break them up too much. Remove from the heat.

Set two tortillas on individual plates, divide the chorizo and eggs among them and sprinkle with cilantro. Serve right away, with hot sauce alongside.

Easy Homemade Chorizo

Makes about 1 ¼ pounds

This version of chorizo is easy to make at home, as it calls for chili powder and ground spices. If you know your way around dried chilies, feel free to use them instead. A mixture of 5 guajillo, 4 arbol, 2 New Mexico, and 1 pasilla is what you'll need for a pound or so of pork, which must contain a fair amount of fat. If the pork you buy is lead, ask that 4 or 5 ounces of fat be added to it.

6 to 7 garlic cloves, peeled and crushed
1 tablespoon kosher salt, plus more to taste
2 tablespoons ground ancho chili powder
1 tablespoon hot Spanish paprika
1 tablespoon smoked Spanish paprika
1 tablespoon sweet Spanish paprika
2 teaspoon dried Mexicano oregano
¼ teaspoon each: ground cinnamon, ground clove, ground coriander, and ground cumin
Black pepper in a mill
⅓ cup red wine vinegar
1 pound pastured pork shoulder with fat, freshly ground or minced

Put the crushed garlic into a large mortar or suribachi, add the tablespoon of salt and use a large wooden pestle to pound and grind the garlic until it forms a smooth paste. Add the spices and several very generous turns of black pepper and mix thoroughly. Stir in the vinegar, taste and correct for salt.

Put the pork into a large mixing bowl and add the garlic mixture. Use your hands to knead the meat and spices together until evenly mixed.

Portuguese-Style Marinated Pork

Serves 6 to 8

You have to plan ahead to make this spicy, succulent dish. You can marinate it for a single day if you're pressed for time, but it's much better if it sits in the marinade for the full four days. Serve it with roasted potatoes or steamed rice.

1 cup peeled garlic cloves
1 teaspoon sweet Spanish paprika
1 teaspoon smoked Spanish paprika
1 teaspoon hot Spanish paprika or ground cayenne
2 tablespoons kosher salt
1 cup red wine vinegar, medium acidity
1 cup water
4 to 5 pounds pork shoulder
¾ cup pitted and sliced green olives
½ cup chopped fresh cilantro or Italian parsley

Using a large suribachi or other mortar and pestle, pound together the garlic, cayenne pepper, and salt to form a smooth paste. Add the vinegar and the water and stir until smooth. Put the pork in a nonreactive dish, pour the marinade over it, and turn the pork to coat it thoroughly. Cover, refrigerate, and marinate for 3 to 4 days, turning the pork in the marinade several times each day.

To cook, preheat the oven to 300 degrees. Put the pork and its marinade in a deep roasting pot, cover with its lid or aluminum foil, and bake until the pork is very tender, about 3 to 3 ½ hours.

Remove from the oven and let rest, covered, 10 to 30 minutes.

Transfer the pork to a serving platter. Stir the olives and cilantro or parsley into the sauce, correct for salt and heat the sauce, if needed.

Spoon some of the sauce over the pork, pour the rest in a small pitcher and serve right away.

Pork Adobo in a Slow Cooker

Serves 6 to 8

This is my personal version of a traditional dish from the Philippines, pork adobo. It is fairly traditional, though I've added fresh cilantro and lime wedges because I think they make the flavors soar beautifully. Serve this with either potatoes, such as Smashed New Potatoes with Vinegar, page 296, or Olive Oil Mashed Potatoes, page 297, or with your favorite fried rice.

1 pork shoulder roast, bone in, about 4 to 4 ½ pounds
Kosher salt
1 large white onion, peeled and very thinly sliced
2 bay leaves
2 chilies, such as Thai chilies or serranos, split open
8 garlic cloves, peeled, crushed, and minced
½ cup soy sauce
⅓ cup white wine vinegar
2 tablespoons palm sugar or brown sugar
2 tablespoons grated fresh ginger
Black pepper in a mill
Chopped fresh cilantro
Lime wedges

Set the pork shoulder on a work surface, cover and bring to room temperature.

Rub the pork all over with about a tablespoon of kosher salt.

Connect a slow cooker to its power source and set it on "high." Spread half the onions over the bottom of the cooker, add a bay leaf and a chili and scatter half the garlic on top. Set the pork, fat side up, on this bed of aromatics and top it with those that remain.

In a small bowl, combine the soy sauce, vinegar, sugar, ginger, and a very generous amount of black pepper (at least 2 tablespoons). Add ¾ cup of water, still well and pour over the pork.

Cook the pork, covered, on high for 1 hour. Reduce to low and cook for 7 to 8 hours more. Take a look at it every now and then and spoon sauce over the meat if it seems at all dry.

About an hour before serving, use tongs to remove the pork form the cooker and set it on a clean work surface. Let it cool briefly and then remove the bone. Use a cleaver to chop the pork into chunks (my preference) or use two forks to shred it, as you would shred kalua pig.

Stir the pork back into the cooking juices, increase the heat to high and cook for 1 hour.

Remove from the heat and serve right away, with potatoes or frlend rice and garnish with chopped cilantro and lime wedges.

Hanger Steak with Salsa Verde & Farro

Serves 2 to 3

This is one of my favorite fallback dishes when I'm suddenly fixing dinner for unexpected guests. Sometimes I use skirt steak and when I can't find it, I use hanger steak. If you don't have farro, serve with Olive Oil Mashed Potatoes, page 294, or Smashed Potatoes with Olive Oil and Herbs, page 297, but replace the herbs with the salsa verde.

Salsa Verde, page 291
½ cup farro, rinsed
Juice of ½ lemon
2 garlic cloves, crushed
Kosher salt
1 teaspoon ground coriander seed
1 teaspoon smoked Spanish paprika
Black pepper in a mill
1 tablespoon extra virgin olive oil
1 hanger steak, 1 to 1 ¼ pounds, preferably grass fed

First, make the Salsa Verde and set it aside.

Cook the farro in plenty of boiling salted water until tender but not mushy. Drain off excess water, transfer to a wide, shallow bowl and squeeze the lemon juice over it. Toss gently with a fork and set aside.

While the farro cooks, put the garlic into a suribachi or other mortar, add a generous pinch of salt and use a wooden pestle to grind the garlic into a smooth paste. Add the coriander, paprika, and several turns of black pepper. Taste and add more salt if it seems a bit flat. Stir in the olive oil.

Rub the garlic paste all over the steak, set it on a plate and cover loosely with a sheet of wax paper. Let rest for 30 minutes.

Heat a stove top grill or a grill pan until very hot. Set the steak on the grill, cook for 90 seconds, rotate it 90 seconds and turn it over. This rotation makes nice grill marks. Cook the steak 90 seconds more, then rotate it 90 degrees and cook until it reaches an internal temperature of 130 degrees for medium rare. Warm the plate the steak rested on and when done cooking, transfer the steak to it, cover and let rest about 10 minutes.

While it rests, divide the farro among individual plates.

Use a sharp knife to cut the steak into ⅓-inch-wide crosswise slices, cutting on a slight diagonal. Drape half on and half off the farro, top with a generous dollop of salsa verde and serve right away.

To drink:

The farro and steak suggest an earthy red wine but the salsa verde cries out for something bright and acidic. A sparkling wine, such as Iron Horse Brut Rosé or another dry sparkling red will settle the argument. A Rosé of Pinot Noir works well, too.

Grilled Beef with Chimichurri Marinade

Serves 6

A friend from Argentina gave me this recipe many years ago, when I was writing the first edition of this book. It was from his father, he told me, who still lived in Argentina. When I asked if there should be any cilantro or parsley, he rebuffed the idea gruffly. "What do you need those things for? We've always done it like this and it's good so don't mess with it!" You have been warned! If you follow these instructions, which are exactly how he told me to prepare the dish, you'll have great results.

2 cups extra virgin olive oil
1 cup red wine vinegar
5 or 6 garlic cloves, minced
2 teaspoons crushed red pepper flakes
1 tablespoon crushed dried oregano
2 teaspoons kosher salt
Black pepper in a mill
3 pounds beef, round steak, top sirloin, or market steak, cut into ¼-inch slices
Salsa (recipe follows)
3 ½ cups steamed white rice

Put the olive oil into a large bowl, add the vinegar, garlic, red pepper flakes, oregano, salt, and several turns of black pepper. Stir to combine, add the meat and turn to coat it evenly. Cover and refrigerate for several hours or overnight. Remove the meat from the refrigerator 30 minutes before cooking.

Shortly before cooking the meat, make the salsa and steam the rice.

Heat a stove top grill until very hot, lift the meat out of its marinade with tongs and cook for just a minute or two, turning it all the while. Serve immediately, with salsa and rice alongside.

Tomato and Green Pepper Salsa

Makes about 1 cup

1 large tomato, cored and cut into small dice
1 large green pepper, stemmed, cored, and cut into small dice
1 tablespoon chopped fresh Italian parsley
1 teaspoon chopped oregano
Kosher salt
Black pepper in a mill
3 tablespoons olive oil
2 tablespoon red wine vinegar

Put the tomato, green pepper, parsley, and oregano into a bowl and toss together. Season with salt and pepper. Add the olive oil and vinegar, stir, taste and correct the seasoning. Cover and refrigerate until ready to serve.

To drink:

Cold beer of choice.

Red Chimichurri

Makes about 1 ¼ cups

4 to 5 large garlic cloves, crushed
Kosher salt
1 small shallot, chopped
½ cup chopped fresh Italian parsley
¼ cup chopped fresh cilantro
1 tablespoon fresh oregano
1 medium tomato, peeled, seeded, minced, and drained
1 Gypsy pepper, seared, peeled, seeded, and minced
1 tablespoon smoked Spanish paprika
A few pinches of crushed red pepper, chipotle powder, or piment d'Esplette
¼ cup red wine vinegar
⅓ to ½ cup extra virgin olive oil
Black pepper in a mill

Put the garlic into a suribachi, sprinkle with salt and use a wooden pestle to grind to a paste. Add the shallot and pound and grind into the garlic.

Using a rubber spatula, fold the parsley, cilantro, and oregano into the paste. Stir in the tomato and Gypsy pepper, add the paprika and hot pepper of choice and stir in the vinegar and olive oil.

Add several turns of black pepper, taste and correct for salt and acid.

To drink:

An Argentine Malbec or an American Malbec, such as Coppola.

Carbonnade Flamande

Belgian-Style Beef, Onion & Beer Stew

Serves 4 to 6

To make this rich and tangy stew without a slow cooker, consult the variation that follows the main recipe.

3 ½ pounds beef short ribs
Kosher salt
Black pepper in a mill
4 tablespoons butter
3 large yellow onions, peeled and cut into ¼-inch-thick rounds
4 tablespoons all-purpose flour
2 cups beef stock, hot
1 bottle (12 ounces) Belgian red ale, Newcastle Brown Ale or Anchor Steam Beer
2 bay leaves
3 teaspoons fresh thyme leaves or 4 thyme sprigs, about 3 inches long
½ star anise
3 tablespoons apple cider vinegar
2 tablespoons double-concentrated tomato paste
Cooked egg noodles, cooked spaghetti squash, roasted creamer potatoes, or homemade fries

Season the short ribs all over with salt and pepper.

Melt 2 tablespoons of the butter in a heavy skillet set over medium heat, add the beef ribs and brown all over, about 3 minutes per side. Transfer the browned ribs to a slow cooker.

Add the remaining 2 tablespoons of butter to the skillet and return it to medium heat. Add the onions, toss to coat them in butter and reduce the heat to low. Cook until the onions are limp and fragrant, about 15 minutes. Turn occasionally and do not let the onions brown.

Sprinkle the flour over the onions, stir and cook about 2 to 3 minutes, stirring or turning gently all the while. Season with salt and pepper, stir and remove from the heat.

Transfer the onion mixture to the slow cooker. Set the temperature on "low" and the timer for 6 hours.

Add the hot stock, the beer, the bay leaves, the thyme, and the star anise. Stir gently a time or two, cover and let cook undisturbed.

Turn off the slow cooker.

Use tongs to transfer the short ribs to a platter and use a slotted spoon to transfer the onions; keep warm.

Use tongs to remove and discard the bay leaves, thyme sprigs, and, if you can find it, the star anise. Stir in the vinegar and tomato paste. Taste and correct for salt and pepper. Return the ribs and onions to the pot.

To serve, ladle into soup plates over or alongside your accompaniment of choice.

Variation:

To make on top of the stove, set the browned short ribs aside while cooking the onions and the flour. Return them, along with any collected juices, to the pan, add the stock, beer, bay leaves, and star anise, bring to a boil over high heat and reduce the heat to very low. Cover and simmer very gently for about 3 hours, or until the short ribs are fork tender and fall off the bone; stir now and then as the stew cooks. Continue as directed in the main recipe.

Argentine-Style Short Ribs with Red Chimichurri

Serves 3 to 4

Chimichurri, an Argentine sauce with both olive oil and vinegar is one of the world's best condiments with beef. There are many styles, some with cilantro and parsley, some, like this one, with tomatoes, and others without any herbs at all. As long as the balance between the olive oil and vinegar is right and the sauce is properly salted, it will be delicious.

Red Chimichurri (recipe follows)
2 pounds beef short ribs, preferably Korean cut (also known as flanken-style)
Coarse salt
Black pepper in a mill

First, make the chimichurri and set it aside.

Set the short ribs on a clean work surface and season all over with coarse salt, rubbing the salt into the meat. Cover with a sheet of wax paper and let rest for about 20 minutes.

Start a fire in a charcoal grill or heat a stove top grill.

Grill the ribs for 5 to 6 minutes or a little less for very rare, turn and grill 4 to 6 minutes more. Do not overcook or the meat will be tough.

Transfer to a serving platter, drizzle a little chimichurri on top and serve immediately, with the remaining chimichurri alongside.

Vegetables

A good vinegar adds sparkle to all manner of sautéed greens and roasted root vegetables and it is a good idea to keep a bottle of a favorite vinegar on the dining table to add to them whenever you want that spark. Olive oil, too, is a welcome condiment to a panorama of vegetables, from asparagus in the spring, summer tomatoes, fall peppers, and winter's delicious cabbages.

For the best vegetables, you probably know what I am going to recommend: Grow your own if you can and, if you can't, shop at your local farmers market and consider joining a CSA program. Wean yourself off out-of-season vegetables and you'll find you enjoy them more than eating the same things year round. Delayed gratification—longing for a local ripe tomato, waiting to enjoy cabbage until after the first cold snap—heightens our pleasure and our satisfaction.

Fresh Artichokes with Olive Oil & Lemon

Serves 4

A second-generation California girl, I have been eating fresh artichokes my entire life. I love them and during the primary season, late winter and early spring, cannot get enough of them. There is often a bumper crop in the fall and I enjoy them then, too, though they are not as good as in late winter and spring, when cold weather—with luck, a frost—sweetens them. The new olive oil is available then, too, and it makes the very best condiment for dipping.

4 large artichokes, preferably Green Globe variety (and not thornless)
Olive oil
Kosher salt
½ cup best-quality extra virgin olive oil, Olio Nuovo, or Meyer lemon olive oil
Juice of ½ lemon, plus more to taste, or best-quality white wine vinegar, such as Vinaigre de Banyuls
Black pepper in a mill

Trim the stem ends of the artichokes so that they are flush with the thistle (the artichoke).

Next, set one artichoke on its side on a work surface with its stem end pointing towards 9 o'clock (if you are right handed; point it towards 3 o'clock if left handed). Using a very sharp knife, make a cut across the artichoke about ¾ of an inch from its tip. (If you like, you can use kitchen shears to snip off the tip of each leaf but this is a decorative step and not necessary.)

Put the artichokes tip-side up into a deep saucepan that holds them snuggly and drizzle about half a teaspoon of olive oil in the center of each one. Fill the pot with water, season it very generously with salt and bring to a boil over high heat; lower the heat so that the water simmers, cover and cook for 12 minutes. After 12 minutes, check the artichoke by using tongs to pull out an inner leaf. If it comes loose with just a bit of resistance, remove the artichokes from the heat. If not, continue to cook, testing the artichokes every 5 minutes. If you are not sure if the artichokes are done, remove one from the liquid, turn stem side up and press a bamboo skewer through the stem end. If it goes in with just a bit of resistance, the artichokes are ready.

Do not let them overcook.

Use tongs to transfer the artichoke to a colander or bowl and let cool slightly. Pour the olive oil into a wide bowl, add the lemon juice or vinegar and season with salt and pepper.

Enjoy immediately, by pulling off a leaf at a time and dipping it into the olive oil mixture. (You may need more of the dipping oil; it really depends on the artichoke itself, its size and flavor, and your preferences.) To enjoy the heart, use a spoon to scoop out and discard the choke, swirl the heart in the oil, season with a little extra salt and enjoy.

Variation:

To serve the artichokes with mayonnaise, page 327, or aïoli, page 332, chill thoroughly, set on individual plates, add a very generous dollop of your preferred sauce, season with salt and pepper and enjoy.

Wilted Lettuce

Serves 2

When I was a little girl, my grandmother made this for my step-grandfather, her fifth husband, nearly every time I had dinner with them. The shredded lettuce sat in a cream-colored serving bowl next to his plate and my grandmother, already bent from osteoporosis, would lift her heavy cast iron pan, the one I cook with today, and pour the bubbling mixture of bacon and vinegar over the lettuce. I loved listening to its sizzle and always breathed in the heady aromas but never asked for a taste, fearing another of the harsh reprimands that came so frequently from this intriguing and mysterious man. I have no way of knowing if this is how she made it, though the scent of my version is evocative of those early years.

1 large head red leaf lettuce, cleaned and cut into ¼-inch-wide crosswise slices
Kosher salt
3 bacon slices, diced
1 tablespoon sugar
⅓ cup red wine vinegar
Black pepper in a mill
Hearth bread, heated

Put the lettuce into a heat-proof bowl and set it aside.

Sauté the bacon until it is crisp. Reduce the heat and when the bacon fat has cooled a bit, carefully add the sugar and vinegar and stir gently as the sugar dissolves. When the mixture is bubbling hot, pour it over the lettuce. Season with black pepper and serve right away, with hot bread alongside for sopping up the delicious juices.

Radicchio Braised in Vinegar, with Bacon & Chévre

Serves 4 to 6

I enjoy this dish with Vinegar Eggs, page 163 and 169, and also alongside chicken and pork.

4 ounces bacon or pancetta, diced (see Note below)
1 small red onion, cut into small dice
2 pounds radicchio
Kosher salt
¼ cup red wine vinegar or sherry vinegar
Black pepper in a mill

Put the bacon or pancetta into a heavy sauté pan set over medium heat and cook until it is just crisp. Add the onion, reduce the heat to low and cook 10 minutes more.

Meanwhile, trim the radicchio and cut it into lengthwise quarters. Add it, cut side down, to the pan and cook for about 2 minutes; turn and cook on the other cut side. Season with salt, add half the vinegar, cover the pan and cook until tender, about 5 minutes.

Uncover, transfer the radicchio to a serving bowl, return the pan to the heat and add the remaining vinegar. Swirl the pan to pick up any juices, season with salt and pepper and pour over the radicchio.

NOTE

If you use pancetta, add 2 tablespoons of olive oil to the pan when it fry it.

Variation:

Top the braised radicchio with 4 ounces crumbled chévre, such as chabis, before adding the sauce.

Serve right way.

Pea Shoots in Peanut Oil, with Garlic & Vinegar

Serves 4

Pea shoots were once available primarily in Asian markets and restaurants but in the last few years they are increasingly found at farmers markets, putting them within easy reach of home cooks. They are delicious, nutritious, and very easy to prepare.

2 tablespoons peanut oil
1 or 2 garlic cloves, crushed
8 to 10 ounces fresh pea shoots
1 tablespoon soy sauce
1 teaspoon rice vinegar or Chinese black vinegar

Put the peanut oil into a wok or sauté pan and set over medium-high heat, add the garlic and cook for 10 seconds. Add the pea shoots, toss and turn in the oil and cook until just wilted, 2 to 3 minutes. Transfer to a serving bowl, sprinkle with soy sauce and vinegar and serve right away.

Glazed Baby Bok Choy

Serves 4

I have always found bok choy, tat soi, and similar greens a bit cloying without a healthy shake of vinegar or generous squeeze of lemon or lime juice, which perks up everything and brings the flavors into harmony.

3 tablespoons peanut oil
2 garlic cloves, pressed
1 tablespoon freshly grated ginger
8 small or 4 medium baby bok choy, rinsed and dried
¾ cup white wine or chicken stock
2 tablespoons black vinegar or rice vinegar, plus more for the table
1 tablespoon soy sauce
Toasted sesame oil
Black pepper in a mill
1 tablespoon toasted sesame seeds

Pour the vinegar into a deep sauté pan set over medium-low heat, add the garlic and ginger and sauté for 1 minute. Add the bok choy, the wine or stock, and the vinegar, cover and cook until almost tender, about 5 minutes.

Uncover, add the vinegar and continue to cook until the juices are reduced to a glaze. Add the soy sauce, toss and transfer to a serving bowl. Season with a few shakes of sesame oil, a few turns of black pepper and scatter the sesame seeds on top. Serve right away, with vinegar alongside.

Sautéed Greens with Garlic, Olive Oil & Vinegar

Serves 4 to 6

You can use kale, chard, collards, or any other sturdy winter green in this recipe but you will need to make adjustments in cooking times. Chard will need less time on the heat, collards quite a bit more. The timing here is for Lacinato kale, also known as black cabbage, which is one of my favorites. If you have found winter greens a bit dull, you'll find that garlic and vinegar typically perk them right up. The basic recipe makes an excellent side dish and can also be used as part of a more complex dish.

2 pounds (2 bunches) kale or other braising greens, stems and ribs removed
¼ cup plus 1 tablespoon olive oil
Kosher salt
Black pepper in a mill
6 to 8 garlic cloves, minced
¼ teaspoon red pepper flakes
2 tablespoons best-quality extra virgin olive oil
1 tablespoon red wine vinegar or Tabasco sauce

Stack several leaves and cut them crosswise into ¾-inch strips. Rinse them in cool water and shake off most but not all of the water. Heat the ¾ cup olive oil in a large, heavy skillet set over medium-high heat. Add about a third of kale and sauté, tossing and stirring the kale until it is wilted. Add another third of the kale, stir and cook until wilted, add the remaining kale, and stir and cook until it is wilted. Season with salt and pepper and reduce the heat to medium low. Add ¼ cup of water, cover the pan, and cook until the kale is completely tender, about 7 or 8 minutes. Remove the lid and push the kale to one side. Add the tablespoon of olive oil and the garlic and sauté until the garlic is fragrant, about 30 seconds. Toss the kale with the garlic and the red pepper flakes. Taste, correct the seasoning, and remove from the heat.

Transfer to a serving bowl, drizzle with the extra virgin olive oil and vinegar or Tabasco, and serve immediately.

Variations:

- Greens with White Beans: After seasoning the kale with red wine vinegar, toss it with 1 ½ cups cooked white beans and 2 tablespoons minced Italian parsley. Top with freshly grated Parmigiano cheese or toasted bread crumbs and serve hot.

- Greens with Potatoes: Clean and slice 6 medium Yellow Finn or Yukon Gold potatoes, place in a pot, cover with cold water, season with salt, and simmer until tender, about 12 minutes. Mash the hot potatoes lightly with a fork, add the seasoned greens, mix gently (do not overmix), add the extra virgin olive oil and vinegar and serve immediately.

- Greens with Winter Squash: Use the kale as a bed for roasted winter squash. Cut peeled squash into 2-inch chunks, toss it with a little olive oil, salt, and pepper, place it on a baking sheet, and roast it at 375 degrees until it is completely tender. Set the squash on top of the cooked kale, season with salt and pepper, and serve hot.

- Greens with Pork: Use the kale as a bed for slow-roasted pork shoulder.

Tangy Glazed Onions

Serves 4 to 6

You can use any small bulb onion in this recipe, but it is best when you use cippoline, a small flat Italian onion that has become increasingly common in the United States. Look for cippoline at farmers markets and in speciality stores.

Kosher salt
12 small (1 to 1 ½ inches) onions, unpeeled
3 to 4 fresh thyme sprigs
3 to 4 Italian parsley sprigs
4 tablespoons butter
1 tablespoon sugar
4 tablespoons red wine vinegar
Black pepper in a mill
2 teaspoon minced fresh thyme leaves

Fill a medium saucepan half full with water, add 2 tablespoons kosher salt, the onions, and the sprigs of thyme and parsley. Bring to a boil over high heat, reduce the heat to medium low, and simmer until the onions are just tender when pierced with a bamboo skewer. Drain, discard the herb sprigs, and set the onions aside.

Shortly before serving, melt the butter in a medium sauté pan, add the onions, and set over medium heat. Cook until the onions are heated through, sprinkle with sugar, and continue to cook until they are lightly browned, about 5 to 7 minutes. Increase the heat to high, add the vinegar, and cook, shaking the pan gently and continuously, until the vinegar is reduced and forms a glaze over the onions. Season with salt and pepper, toss with thyme leaves, and transfer to a pretty dish.

Serve right away.

Roasted Peppers in Red Wine Vinegar, with Variations

Serves 4 to 6

Roasted peppers are now everywhere, sold freshly seared at farmers markets and freshly seared and peeled in supermarkets. It is easy to roast them at home, too, of course. They are delicious as an appetizer, a salad, or a side dish and need nothing more than vinegar, salt, and pepper, though feel free to gild the lily, as I suggest here.

6 fresh sweet peppers in a combination of colors, roasted, peeled, stemmed, seeded, and cut into 1-inch-wide strips
⅓ cup red wine vinegar
Black pepper in a mill
Flake salt
1 tablespoon chopped fresh herbs
2 teaspoons finely minced fresh herbs such as oregano, Italian parsley, marjoram, and thyme

Put the peppers into a wide shallow serving bowl, add the vinegar and season very generously with black pepper. Season lightly with salt, scatter the herbs on top and serve right away.

Variations:

- Add 8 ounces crumbled feta cheese and 3 or 4 garlic cloves, peeled and thinly sliced, and toss with the pepper and vinegar. Serve with hot bread.
- Put 4 or 5 medium-ripe garden tomatoes into a baking dish, set in a 350-degree oven and cook until very tender, about 20 to 25 minutes. Remove from the oven, cool until easy to handle and then remove the skins and stem core. Add to the sweet peppers.
- Add 2 tablespoons of capers to any version of this dish.

Roasted Peppers with Eggplant, Zucchini & Whipped Feta

Serves 4 to 6

Although this summer vegetable stew is neither a ratatouille nor a caponata, it shares qualities with both. One of the main differences is that there are no olives, as there are in a caponata, and there are no tomatoes, an ingredient in both traditional dishes. I wanted something that let the other vegetables shine through, so that I could use tomatoes in other recipes. The feta adds a delightful spark so do not omit it; if you don't feel like making the whipped feta, consult the variation at the end of the recipe. This recipe shows another way to roast peppers, the way it is typically done in France.

4 to 6 bell peppers, cut in half lengthwise, seed cores and stems removed
Olive oil
2 medium-small or 1 large eggplant, cut into 2-inch by ½-inch batons
Kosher salt
1 medium large zucchini, cut into 2-inch by ½-inch batons
4 to 5 garlic cloves, crushed and minced
¼ cup red wine vinegar
6 large basil leaves, thinly shredded
2 tablespoons capers
Black pepper in a mill
Whipped Feta, page 85
4 thick slices country-style bread

Preheat the oven to 325 degrees. Put the peppers in a baking dish, drizzle with a little olive oil, and turn them so they are lightly and evenly coated. Arrange in a single layer, cut sides down. Bake the peppers until the skins blister, about 25 to 35 minutes. Remove from the oven, transfer to a bowl, and cover with a tea towel.

Meanwhile, pour enough olive oil in a heavy sauté pan to coat the bottom of the pan with a layer not quite ⅛ inch deep. Set over medium heat, add the eggplant, season generously with kosher salt, and toss several times. Reduce the heat to very low, cover the pan, and cook for 20 minutes, until the egg-plant is very soft and tender. Transfer to a wide shallow bowl and return the pan to medium heat. Add a teaspoon of olive oil and the zucchini. Season with salt and pepper and cook, stirring or tossing frequently, until it is just barely cooked, about 3 to 4 minutes; the zucchini should be somewhat crunchy. Add to the bowl with the eggplant.

Use your fingers to pull the skins off the peppers and cut them into ½-inch-wide lengthwise strips; add to the bowl with the other vegetables. Add the garlic, vinegar, basil, and capers, if using. Season with salt, add several generous turns of black pepper, and toss gently. Let rest at room temperature for at least 30 minutes and up to 1 hour before serving.

To serve, toast the bread until it is lightly browned. Cut each piece in half and arrange it around the outside of the vegetables. Serve family style, with the whipped feta alongside.

Variation:

Instead of the whipped feta, cut 8 ounces feta cheese into ½-inch cubes and toss it with the vegetables just before serving.

Eggplant with Salsa Verde

Serves 4 to 6

Here is an ideal example of using two grades of olive oil in the same dish. First, olive oil is used to lubricate the eggplant and facilitate the transfer of heat. Next, a full-flavored olive oil makes the Italian-style salsa verde, one of the most delicious and versatile condiments there is, blossom. Meat lovers will enjoy the recipe for hanger steak with this salsa verde on page 291.

Olive oil
2 large eggplant
Kosher salt
Black pepper in a mill
1 bunch fresh Italian parsley, stems removed
2 large garlic cloves, minced
Zest of 2 lemons
Juice of 1 lemon, plus more to taste
⅓ cup extra virgin olive oil, plus more to taste

Preheat the oven to 375 degrees.

Remove the stem end of the eggplant. Using a sharp knife, cut the eggplant into ½-inch-thick lengthwise slices.

Pour enough olive oil onto a baking sheet so that there is a layer of oil about ⅛ inch thick. Arrange the eggplant on top of the oil, fitting the slices close together. Quickly turn over each slice, season with salt and pepper and bake until tender, about 25 minutes. To test the eggplant, press a slice quickly with your thumb; if the eggplant gives, it is done.

Transfer the eggplant to a wide shallow serving dish and allow to cool slightly.

Meanwhile, make the salsa verde. Use a sharp knife to chop the parsley and put it in a medium bowl. Add the garlic, lemon zest, and juice of 1 lemon. Season generously with salt and pepper. Add the olive oil. Taste the salsa verde for both flavor and texture; if it is too dry, add the remaining lemon juice and enough olive oil to balance the acid.

Correct the seasoning and set aside.

Spoon the salsa verde over the eggplant and serve within 45 minutes.

Variations:

- Add ¾ diced Armenian cucumber to the salsa verde.
- Crush 2 teaspoons brined green peppercorns and add to the salsa verde.
- Rinse 2 tablespoons salted capers in water and fry in a small amount of olive oil until they just open. Scatter over the eggplant after adding the salsa verde.
- Toast ¼ cup pine nuts and scatter over the eggplant after adding the salsa verde.
- Grate 2 hard-cooked eggs and scatter over the eggplant after adding the salsa verde; top with fried capers.

Zucchini Ribbons with Cherry Tomato Vinaigrette

Serves 3 to 4

The dish, served either hot or cold, is like summer in a bowl: light, pretty, a little sweet, and very good for you. Serve it as a main course on a hot day or as a side dish with a more elaborate meal.

5 to 6 small zucchini, ends trimmed
Kosher salt
1 pint very small cherry tomatoes, preferably mixed colors, cut in half
2 garlic cloves, minced
3 tablespoons minced red onion
1 serrano, seeded and minced, optional
5 tablespoons extra virgin olive oil
Juice of 1 lime
Black pepper in a mill
4 or 5 mint leaves, cut into very thin ribbons
3 tablespoons minced fresh Italian parsley

Use a mandoline to cut the trimmed zucchini into very thin lengthwise pieces, making long ribbons.

Fill a medium pot half full with water, add a tablespoon of kosher salt and bring to a boil over high heat.

While waiting for the water to boil, put the tomatoes, cloves, onion, and serrano, if using, into a medium bowl and toss together gently. Add the olive oil and lime juice, season with salt and pepper, taste and correct the seasoning. Set aside.

When the water boils, reduce the heat to medium, add the zucchini and cook for 2 minutes, until the zucchini is just limp. Drain and immediately put into a wide shallow bowl. Add the cherry tomato vinaigrette, toss very gently, scatter the mint and parsley on top and either serve hot or at room temperature.

Olive Oil Mashed Potatoes

Serves 3 to 4

When you drain the potatoes, don't try to shake off all the water; you want some of it to remain, so that the potatoes are not dry. When making mashed potatoes with butter, one typically adds milk or cream so it is crucial that some of the cooking water clings to the potatoes as you puree them.

3 large russet potatoes, peeled and sliced
Kosher salt
1 teaspoon lemon juice
⅓ cup best-quality extra virgin olive oil, warmed
¼ cup chopped fresh Italian parsley or snipped chives
Black pepper in a mill
Flake salt

Put the potatoes into a medium saucepan, covered with water by at least 2 inches and season generously with salt. Bring to a boil over high heat, reduce the heat to low and simmer gently until the potatoes are tender when pierced with a fork, about 12 to 15 minutes.

When done, use a slotted spoon to transfer the potatoes to a food mill fitted with its large blade and set over a deep bowl. Pass the potatoes and whatever liquid clings to them through the mill.

Working quickly, add about a teaspoon of kosher salt to the potatoes, squeeze lemon juice on top of the salt to dissolve it and use a rubber spatula to fold it into the potatoes. Fold in the olive oil and the parsley or chives. Taste, correct for salt and season with black pepper.

Transfer to a serving bowl, sprinkle with a little flake salt and serve right away.

Smashed New Potatoes with Vinegar

Serves 4 to 6

These potatoes are delicious with Portuguese-Style Pork, page 263, and any other tangy meat or poultry dish. I prefer a rich artisan vinegar, such as B. R. Cohn Cabernet Sauvignon vinegar or O Zinfandel vinegar.

1 ½ pounds very small new potatoes
Kosher salt
Best-quality red wine vinegar
Black pepper in a mill

Cook the potatoes in plenty of rapidly boiling salted water until they are tender when pierced with a fork. Drain and transfer to a bowl.

Using a dinner fork, gently smash each potato, leaving it squashed but intact. Set on a baking sheet, cover and set aside until ready to serve.

To serve, warm the potatoes for 15 minutes in an oven preheated to 350 degrees. Transfer to a serving bowl, sprinkle generously with vinegar, season with salt and pepper and serve right away.

Smashed Potatoes with Olive Oil & Fresh Herbs

Serves 4 to 6

In this dish, the olive oil you use must be the very best, an ultra-premium oil valued for its flavor and texture. Otherwise, they potatoes will just be oily and you'll wonder why you bothered. I like these alongside Chicken au Vinaigre, pg. 248, Roasted Chicken, 249, or almost any other chicken dish. And sometimes I enjoy them solo, for lunch.

1 ½ pounds very small new potatoes, such as creamers
Kosher salt
Best-quality extra virgin olive oil
3 tablespoons chopped fresh herbs (any combination of thyme, oregano, chives, and Italian parsley)
Black pepper in a mill

Cook the potatoes in plenty of rapidly boiling salted water until they are tender when pierced with a fork. Drain and transfer to a bowl.

Using a dinner fork, gently smash each potato, leaving it squashed but intact. Set on a baking sheet, cover and set aside until ready to serve.

To serve, warm the potatoes for 15 minutes in an oven preheated to 350 degrees. Transfer to a serving bowl, drizzle with olive oil, scatter the herbs on top and season with salt and pepper. Enjoy right away.

Baked Potatoes with a Very Special Olive Oil

When I wrote the first edition of this book in 1991, I had become enchanted by a late harvest olive oil from Liguria, Ardoino's Biencardo. It is produced only in those years when the weather allows the olives to remain on the trees until mid to late winter before harvest. In most years, the olives drop to the ground before they have developed their richest flavors. But when the conditions are perfect, the resulting oil is luscious and buttery with a color like liquid sunlight.

This oil, which I have found at one store in New York City, should never be used in cooking. Drizzle it over great bread, toss it with premium pasta, or drizzle it over a perfectly baked potato and add a bit of flake salt and the best pepper you can find. It is a treat and a treasure.

Flavored & Seasoned Oils, Vinegars & Sauces

As I worked on photos for this book, a dear friend, Fabiano Ramaci, a chef and winemaker, arrived to help with food preparation early one morning but he did not come empty handed.

"Try this," he said, handing me a beautiful bottle that had been hand painted by his wife Lanie. "It's my habañero oil."

As I worked to finish the manuscript, his delicious oil served me well. I sprinkled it over rice and chorizo, dipped bread in it, and added a bit to scrambled eggs. It made me think of the delicious paella he made at some of our local farmers markets when we first met, as he'd sprinkle a bit of harissa oil over the paella just before handing it to me.

The right flavored oil adds a delicious spark to all manner of foods, from simple steamed rice to an elaborate slow-cooked stew. Vinegars, too, can excite the palate and the appetite when combined thoughtfully and carefully with herbs, spices, fruits, and even vegetables.

In this chapter, I share the ones that I feel are the most reliable for home cooks to make. Always remember to start with a good-quality product, not a cheap oil, not an inferior vinegar. Also included in this chapter are classic sauces that rely upon an oil or a vinegar for its essential character.

Flavored Olive Oil, How to & How Not to Make Them

In my opinion, which is based on years of experience, most flavored oils are overrated. They are typically made with chemical approximations of the flavoring agent and the oils are not necessarily of the highest quality. Some are sweetened, which I find insipid. There are exceptions to this, of course, and there are a handful of excellent flavored oils on the market. The best are citrus olive oils made with fresh fruit that is crushed and and pressed with the olives. Meyer lemon olive oil is the most popular and for good reason; it is delicious and versatile. Olive oils infused with lime, blood orange, grapefruit, and citron are also quite good and ideal as condiments.

If you want to make flavored oils at home, prepare them in small quantities that you will use fairly quickly. And guard against contamination, including with spores of botulinum, which are naturally present in soil and require an anaerobic environment to grow. Oil is the perfect medium and garlic is the most common source of contamination so do not simply drop a clove or two into a bottle of oil and don't ever chop the garlic, which increases the risk of contamination. To make garlic oil, peel fresh garlic, wash it and score it in 2 or 3 places and then soak it overnight in vinegar. Dry it thoroughly, add it whole to a small bottle of olive oil. It will, after a few days, infuse the oil with its flavor, though I think simply using fresh garlic and a great olive oil produces better results.

Herb-Infused Olive Oil

Makes about 1 ½ cups

If you feel compelled to infuse an olive oil with your favorite herb, this technique works quite well and is entirely safe. However, refrigerations degrades the flavor of the oil and leaving it at room temperature risks contamination by tiny specks of vegetable matter.

1 cup, loosely packed, fresh herb leaves (basil, sage, or thyme), rinsed, blanched in salted water for 15 seconds, and pressed dry on a tea towel
1 ½ cups good-quality extra virgin olive oil

Put the herbs into the work bowl of a blender or food processor fitted with its metal blade and pulse several times. Add half the olive oil, pulse again and scrape into a Mason jar. Add the remaining oil, stir, cover and refrigerate for at least 1 day and up to 2 days.

Strain the mixture through a fine sieve lined with several layers of cheese-cloth. Pour into a bottle, close and store in the refrigerator. Use within a week or two.

Chili Oil

Makes about 1 ½ cups

The easiest flavored oil to make successfully is a spicy one.

2 tablespoons crushed red pepper flakes
1 ½ cups good-quality extra virgin olive oil

Put the pepper flakes into a Mason jar, add the oil, close with the jar's lid and set in a cool, dark pantry for several days. Taste the oil and begin to use it when its flavors have blossomed. Discard after 1 month.

About Flavored Vinegars

Flavored vinegars fall into five general categories: fruit, herb, spice, vegetable, and blends. The reason to make them is because you like them, have an abundance of ingredients, and find it fun. If you have to buy, say, raspberries, it is probably better to purchase a commercial raspberry vinegar, almost all of which are quite good. If you have a raspberry patch, you are set to make your own.

A flavored vinegar will not be any better than the vinegar you begin with, so use one of good quality, one with a pleasing flavor on its own.

When working with vinegars in any capacity, keep in mind its corrosive nature. Use stainless steel implements, glass or porcelain containers, and lids of cork or plastic. If using canning jars, add a double layer of wax paper or a round of parchment on top of the jar before closing it with its lid and ring. Stir vinegars with a wooden spoon. Wine bottles, especially 375ml bottles, are perfect for bottling your vinegars.

Flavored vinegars are delicious sprinkled on fresh fruit, steamed vegetables, soups, and stews. They can also be used in any recipe calling for vinegar; just be sure flavors that are compatible with the other foods in the meal. Spaghetti and meatballs is lovely with a salad dressing with oregano vinegar and good olive oil. Basil vinegar works best with summer tomatoes. My favorite is sage vinegar, which I use throughout late fall and early winter.

Fruit Vinegar

Makes about 2 ½ to 3 cups

The amounts here yield rich, voluptuous, and full-flavored vinegar, which is my preference. My favorite is Cranberry Vinegar, which I make every fall when the new crop of cranberries arrives.

4 cups chopped fruit
2 cups good-quality vinegar, no more than 6 percent acidity, plus more as needed

Put the fruit into a glass jar or crock and pour the vinegar over it. There should be just enough vinegar to completely cover the fruit; add more if necessary. Place the chopped fruit in a glass jar or crock and pour the vinegar over it. You should have just enough vinegar to cover the fruit; add more if necessary. Store the mixture, covered, in a cool pantry or refrigerator for at least 2 days or up to 10 days, tasting frequently to determine when your vinegar is sufficiently flavored. Strain the mixture through several layers of cheesecloth or through a paper or cloth coffee filter until the liquid is absolutely clear, pressing the fruit to remove all of the liquid. Bottle, close with a cork, and store in a cool, dark cupboard. Use within 6 months.

Recommended Combinations:

- Gold raspberries with Champagne vinegar or apple cider vinegar
- Red raspberries, strawberries, gooseberries, cranberries with white wine or Champagne vinegar
- Black raspberries, blackberries, boysenberries, olallieberries, blueberries with red wine vinegar
- Stone fruit (apricots, peaches, nectarines) with white wine or Champagne vinegar
- Pears, Asian pears with Champagne vinegar
- Papaya, mango, persimmons, pineapple with rice wine or apple cider vinegar; add 2 tablespoons of grated ginger root if you like
- Peaches, apricots, nectarines, pits removed, and persimmons with apple cider vinegar
- Citrus (use just the zest) with white wine or Champagne vinegar; add a sprig of lemon thyme if you like

Garlic Vinegar

Makes 4 cups

Garlic vinegar is a staple in many pantries and can be made with either red wine vinegar or white wine vinegar; if you love it, consider making both. Use the vinegar wherever the flavor of garlic will enhance a dish, and try it as a condiment on soups, stews, and pizza.

1 head garlic
4 cups red or white wine vinegar, any strength

Separate the cloves of garlic, discard the root, and cut the cloves in half. You need not peel them. Place the cloves in a glass jar or crock, pour the vinegar over them, and close the container with a cork. Let the vinegar sit in a cool, dark cupboard for a week before using it. Use the vinegar directly from the container, and replenish it as you use it. It should continue to provide lusty garlicky flavor for about 6 months.

Variation:

Add a large sprig of culinary rosemary to the jar.

Herb Vinegar

Makes 3 cups

My favorite herb vinegar is rosemary made with a rich red wine vinegar: It is the only one I use regularly, preferring to add other herbs fresh to specific dishes. You should experiment until you find your favorite combinations.

1 cup fresh herbs
3 cups vinegar, no more than 6 percent acidity
Sprigs of fresh herbs with their flowers, if available when bottling

Lightly crush the herbs, put them in a glass jar or crock, and cover with the vinegar. Let the mixture steep in a cool pantry for up to 1 month, tasting now and then to determine when your vinegar is sufficiently flavored. Strain through cheesecloth or a coffee filter. Bottle, add a fresh sprig of the herb, and close with a cork. Store in a cool, dark cupboard.

Suggested Combinations:

- Chives, summer savory, sage, thyme, tarragon, chervil with white wine or Champagne vinegar
- Rosemary, marjoram, oregano with red wine vinegar

Peppercorn Vinegar

Makes 3 cups

Peppercorns add a seductive flavor the a vinegar, which in turn makes a delicious condiment.

3 tablespoons peppercorns, black or a mixture of black, white, and green
3 cups white wine vinegar

Put the peppercorns into a glass jar, pour in the vinegar and close with a non-metalic lid. Store in a cool, dark cupboard for 2 to 3 months, tasting now and then to determine strength. Strain through cheesecloth or a coffee filter into clean bottles, add a few fresh peppercorns and close with corks.

Ginger Vinegar

Makes 3 cups

Rice vinegar and ginger often appear in recipes together, as their flavors merge beautifully.

1 large piece of ginger root, about 3 inches long, minced or grated
3 cups rice vinegar, 5 percent acidity

Put the ginger into a glass crock or jar, cover with the vinegar, seal with a non-metallic lid and steep for 2 to 3 weeks, until the flavor suits you. Strain the mixture through cheesecloth or a coffee filter into clean bottles and close with a cork. Use within about 6 months.

Spice Vinegar

Makes 4 cups

Some cooks suggest heating the vinegar when you add spices but I find it can degrade the flavor. I prefer to lightly toast the spices.

1 tablespoon each whole cloves, allspice, and black peppercorns
2-inch piece of cinnamon
1 teaspoon cardamom seeds
1 whole nutmeg, cracked
1 whole star anise
½ teaspoon juniper berries
4 cups red wine vinegar, no more than 6 ½ percent acidity

Put the spices into a sauté pan set over medium heat and toast, agitating the pan gently, until they give off an aroma. Remove from the heat and cool.

Put the spices into a glass jar or crock, cover with the vinegar, seal with a non-metalllic lid and steep for 1 to 2 months. Strain into clean bottles and close with corks.

Rose Petal Vinegar

Makes 3 cups

This is an almost heartbreakingly delicate vinegar, full of transcendent aromas. Sprinkle it on fresh melon or use it in a subtle, fragrant mayonnaise or a hazelnut vinaigrette. Because it is so beautiful, it also makes a lovely gift. Remember, the deeper the color of the rose petals you use, the more vibrantly colored your vinegar. Be certain that the roses you use have not been sprayed with any sort of fungicide or pesticide.

4 cups rose petals, lightly crushed
3 cups Champagne vinegar, no more than 6 percent acidity
10 drops rosewater, optional, when bottling
1 perfect rosebud, when bottling

Put the rose petals into a glass jar or crock, cover with vinegar, seal with a non-metallic lid and set in a cool, dark pantry for 4 weeks.

Strain the vinegar into a tall glass jar, add the rosewater, if using, and the rosebud, seal with a cork and use within 4 to 6 months.

Cucumber-Chive Vinegar

Makes about 2 ½ to 3 cups

Cool and refreshing, this vinegar is wonderful with seafood salads, either in a vinaigrette or in a mayonnaise.

4 cups cucumber, peeled and chopped (see Note below)
2 tablespoons minced fresh chives
2 cups Champagne vinegar, no more than 6 percent acidity
2 or 3 blades of chives
1 chive flower

Put the cucumber and chives into a glass jar or crock, pour the vinegar over it, seal the jar with a non-metallic lid and store in a cool, dark pantry for about 3 weeks, tasting now and then. When the vinegar suits you, strain it through several layers of cheesecloth or a coffee filter until the liquid is very clear. Pour it into a clear glass bottle, add the blades of chive and the chive flower, seal with a cork and store in a cool, dark cupboard. Use within 4 to 6 months.

About Mignonette

"A loaf of bread," the Walrus said,
"is what we chiefly need:
Pepper and vinegar besides
Are very good indeed—
Now if you're ready, Oysters dear,
We can begin to feed."
—Lewis Carroll, *Through the Looking-Glass*

Ice-cold oysters on the half shell are among the simplest, purest joys in the world and they require nothing more than a squeeze of lemon. Sometimes, though, it is nice to dress them up with a lovely mignonette, a classic French sauce of vinegar, shallots, and pepper, and, sometimes, a spritz of citrus.

Classic Mignonette

Makes about ½ cup, enough for 12 to 18 oysters

This is the basic mignonette, the one served wherever oysters on the half shell are enjoyed. The most common variations are simply the use of different vinegars, sherry vinegar, perhaps, or balsamic vinegar. If you have a favorite vinegar, homemade or commercial, give it a try here.

½ cup white wine or red wine vinegar, medium acidity
1 small shallot, minced
Black pepper in a mill

Put the vinegar in a bowl, add the shallot and several turns of black pepper, stir and serve alongside raw oysters.

Cranberry Mignonette

Makes about 1 cup, enough for up to 4 dozen osyters

I love this during the winter holidays, when oysters are bright and crisp and there is, if we're lucky, time to indulge. For years, several friends and I spent New Year's Eve together eating Dungeness crab and then gathered the next morning for raw oysters and crab cakes, which I would make from the leftover crab.

2 tablespoons fresh cranberries, minced
½ teaspoon grated orange zest
1 small shallot, minced
¾ cup cranberry vinegar
1 tablespoon fresh orange juice
Freshly ground black pepper

Put the cranberries, orange zest, shallot, vinegar, and orange juice in a small bowl, stir, season with several turns of black pepper, cover and refrigerate until ready to use. Serve alongside raw oysters.

Ginger Mignonette

Makes about 1 ¼ cups, enough for 5 to 6 dozen oysters

The combination of ingredients in this spicy sauce is absolutely seductive. Make sure you have plenty of oysters on hand and be sure that the sauce is well chilled.

1 cup rice vinegar or homemade ginger vinegar
Juice of 2 limes
1 shallot, finely chopped
1 serrano, minced
1 teaspoon grated fresh ginger, strained
2 tablespoons chopped cilantro
½ teaspoon kosher salt

Put the vinegar, lime juice, shallot, serrano, ginger (you can omit if using ginger vinegar), and cilantro in a small glass bowl. Add the salt, stir until it is dissolved, cover and chill until ready to serve alongside raw oysters.

Black Raspberry Mignonette

Makes about 1 cup, enough for up to 4 dozen oysters

Fragrant and tangy, this mignonette highlights the natural sweetness of the oysters.

1 cup low-acid black raspberry vinegar
1 shallot, minced
Juice of 1 lemon
Kosher salt
Black pepper in a mill

Put the vinegar, shallot, and lemon juice in a small glass bowl. Add a few minutes of salt and stir until it dissolves. Add several turns of black pepper, cover and chill until ready to serve alongside raw oysters.

About Beurre Blanc & Beurre Rouge

Beurre blanc and beurre rouge—literally, white butter and red butter—depend upon both wine and vinegar for their flavor and butter for their voluptuous texture. There are many versions of these classic mother sauces and endless disagreements about how they are best made. At their most basic, they are simple emulsions, with a large amount of fat suspended in a small amount of acid. Some versions call for the addition of cream, when served with seafood a fish fumet may replace the wine and spices may be added to resonate with the overall meal.

Beurre Blanc

Makes about 1 cup, enough for 4 to 6 servings

If you worry about the sauce breaking as you make it, use a double boiler with barely simmering water when you incorporate the butter.

½ cup dry white wine
⅓ cup white wine or Champagne vinegar
Spritz of lemon juice, optional
1 small shallot, minced
Kosher salt
White pepper in a mill
8 ounces (2 sticks) best-quality butter, cut into pieces and chilled

Put the wine, vinegar, lemon juice, if using, and shallot in a small heavy saucepan, set over medium heat, season generously with salt and a few turns of pepper and simmer until the liquid is reduced to just 3 tablespoons. Remove from the heat and let cool a bit. Lower the gas flame so that it barely flickers or set an electric vinegar on its lowest setting.

Return the pan to the heat and begin to add butter, a piece at a time, whisking all the while. Do not add a second piece until the first has been incorporated. Continue until all the butter has been added. Lift the pan if necessary to ensure that the emulsion does not break, i.e., separate. The butter should never rise above 130 degrees. Taste, correct for salt and pepper and strain into a small pitcher. Serve immediately or hold the sauce in a warm place for up to 30 minutes; if necessary to hold it a bit longer, pour it into a wide-mouthed thermos.

Best Uses: With sautéed, pan-fried, or roasted fish, such as Petrale sole, sanddabs, Branzino; with lobster; with chicken; with vegetables.

Beurre Rouge

Makes about 1 cup, enough for 4 to 6 servings

I like to make this sauce using a varietal vinegar, such as B. R. Cohn Cabernet Sauvignon Vinegar or O Zinfandel Vinegar. Both have more character, more richness, and more depth of flavor than most generic vinegars. It is also excellent made with Spice Vinegar, pg. 311.

½ cup dry red wine
⅓ cup best-quality red wine vinegar
1 small shallot, minced
Kosher salt
Black pepper in a mill
8 ounces (2 sticks) best-quality butter, cut into pieces and chilled

To make beurre rouge, follow the instructions for beurre blanc. The technique is identical for both.

Best Uses: With grilled, broiled, or pan-fried steak; with wild Pacific King salmon; with roasted beets.

Dressings, Salsas & Condiments

Certain sauces rely on vinegar, oil, or both for their essential flavors and textures and here you'll find the classics, from vinaigrettes—for which I offer two template recipes—mayonnaise and its cousins, traditional basil pesto, and chutney, that delightful sweet and spicy condiment essential in Indian cuisine.

It is a very good idea to learn to make your own sauces, including mayonnaise and even ketchup—which wasn't always made with tomatoes as most is today—salad dressings, and such, as you then have complete control over the ingredients and need neither binders to maintain emulsification or preservatives to create self-stability. Follow the seasons—make apricot chutney and blueberry chutney in June, for example—for those sauces that need lengthy cooking, as chutneys do, and understand that even the very best vinaigrette can be made in five minutes or less.

Basic Vinaigrette
Nut Oil Vinaigrette
Vanilla Vinaigrette
Handmade Mayonnaise
Mayonnaise by Machine
Flavored Mayonnaise
Aïoli by Hand
Aïoli by Machine
Romesco Sauce
Rouille
Traditional Basil Pesto
Spicy Garlic Cilantro Relish
Pickled Onions & Grapes
Apricot Chutney
Blueberry Chutney
Peach & Currant Chutney Cranberry Pear Chutney
Peach Ketchup

About Vinaigrettes

Have you ever wondered where the term vinaigrette came from? It is, of course, a French word, but was it always a dressing?

It was not.

Before humans developed enclosed sewer systems and figured out how to dispose of garbage, sewage ran open through city streets and trash was typically dumped out of windows. The stench, we can imagine, was overpowering. In France, upperclass women carried tiny sponges in little silver boxes and when they encountered the unpleasant aromas, they held the sponges to their noses, which effectively eclipsed the facts of life that surrounded them. These little boxes and their sponges were known as *vinaigrettes*.

When I wrote the first edition of this book, I was just exploring the remarkable diversity of this group of sauces, which I have always loved. Eventually, I wrote an entire book on the topic, *Vinaigrettes and Other Dressing*, published by Harvard Common Press in 2013. Thus, I have reduced the number of recipes here and instead offer two template recipes along with a couple of others.

I encourage you to think of vinaigrettes outside the salad bowl, so to speak. You can use them in every course and even before you sit down to eat by employing one as a marinade for vegetables, fruit, fish, or meat.

When adjusting a vinaigrette for acid balance, let your palate guide you. If you prefer things on the tart side, you'll likely want a ratio of 1 part vinegar to 3 parts vinegar. If you prefer a milder vinaigrette, you'll want that ratio closer to 1 part acid to 4 parts oil. If using a fruit vinegar and don't feel the taste of the fruit is bright enough, do not add more vinegar; instead, add a pinch or two of sugar, which will make the fruit flavor blossom. You can use citrus juice instead of vinegar in almost any vinaigrette, which is then, technically, a citronette. I often use both, about ⅔ vinegar and ⅓ citrus juice.

Basic Vinaigrette

Makes about 1/3 cup

A vinaigrette takes just a few minutes to make and produces such good results that there is no reason to buy a commercial one and no reason to make one in quantities larger than what you will use in a single meal. You can easily vary the type of acid, the kind of oil, and other additions to suit your fancy and your menu.

1 small shallot, minced, or 1 tablespoon minced red onion
1 tablespoon vinegar of choice
Kosher salt
3 to 4 tablespoons extra virgin olive oil
Black pepper in a mill

Put the shallot into a small bowl, add the vinegar and season with kosher salt. Let sit a few minutes. Stir in the olive oil and add several turns of black pepper. Taste, correct for salt and acid, and use right away.

Nut Oil Vinaigrette

Makes about ½ cup

Nut oils are delicately flavored and fairly perishable. They should be purchased in small quantities and stored in the refrigerator.

1 small shallot, minced
2 tablespoons white wine, Champagne or pear vinegar
Kosher salt
3 tablespoons hazelnut, walnut, or roasted peanut oil
2 tablespoons peanut oil or mildly flavored olive oil
Black pepper in a mill

Put the shallots into a small bowl, add the vinegar and season with kosher salt. Let sit a few minutes. Stir in the two oils, season with several turns of black pepper, taste and correct for salad and acid.

Vanilla Vinaigrette

Makes about 1 cup

This dressing was inspired by Diane Ackerman's book Natural History of the Senses *(Random House, 1990), which includes an astonishingly seductive essay on vanilla. I've used balsamic vinegar because vanilla is one of its flavors, naturally in aceto balsamico tradizionale and by addition in commercial approximations. Use this dressing on wild rice salads and with quail, chicken, and duck.*

1 medium shallot, minced
3 tablespoons good-quality balsamic vinegar
1 tablespoon white wine vinegar
Kosher salt
½ teaspoon sugar, plus more to taste
1 teaspoon pure vanilla extract
4 tablespoons walnut oil
6 tablespoons roasted peanut oil
Black pepper in a mill
3 tablespoons chopped fresh Italian parsley

Put the shallot into a medium bowl, add the vinegars, season with salt and set aside for a few minutes.

Add the ½ teaspoon of sugar, along with the vanilla, oils, and several turns of black pepper. Taste and correct for salt and acid balance. Stir in the parsley and use within a day.

Mayonnaise, the Mother Sauce

Mayonnaise is the classic cold emulsion, an oil-in-liquid mixture, the oil suspended in raw egg yolks with the help of a small quantity of lemon juice and vinegar. It is the mother of a panorama of other sauces, from humble "secret sauce" and Thousand Island Dressing to Remoulade sauce, Tartar sauce, and the suave sauces that accompany chilled seafood in the finest French restaurants. It is the easiest thing in the world to grab a jar off a supermarket shelf—Best Foods or, as it is called on the East Coast, Hellman's, is the generally agreed-upon mayonnaise of choice—but there are reasons to make it at home. Most importantly, you have complete control over all the ingredients and don't have to turn a blind eye to undesirable and potentially toxic ingredients in all commercial brands.

Oil is by quantity the primary ingredient in mayonnaise. Many recipes call for canola oil, which I do not recommend in any recipe, or another neutral oil. I typically make mayonnaise with olive oil, choosing a mildly flavored one at times and a boldly flavored one when the menu calls for it. If you don't want to use olive oil, avocado oil and grape seed oil are your best options.

I also typically use lemon juice as the acid for the simple reason that it suits me. I'll sometimes add a nut oil or a toasted sesame seed oil to go with a specific dish.

Classic mayonnaise does not contain mustard but I sometimes add it for the depth of flavor it contributes. Many published recipes include instructions to "bind" the sauce with the addition of boiling water as the final step in preparation. My experimenting has never proven this to be necessary, and my experience is backed up by Harold McGee, who writes on the science of food, and tells us that the only reason to add water is to adjust the consistency of an overly stiff mayonnaise.

When discussing cold emulsions that are made with egg yolks, it has become necessary to address questions of safety. The best advice is always to know the source of your ingredients. Use eggs from backyard chickens or pastured chickens, as problems with contamination, which have been quite rare, come from mass-produced eggs laid by hens who live in crowded and appalling conditions. Try to find a good egg farmer at your local farmers market or roadside stand, which are increasingly common these days, even in cities.

Properly refrigerated, homemade mayonnaises and their cousins will maintain their peak flavor for 5 or 6 days.

Handmade Mayonnaise

Makes 1 ½ cups

If you like to make mayonnaise and other emulsified sauces, get yourself a balloon whisk, which is most efficient for this process. A balloon whisk is simply a whisk with wires that form a balloon. They incorporate air more quickly and efficiently than most other whisks.

2 egg yolks, at room temperature
1 teaspoon kosher salt
¼ teaspoon ground white pepper
3 tablespoons extra virgin olive oil
¾ cup mildly flavored olive oil, avocado oil, or grape seed oil
2 teaspoons Champagne vinegar
1 to 2 tablespoons lemon juice
1 tablespoon water, if needed

Put the egg yolks, salt, and pepper into a wide, deep bowl and use a balloon whisk to beat the mixture until the eggs turn pale and thick. Begin adding the oil a teaspoon at a time, whisking it in completely before adding more. As the sauce thickens, you may add progressively more oil and, finally, the vinegar and lemon juice. If the mixture seems to stiff, thin with the tablespoon of water.

Refrigerate for 2 hours before using.

Mayonnaise by Machine

Makes 1 ½ cups

The trouble with emulsions made in the blender is that the air incorporated into them acts as a cushion on the tongue, dulling the flavors a bit. It is often necessary to increase the flavoring agents, so you should taste the emulsion frequently until you find the proportions that suit your palate. If you are making mayonnaise during a hot summer, you probably should use a blender or food processor, as hand-whipped emulsions are less stable and can separate in hot weather.

1 whole egg, at room temperature
1 egg yolk, at room temperature
2 to 3 teaspoons vinegar
1 teaspoon kosher salt
¼ teaspoon ground white pepper
1 teaspoon prepared Dijon mustard
¼ cup extra virgin olive oil
1 cup mildly flavored olive oil, avocado oil or grape seed oil
1 to 2 tablespoons lemon juice
1 tablespoon boiling water, if needed

Put the whole egg, egg yolk, vinegar, salt, pepper, and mustard into the work bowl blender or food processor fitted with the metal blade and pulse for 30 seconds.

With the machine operating, slowly drizzle in the oils in a steady stream. Add lemon juice to taste.

Thin with boiling water if the mayonnaise is too thick.

Transfer to a glass bowl or jar and refrigerate, covered, for at least 2 hours.

Flavored Mayonnaise

Using either basic recipe as a template, you can create a kaleidoscope of flavored mayonnaises by changing the vinegar and oil, by eliminating the lemon juice, and by varying the type of mustard. These are my favorite combinations.

Cranberry: Use cranberry vinegar and replace the lemon juice with orange juice.

Pomegranate: Use homemade or commercial pomegranate vinegar and omit the lemon juice.

Red Raspberry: Use red raspberry vinegar and omit the lemon juice.

Blueberry: Use blueberry vinegar, omit the lemon juice, and add a healthy pinch of ground clove.

Black Raspberry: Add 2 cloves minced garlic and 1 teaspoon sugar to the egg yolks, use black raspberry vinegar, and omit the lemon juice.

Toasted Sesame: Use rice vinegar, toasted sesame oil (for the smaller amount), peanut oil (for the larger amount), and replace the lemon juice with the juice of a lime.

Herb: To the eggs in the blender, add 2 cloves garlic and use champagne vinegar. After completing the mayonnaise, stir in by hand 3 tablespoons finely chopped fresh herbs.

Aïoli and Its Cousins

Aïoli is the peasant cousin of mayonnaise, robust where mayonnaise is subtle, wild where mayonnaise is tame. Some variations are full of fire where the mellow mother sauce is mild, soothing, and, it might be said, bland. It is a short leap from homemade mayonnaise to this family of velvety garlic sauces known as aïoli, allioli, rouille, romesco, and even skordalia, which you'll find on pages 97 to 100. Throughout the Mediterranean, versions of this paste of olive oil and garlic have been used to garnish fish stews and dozens of other dishes. The specific ingredients vary with the region, but the basic concept and the technique for producing are simple: Crush garlic, add eggs, add oil. There you have it.

Traditionally, garlic is ground into a paste with a small quantity of salt and egg yolks in a mortar with a pestle. Olive oil is slowly added to form a thick, rich emulsion. Potatoes, breadcrumbs, tomatoes, peppers—hot and sweet, ground and fresh—monkfish liver, sherry vinegar, lemon juice, and almonds all make appearances in the regional panorama of sauces, depending on the local flair.

Aïoli itself comes to us from Provence, where it is so ubiquitous that it is sometimes called the Butter of Provence. Huge feasts known as *Grand Aïoli and Aïoli Monstre* are held in villages throughout Provence when the new crop of garlic is ready. Gallons of freshly made aïoli are served with seasonal vegetables, stewed octopus, hard-cooked eggs, escargots, and more, with plenty of chilled rosé and rustic red wine alongside.

A well-kept secret of aïoli is that the version of the sauce served to locals is much more garlicky than the version served to tourists, especially from America. I make mine in the Provençal way, with a full head of garlic for each batch.

For many years, I made my aïoli in a blender and wrote, rather foolishly, in the first edition of this book that the time to make it by hand is a luxury we don't have. I blush at my own words. I almost always make aïoli by hand, unless there's a heat wave. For several years, I hosted a Grand Aïoli at Preston Farm and Vineyards in Healdsburg, California, an annual celebration of the Sonoma-Provence Exchange, which I founded in 1994. Each year, I would make six gallons of aïoli, all of it by hand. One year, we had to quickly re-emulsify it in a food processor because the temperature soared past 100 degrees and the emulsion began to separate. Electricity saved the day!

Aïoli by Hand

Makes 1 ¾ to 2 cups

If you are nervous about making an emulsified sauce by hand, here's what I recommend. Sit outside if you can and if you can't, sit inside where there is a good view. Put on some favorite music, relax, and enjoy the process. Let it mesmerize you without much thought for the final outcome. You'll be amazed at how quickly time passes. I've made gallons of aïoli while listening to Puccini arias, the Ramones, Nirvana, Hole, and Roxy Music, sometimes while sitting on my deck and watching the crows doing somersaults in the warm air.

1 garlic bulb, cloves separated, peeled and lightly crushed
1 teaspoon salt, plus more to taste
2 egg yolks from farm eggs, at room temperature
1 to 1 ¼ cups best-quality olive oil
2 tablespoons lemon juice

Put the crushed garlic into a large suribachi or mortar, add the teaspoon of salt and use a wooden pestle to crush and pound the garlic until it forms a very smooth paste. Mix in the egg yolks.

Switch from the pestle to a balloon whisk and begin adding oil a few drops at a time, gradually increasing the amount as the emulsion increases in volume.

After all the oil has been incorporated, taste the mixture. If it is flat, add a few generous pinches of salt, placing it in one area; slowly pour the lemon juice over it so that it dissolves and then whisk well.

The texture of the aïoli should be similar to that of mayonnaise; if it seems too stiff, thin with up to 1 tablespoon of water.

Cover and refrigerate for at least 2 hours before serving.

Aïoli by Machine

Makes 1 ¾ cups

Although it may seem counterintuitive, a machine-made aïoli will never be as velvety as one made by hand because a metal blade reduces the garlic into smaller and smaller pieces but does not pulverize them into a smooth paste. Still, use good ingredients and you'll have a great sauce.

1 whole egg, at room temperature
2 egg yolks, at room temperature
1 teaspoon Dijon-style mustard or 1 teaspoon powdered mustard
1 garlic bulb, cloves separated and peeled
1 teaspoon kosher salt
¾ cup extra virgin olive oil
¾ cup mildly flavored olive oil
1 to 2 tablespoons lemon juice, to taste
Pinch of Piment d'Esplette or ground cayenne

Put the egg, egg yolks, mustard, garlic, and salt into the work bowl of a food process or and pulse until the garlic is pulverized and the mixture uniform. With the machine operating, slowly drizzle in the extra virgin olive oil. When it is fully incorporated, slowly drizzle in the second olive oil.

Add the lemon juice, taste and correct for salt and acid, add the Piment d'Estplette or ground cayenne and pulse again. Place the egg, egg yolks, mustard, garlic, and salt in a food processor. Process until the mixture is pulverized. With the machine running, slowly drizzle in the extra virgin olive oil. Add the lemon juice. With the machine still running, drizzle in the olive oil. Taste the mixture, add the cayenne, and more salt or lemon juice to taste.

Transfer the aïoli to a bowl or jar, cover and refrigerate for at least two hours before using.

Romesco Sauce

Makes about 2 cups

Romesco sauce has its roots in Catalunya in northeastern Spain, where almond trees thrive alongside olive trees. This sauce is delicious on seafood stew, with grilled spring onions, and as a dip for grilled vegetables, shrimp, and scallops.

2 small dried red chilies
2 egg yolks, at room temperature
5 garlic cloves
¼ cup toasted, slivered almonds
1 teaspoon kosher salt, plus more to taste
1 sweet red bell pepper, roasted, peeled, and seeded
1 small tomato, peeled and seeded
1 ¼ cup extra virgin olive oil
¼ cup red wine vinegar
Juice of 1 lemon

At least 2 hours before making the sauce, cover the dried peppers with boiling water and let them rest.

Drain, scrape the flesh from the skin and put the paste into the work bowl of a food processor fitted with the metal blade. Add the egg yolk, garlic, almonds, and salt and process to form a smooth paste. Add the sweet pepper and tomato and pulse again until smooth.

With the machine operating, slowly drizzle in half the olive oil. Stop the machine and use a rubber spatula to scrape ingredients off the side of the bowl, if necessary. With the machine operating, add the vinegar followed by the remaining olive oil. When all have been incorporated, stop the machine, taste, correct for salt and add as much of the lemon juice as needed to suit your palate; taste after adding half of it.

Scrape into a bowl or jar, cover and refrigerate for at least two hours.

Rouille

Makes approximately 1 ½ cups

This smoldering garlic sauce will wake up the sleepiest, most jaded palate in record time. I have come across several versions of this Mediterranean condiment, some that use bell pepper and a mere 2 cloves of garlic, some that call for pimientos instead of hot peppers. The timid palate may not concur but when it comes to pepper and garlic, I say why hold back? This version, adapted from the inimitable Book of Garlic *by Lloyd J. Harris, does not know the meaning of the word restraint.*

¼ cup red wine vinegar
½ cup, packed, fresh breadcrumbs
10 garlic cloves, peeled and chopped
1 teaspoon salt, plus more to taste
2 teaspoons Piment d'Esplette or dried hot red pepper flakes
½ cup extra virgin olive oil

Pour the vinegar over the breadcrumbs and let the mixture sit for 30 minutes. Squeeze out the vinegar and discard it. Set the bread aside.

Put the garlic in a large mortar, add the salt and use a wooden pestle to pound the garlic into a fine, smooth paste.

Add the Piment d'Esplette or pepper flakes and the bread crumbs and pound until the mixture is once again smooth. Add a tablespoon of oil and mix thoroughly. Continue adding oil, a tablespoon at a time, until all of it has been incorporated. The sauce should be quite thick, a smooth paste that keeps its shape on a spoon.

Taste, correct for salt, cover and refrigerate until ready to use.

Traditional Basil Pesto

Makes about 1 ½ to 2 cups, enough for 1 to 1 ½ pounds of pasta

Do you ever feel like you've eaten your fill of something you once craved? I feel that way about pesto, likely because I've been served blender versions too many times in the cooler months, when basil is not in season. The worst is when this out-of-season pesto is slathered onto a pizza skin before cooking. When it comes out of the oven, it is nearly black and has an unpleasantly cloying taste. For years, I couldn't even look at it.

Now I make it by hand and only when it is growing in my own backyard or is fresh at my local farmers market. I serve it traditionally, with pasta. The best way to do this is to leave the pesto in the suribachi or mortar, and add a couple of tablespoons of cooking water just before you drain the pasta. Put the hot pasta into a serving bowl, add a couple of big spoonfuls of pesto to it, stir and then set the rest on the table so guests may add as much or as little as they like.

4 cups fresh small basil leaves, loosely packed, chopped
8 garlic cloves, peeled and crushed
1 teaspoon kosher salt
¾ cup fresh Italian parsley leaves, chopped
4 ounces butter, at room temperature
4 ounces (1 cup) Parmigiano-Reggiano, grated
¾ cup best-quality extra virgin olive oil
3 tablespoons pine nuts (please read Note about pine nuts on page 82) or walnuts, lightly toasted

Do not wash the basil; brush off any dust or dirt. Remove all stems and tough central veins.

Put the garlic and salt in a large suribachi or mortar and, using a wooden pestle, begin to grind in a circular motion, pounding now and then to break up the garlic. When the garlic has been reduced to a smooth paste, add a small handful of basil and parsley and continue to grind in a circular motion. Repeat until all the leaves have been incorporated into a slightly rough but even mixture.

Add the butter and mix thoroughly. Fold in the cheese and use a rubber spatula to scrape the pesto from the sides of the mortar. Slowly drizzle in the olive oil, mixing continuously to incorporate it into the mixture. Taste and correct for salt. Fold in the pine nuts or walnuts.

Cover with a plate until ready to use.

Spicy Garlic Cilantro Relish

Makes about 2 cups

This is a favorite condiment, one that is quite versatile, easy to make, and irresistibly delicious. However, if you don't like cilantro just move long, nothing to see here, bye-bye!

6 garlic cloves, peeled and crushed
Kosher salt
1 tablespoon chipotle powder
3 cups cilantro leaves, chopped
¼ cup freshly squeezed lime juice
⅔ cup extra virgin olive oil
6 to 8 ounces best-quality feta cheese, crumbled
Black pepper in a mill

Put the garlic cloves into a large suribachi or mortar, season generously with salt and use a wooden pestle to crush and pound the garlic until it is reduced to a smooth paste. Mix in the chipotle powder.

Add the cilantro and mix it into the paste, pounding it a bit as you do. Stir in the lime juice and olive oil. Use a rubber spatula to fold in the cheese. Taste, correct for salt as needed and season with a few turns of black pepper. Cover and let rest for 30 minutes before using.

Best Uses: On grilled ahi tuna; in quesadillas and on tacos; with roasted meats; on Mexican-style stews and braises; on crackers; with pasta.

Pickled Onions & Grapes

Makes 8 to 10 pints

The late Stanley Eichelbaum, a food writer and chef who lived in San Francisco, loved this condiment, especially with grilled fish or poultry. It is also excellent with smoked salmon, on sandwiches, and alongside roasted meats. It is a welcome addition to cheese boards and Ploughman's Lunch, too. The time to make this is in late summer and early fall, when grapes are in season.

3 ½ cups raspberry vinegar
1 bottle (750ml) red wine
1 ½ cups sugar, plus more to taste
10 whole allspice berries, crushed
10 whole cloves, crushed
1 teaspoon black peppercorns
1 teaspoon white peppercorns
1-inch piece of cinnamon
8 to 10 cardamom seeds
Kosher salt
Black pepper in a mill
2 pounds organic seedless red grapes, removed from their stems
3 pounds small red onions, peeled and very thinly sliced

Put the vinegar, red wine, sugar, and all the spices into a heavy saucepan set over medium heat and stir until the sugar melts. Taste and correct for sugar balance. Season with salt and pepper, remove from the heat and let cool.

While the mixture cools, cut the grapes in half lengthwise.

Put the grapes and onions into a large bowl and toss together. Pack into pint jars. Fill each jar with the marinade and divide the spices among the jars. Seal with lids and rings, refrigerate and let rest for at least a day before using. Use within a month or so.

Apricot Chutney

Makes approximately 6 pints

Apricots have a short season and you must pay attention if you want to make this chutney, as it must be done with fresh local apricots, not those that have traveled from the Southern Hemisphere. This chutney is delicious with pork loin, pork shoulder, and almost any Indian curry.

6 pounds ripe apricots, halved and stoned
3 pounds sugar
1 pound currants
3 heads garlic, cloves separated, peeled, and chopped
5 serranos, seeded and cut into a very thin julienne
5 ounces fresh ginger, peeled and grated or chopped
1 tablespoon crushed red pepper flakes
1 ounce dried hot chilies
3 cups apple cider vinegar
1 to 2 tablespoons salt

Put the apricots and sugar into a heavy pot set over medium heat and stir gently until the sugar dissolves. Add the currants, garlic, serranos, ginger, red pepper flakes, apple cider vinegar, and 1 tablespoon of the salt. Stir and continue to cook very gently for about 1 hour, until the mixture thickens.

Taste and add the remaining salt if the chutney seems at all flat.

Pour the chutney into hot sterilized half-pint or pint jars and process in a water bath according to manufacturer's instructions for 15 minutes. Cool on several layers of tea towel, check the seals and store in a cool, dark cupboard for up to 1 year.

Blueberry Chutney

Makes about 4 cups

Blueberries are abundant where I live in west Sonoma County and during their season it can be hard to keep up with them. I freeze them for making shrub, I make vinegar and, when I have time, I make this chutney, which is delicious with whole milk yogurt, fresh ricotta, mozzarella fresca, grilled polenta, rice pudding, and alongside duck, venison, bison, buffalo, and goat.

4 cups fresh blueberries, rinsed
2 ripe pears, preferably Comice, peeled, cored, and diced
1 small yellow onion, diced
1 or 2 serranos, stemmed, seeded, and cut into very thin julienne
2-inch piece of fresh ginger, peeled and grated
¾ cup sugar
1 teaspoon kosher salt
½ teaspoon ground clove
⅛ teaspoon ground cardamom
Pinch of ground cinnamon
Pinch of ground cayenne
¾ cup best-quality red wine vinegar, such as O Pinot Noir Vinegar

Put the blueberries and pears into a medium heavy saucepan, add the onion, serranos, ginger, sugar, salt, clove, cardamom, cinnamon, and cayenne. Stir gently.

Add the vinegar, set over medium heat, and stir continuously until the liquid boils.

Reduce the heat to very low and simmer until the mixture thickens, about 20 to 25 minutes. Remove from the heat, cool, transfer to glass jars, and refrigerate for up to 3 weeks.

Peach & Currant Chutney

Makes approximately 2 quarts

Make this spicy chutney in midsummer or early fall, when there is an abundance of ripe peaches. Excellent with any curry dish, it is also delicious served with grilled chicken that has been marinated in balsamic vinegar. Homemade curries make wonderful gifts, so you might want to make a double batch to put in half-pint jars for the holidays.

2 pounds dried currants
2 cups balsamic vinegar
4 cups apple cider vinegar
10 pounds peaches, peeled, pitted, and cut into lengthwise slices
2 pounds sugar
3 garlic bulbs, cloves separated and minced
3 to 6 serranos or jalapenos, minced
3-inch piece of fresh ginger, grated
1 tablespoon salt

Put the currants into a medium bowl, cover with balsamic vinegar and 2 cups of apple cider vinegar and set aside. Cover and let rest for several hours or overnight.

Put the peaches into a large, heavy pot and sprinkle the sugar over them. Let rest, covered, until the currants are ready. Add the currants and their liquid, the remaining 2 cups of apple cider vinegar, the garlic, and the serranos to the pot with the peaches.

Set over medium-low heat and stir now and then until the sugar dissolves. Add the ginger and the salt, stir and taste. Add more salt if the chutney seems a little flat and add more sugar if you want it a bit sweeter.

Cook, stirring now and then, very gently until it reduces by about a third and thickens, about 1 to 1 ½ hours.

To use the chutney within a month or 2, cool it and store it Mason jars in the refrigerator.

To preserve it, ladle it into 1 or 2 pint jars that have been sterilized and then process it according to the jar manufacturer's instructions. Cool the processed jars on several layers of tea towel, check the seals and store in a cool, dark cupboard for up to 1 year.

Cranberry Pear Chutney

Makes approximately 4 pints

Cranberry chutney has a deep, rich flavor that is an ideal accompaniment to all types of poultry, including Thanksgiving turkey, duck, and chicken. It is delicious on sandwiches and a lovely addition to a cheese platter.

8 cups cranberries, rinsed and picked through for soft berries
8 garlic cloves, minced
2 red onions, cut into small dice
2 or 3 serranos, stemmed, seeded, and minced
2 cups currants
2 to 2 ½ cups granulated sugar
2 cups cranberry vinegar or apple cider vinegar
2-inch piece of fresh ginger, peeled and minced
½ teaspoon each ground cardamom, cloves, cayenne pepper, and allspice
3 pears, peeled, cored, and minced
2 teaspoons kosher salt

Put the cranberries into the work bowl of a food processor and pulse several times to mince them evenly; work in batches if your processor is a small one.

Transfer the cranberries to a large saucepan and add the garlic, onion, serranos, currants, sugar, vinegar, ginger, spices, and pears. Add the salt and stir.

Set over medium-low heat and simmer gently for about 30 minutes, until the mixture begins to thicken.

Carefully taste the chutney and adjust for acid balance and sugar. If it seems at all flat, add another teaspoon of salt.

Ladle into sterilized half-pint jars, seal, cool and store in the refrigerator. Use within a couple of months.

Peach Ketchup

Makes 5 to 6 cups

Ketchup was not always made with tomatoes, even though for a commercial produce in the United States to call itself "Ketchup" it must contain not only tomatoes but also vinegar and sugar. If it contains no sugar, it must be identified as "Imitation Ketchup." Yet there is evidence it was originally made with mushrooms or pickled fish and then evolved using all manner of fruit until the New World version took hold and became ubiquitous the world around. Thanks, Heinz! Thanks, Del Monte!

This version, inspired by a gift of peaches and a recipe in a sweet little book, The Art of Accompaniment *by Jeffree Sapp Brooks. I like it best with grilled or roasted chicken, but it is delicious with cheeses and with French fries.*

5 pounds ripe peaches, peeled, pitted, and chopped
2 ½ cups unfiltered apple cider vinegar or peach vinegar
1 tablespoon kosher salt
1 pound brown sugar
1 small vanilla bean
Zest of 1 small orange
2 teaspoons mustard seed
1 cinnamon stick, 2 inches long
2-inch piece of fresh ginger, sliced
1 teaspoon whole cloves
1 teaspoon whole allspice berries
1 nutmeg, cracked
1 teaspoon juniper berries

Put the peaches, vinegar, salt, and brown sugar in a large saucepan. Cut a large square of cheese cloth, put the vanilla bean, orange zest, mustard seed, cinnamon stick, ginger, cloves, allspice, nutmeg, and juniper berries in the center of the square, gather it up and tie it with kitchen twine. Tuck the cheesecloth bundle into the pot.

Set over medium heat and simmer, stirring now and then, for 30 minutes, until the peaches are very, very soft.

Remove from the heat, stir, cover and let cool. Use tongs to remove the spice package but do not discard it. Use an immersion blender to puree the peaches, return the spice bag to the pot, set over very low heat and cook until very thick, about 1 hour. Stir now and then and be careful not to let the mixture scorch.

When quite thick, ladle the ketchup into hot sterilized half-pint jars, add the hot lids and rings and process in a boiling water bath for 15 minutes. Cool on several layers of tea towel, check the seals and store in a cool, dark cupboard for up to 1 year. Refrigerate after opening.

Desserts

Just as we are seeing salt and, frequently, pepper in desserts, so, too, are vinegars and olive oils increasingly offered at the end of a meal, in ice creams and other frozen desserts, in pies, cookies, cakes, and even candy. Some of these sweets may seem a bit gymnastic at first—vinegar pie, really?—but many have a long tradition in America. They are being rediscovered, not invented, and shaped by our newly expanded national and international pantry.

Gelato Modena

Makes about 1 quart

Gelato is, traditionally, closely related to ice cream, though it has fewer eggs and less cream. This version has no eggs at all and just a bit of cream, which gives it a lush, smooth texture. I make it this way because this is how I prefer it, with the bright taste of vinegar taking center stage. It is remarkably refreshing, especially on a hot night.

3 cups water
1 ½ cups sugar
⅔ cup good-quality balsamic vinegar
1 teaspoon vanilla extract
1 to 2 teaspoons freshly ground black pepper
¼ cup cream

Combine the water and sugar in a heavy nonreactive saucepan and bring to a boil. Cover the pan and simmer for 5 minutes. Remove from the heat and stir in the vinegar, vanilla, and black pepper.

Cool to room temperature and chill for at least 3 hours.

To freeze, prepare an ice-cream freezer according to the manufacturer's instructions. Stir the cream into the vinegar mixture and freeze, as recommended by the machine's instructions.

Transfer the gelato to a container, cover tightly and freeze overnight before serving.

Variation:

Omit the cream for something that more closely resembles a *sorbetto*.

Gelato Modena with Roasted Strawberries & Chocolate Vinaigrette

Serves 4

As the new edition of this book heads to the printer, water kefir is still a niche item, not readily available throughout the United States. The Kefiry, located in Sebastopol where I live, makes delightful water kefirs, including several that contain chocolate. What is amazing about them is that they have the full flavor of chocolate without its thick texture. The first time I tasted one I thought immediately that it would make a delightful dessert vinaigrette. The first time I made it was for 70 guests at a special benefit dinner for Worth Our Weight Culinary Apprenticeship Program in Santa Rosa, California. We served the vinaigrette in little ramekins alongside roasted strawberries topped with this gelato. Some guests tipped the vinaigrette over the dessert and some drank it down, like a special liqueur. There is no substitute for the chocolate kefir.

Gelato Modena, page 350
1 pint small sweet strawberries, stemmed and cut in half
2 tablespoons sugar
2 tablespoons good-quality balsamic vinegar
Black pepper in a mill
½ cup chocolate water kefir
Grated zest of ½ orange
4 or 5 mint leaves, cut into very thin lengthwise slices
1 tablespoon best-quality white wine vinegar, plus more to taste
4 small mint sprigs

Make the gelato the day before serving the dessert and be certain it is well frozen.

Put the strawberries into a bowl, sprinkle with sugar, cover and refrigerate for at least 2 hours and as long as overnight.

Pour the chocolate kefir into a small bowl, add the orange zest, mint, the white wine vinegar, and several very generous turns of black pepper. Taste and adjust for acid. Cover and refrigerate until ready to serve.

About half an hour before serving, preheat the oven to 375 degrees. Put the strawberries and all their juices into a pan or other ovenproof container, add the balsamic vinegar and several turns of black pepper and set on the middle rack of the oven. Cook until hot and bubbly, about 10 minutes. Divide the chocolate vinaigrette among shot glasses or little espresso cups.

To serve, divide the roasted strawberries among dessert cups and top with 2 scoops of gelato. Garnish with a mint sprig and serve immediately, with the chocolate vinaigrette alongside for guests to pour over the gelato. Enjoy promptly!

Olive Oil & Meyer Lemon Cake

Makes one 9- or 10-inch cake

Olive oil
1 cup all-purpose flour
1 cup cornmeal
1 cup sugar
1 teaspoon baking powder
1 teaspoon salt
4 farm eggs, beaten
1 teaspoon vanilla
Grated zest of 2 Meyer lemons
⅓ cup freshly squeezed Meyer lemon juice
1 cup good-quality extra virgin olive oil
Confectioner's (powdered) sugar

Preheat the oven to 350 degrees.

Brush the inside of a spring form pan with olive oil and set it aside.

Put the flour, cornmeal, sugar, baking powder, and salt in a medium bowl and mix with a fork. Set aside.

Break the eggs, one at a time, into a large mixing bowl. Use whisk to whip them until smooth, pale, and creamy. Add the vanilla, lemon zest, lemon juice, and olive oil and whisk again.

Use a large rubber spatula to quickly fold in the dry ingredients; do not over-mix.

Pour the batter into the pan, agitate gently to distribute the batter evenly and set on the middle rack of the oven. Bake until the middle has risen a bit and the cake is lightly browned, about 35 minutes. If you are uncertain if it is done, insert a bamboo skewer into the center; if it comes out clean, the cake is ready. If not, cook for 5 minutes and test again.

Set the pan on a rack to cool until easy to handle. Put a tablespoon or 2 of the confectioner's sugar into a strainer and shake it over the cake.

Remove the spring form and serve warm or at room temperature.

Olive Oil Ice Cream, with Variations

Makes about 1 quart

Olive oil ice cream has grown very popular in the last few years. If you live in an area where olive oil is made, as I do, you might find it as a seasonal delicacy during late fall's and early winter's olive harvest. Screamin' Mimi's, my local ice cream parlor, offers a delicious version from time to time.

You can make it at home, too, of course. In this version, I steep black peppercorns in half-and-half before making the custard. This may seem like an affectation but its roots are in history. In ancient Rome, desserts were once laden with all manner of spices, including black and white peppercorn. I began experimenting with various spices in desserts years ago, when I was writing Salt and Pepper. *I've never had much of a sweet tooth but when spices, especially peppercorns, and salt add additional layers of flavor that punctuate the pure sweetness, my interest perks up.*

1 ½ cups half-and-half
⅔ cup granulated sugar
1 teaspoon kosher salt
2 teaspoons best-quality crushed black pepper
6 large farm egg yolks
1 cup heavy cream
½ cup boldly flavored extra virgin olive oil
Olio Nuovo, optional
Flake salt

Put the half-and-half, sugar, salt, and black pepper into a medium saucepan, set over low heat and stir gently until the sugar dissolves. When the milk just begins to simmer, remove from the heat, cover and let steep for 30 minutes.

Break the eggs, one at a time, into a large mixing bowl. Whisk until thick and pale.

Pour the cream into a deep bowl.

Reheat the half-and-half mixture and when it is hot, remove it from the stove. Pour a little into the eggs, whisking constantly. Continue to pour it into the eggs, whisking all the while. Pour very slowly so that the eggs do not coagulate.

When all of the mixture has been incorporated into the eggs, pour the resulting custard through a strainer into the saucepan. Set over medium heat and stir continuously with a rubber spatula, scraping the bottom and sides of the pan, as the mixture thickens. When it is very thick—it will coat the spatula—remove it from the heat. Slowly pour it into the cream, whisking all the while.

Continue to stir as the custard cools. (Setting it atop a bowl of ice will move the process along more quickly.) When the custard has cooled to room temperature, whisk in the olive oil.

Cover and refrigerate for at least 2 hours and as long as overnight.

Freeze in an ice cream maker, using the manufacturer's instructions as your guide. Transfer to a glass or porcelain bowl, cover and freeze for an hour or two, until quite firm.

To serve, use an ice cream scoop to divide among individual chilled bowls. Drizzle each portion with a little Olio Nuovo, if using, sprinkle with a little flake salt and enjoy right away.

Variations:

You can transform this ice cream simply by using a different oil. A citrus olive oil will add the fruit's flourish. A delicate Grapefruit Olive Oil is particularly lovely. Any expeller pressed nut oil—hazelnut, walnut, toasted peanut, and toasted pistachio oil—makes delicious ice creams.

Vinegar Pie

Serves 6 to 8

Vinegar pie is not a new, trendy invention. Rather, it is an old American tradition, developed during hard times when other flavoring agents—fresh fruit, natural juices, and such—were not at hand. Think of it as a specialty of pioneer housewives, who were quite inventive in feeding their families.

I include the recipe here for both its historical interest and because it is delicious and versatile. You can change the flavor simply by using a different vinegar.

for the crust

1 ¼ cups all-purpose flour
Generous pinch of kosher salt
6 tablespoons unsalted butter, cut in pieces and chilled
2 tablespoons lard, preferably homemade, well chilled
1 tablespoon cold apple cider vinegar, chilled
1 tablespoons ice water

for the filling

4 farm eggs
¾ cup granulated sugar
½ cup brown sugar
1 teaspoon kosher salt
3 tablespoons vinegar of choice (see Note on next page)
1 teaspoon vanilla extract
6 tablespoons unsalted butter
1 cup shelled pecans or walnuts, lightly toasted

To make the pie crust, put the flour and salt into a the work bowl of a good processor fitted with a metal blade. Add the butter and lard and pulse several times. Working quickly, scrape down the sides of the work bowl with a rubber spatula, if needed. Add the vinegar and water, pulse 2 or 3 times and tip out onto a sheet of wax paper.

Press the dough together, wrap it tightly and chill it for 1 hour.

Roll out the dough between 2 sheets of parchment or wax paper or on a floured pastry cloth, making a circle about 11 inches across. Carefully lift the dough onto a 9-inch pie shell, press it to fit and pleat and trim the edges. Set a circle of parchment on top of the dough, add beans or pie weights, and refrigerate for 30 minutes as you preheat the oven to 450 degrees.

Bake the pie shell on the middle rack of the oven for 10 minutes. Remove it from the oven, reduce the heat to 350 degrees, lift out the paper lining and weights and return to the oven. Bake until just barely golden brown, about 8 to 10 minutes. Remove from the oven and let cool.

While the pie shell cools, break the eggs into a medium mixing bowl and whisk until thick and creamy. Add the sugars, salt, vinegar, and vanilla and whisk again. Melt the butter in a small saucepan and slowly whisk into the egg mixture.

Spread the nuts over the bottom of the pie shell and pour in the custard. Set a baking sheet on the middle rack of the 350-degree oven and set the pie on the baking sheet. Cook until the custard is set, about 25 minutes.

Remove from the oven, set on a rack to cool for about 15 minutes and serve warm.

NOTE

Use a boldly flavored vinegar. It was originally made with apple cider vinegar but it is also delicious with a good balsamic vinegar (DaVero is a very good one), almost any fruit vinegar, and with varietal red wine vinegars, such as O Pinot Noir Vinegar, O Zinfandel, and B. R. Cohn Cabernet Sauvignon vinegar. If you use a citrus vinegar, add some zest of the same fruit to the custard.

Variations:

- Serve with a scoop of Gelato Modena, page 350, alongside the pie when it is made with balsamic vinegar.
- Serve with a scoop of Olive Oil Ice Cream, page 355, topped with a little flake salt.
- Use a blueberry vinegar and replace the pecans or walnuts with a layer of fresh blueberries.

Walnut & Black Pepper Biscotti

Makes between 3 ½ and 4 dozen cookies

When the first edition of this book was in the works, there were almost no commercial biscotti, except for a single brand imported from Italy. Now they are everywhere, at farmers markets, bakeries, independent grocery stores, and supermarkets. The first edition of the book included several biscotti recipes and I have removed all but two. Both are delicious with Gelato Modena and Olive Oil Ice Cream.

- 2 eggs
- 2 tablespoons unrefined walnut oil
- 1 cup dark brown sugar, firmly packed
- 1 teaspoon fresh cracked black pepper
- 2 cups all-purpose flour
- 1 teaspoon baking soda
- ½ teaspoon ground cardamom
- ½ teaspoon freshly grated nutmeg
- 1 teaspoon kosher salt
- 1 cup coarsely chopped walnuts, lightly toasted

Preheat the oven to 375 degrees.

Cover a baking sheet with a sheet of parchment paper.

Break the eggs into a mixing bowl and mix thoroughly until thick and pale. Mix in the walnut oil. Add the sugar and pepper and and mix until smooth and creamy. Set aside.

Put the flour, baking soda, cardamom, nutmeg, and salt in another bowl and stir with a fork.

Slowly add the dry mixture to the egg mixture and then fold in the walnuts. The dough will be stiff but a bit sticky.

Flour your work surface, divide the dough in thirds, and roll each piece into a rope about 12 inches long and 2 ½ inches in diameter. Set the ropes on the baking sheet, placing them about 2 ½ inches apart. Using your fingertips, gently flatten each rope just a bit. Bake for 25 minutes.

Remove from the oven, transfer to a rack and cool for about 5 minutes. Cut each loaf diagonally into ½-inch-wide slices. Set the slices on a baking sheet, cut side down, return to the oven, bake for 10 minutes, turn over and bake for 10 minutes more.

Remove from the oven, cool completely and store in an airtight jar or other container. For the best flavor and texture, enjoy within a couple of weeks.

Variation:

To make hazelnut biscotti, replace the walnut oil with hazelnut oil and the walnuts with toasted, peeled, and chopped hazelnuts. Omit the pepper and add 1 teaspoon vanilla extract to the eggs.

Olive Oil & Red Wine Biscotti

Makes about 5 dozen cookies

These cookies, with their rosy hue and subtle hint of wine, have been a favorite around my house for years. Enjoy them at the end of a leisurely meal, while enjoying the last bit of the evening's wine. Stored in a jar or tin, they keep well and make excellent holiday gifts.

2 eggs
1 cup olive oil
1 cup sugar
1 teaspoon pure vanilla extract
5 cups all-purpose flour
2 teaspoons baking powder
1 teaspoon kosher salt
1 cup red wine, such as Cabernet Sauvignon, Zinfandel, Pinot Noir, or Merlot
1 ½ cups chopped walnuts, lightly toasted

Preheat the oven to 375 degrees.

Break the eggs into a mixing bowl until they are thick and creamy. Stir in the olive oil, mix thoroughly, add the sugar and vanilla extract and mix vigorously, until the mixture is thick and slightly foamy. Set aside.

Put the flour, baking powder, and salt into a mixing bowl and stir with a fork.

Add a quarter of the dry mixture to the egg mixture and blend quickly; add a quarter of the wine and mix again. Repeat, alternating dry ingredients with the wine, until all has been added. Fold in the walnuts.

Divide the dough into four equal pieces. Flour a work surface. Roll each piece of dough into a rope about 10 inches long and 1 ½ inches in diameter. Set on a baking sheet lined with parchment, flatten slightly and bake for 25 minutes.

Remove the biscotti loaves from the oven and reduce the heat to 325 degrees. Cool the loaves for 5 minutes, cut them into ½-inch-wide diagonal slices and set, cut side down, on a baking sheet. Cook for 10 minutes, turn over and cook for 5 to 10 minutes more, until fairly firm.

Remove from the oven, let cool on wire racks and store in an airtight glass jar or tin. For the best flavor and texture, enjoy within a couple of weeks.

Pumpkin Bar Cookies

Makes 48 cookies

Sciabica's California Olive Oil has been producing olive oil in California's Central Valley since 1936, when Nicola Sciabica, who was born in Marsala, Sicily, in 1887, moved on from growing grapes. For decades, the company was one of just four producers in California, until the renaissance began in the late 1980s and early 1990s. Then, Nicola's son Joseph and his grandsons Nick and Daniel were extremely helpful to all the newcomers in the business. Even though the new growers were potentially competitors, the Sciabica's were remarkably generous with both their knowledge and their production facilities. The vibrancy of the current industry owes much to this family.

When I was writing the first edition of this book, I called the company and spoke with Nick about the industry for a while. We agreed that at some point in the future we would get together for a tasting of the company's oils. The next day, I had just gotten out of the shower. My hair was wrapped in a towel and I was wearing just a green chenille bathrobe when there was a knock at the door. I was surprised because my little cottage is fairly hard to find and then was even more surprised when I opened the door. There stood Nick, olive oils in hand. I'm not sure who was more embarrassed but I did my best to make us both comfortable and soon we were tasting our way through the family's oils.

Today, Sciabica produces several types of extra virgin olive oils, several flavored oils and other products, including vinegars, tomatoes and tomato sauces, and olive oil–based skin care products.

Nick shared this recipe, from Gemma Sciabica, who has written five cookbooks full of family recipes.

Butter
4 eggs
1 ¾ cups sugar
⅓ cup extra virgin olive oil
1 ¾ cups cooked pumpkin or other winter squash, cooled
2 ¼ cups flour
2 teaspoons baking powder
1 teaspoon baking soda
1 teaspoon kosher salt
1 teaspoon ground cinnamon
¼ teaspoon each ground ginger, ground nutmeg, and ground cloves
½ cup raisins
½ cup chopped pecans

Preheat the oven to 350 degrees. Lightly spray a baking pan that measures about 15 ½ inches by 10 ½ inches by 1 ½ inches.

Break the eggs into a mixing bowl, add the sugar and beat vigorously until the mixture is thick, pale, and foamy. Mix in the olive oil and pumpkin. Set aside.

Put the flour, baking powder, baking soda, salt, and spices into a bowl and mix with a fork.

Quickly add the dry ingredients to the egg mixture, being careful not to over-mix. Fold in the raisins and nuts.

Pour the batter into the buttered pan, spread it evenly and set on the middle rack of the oven. Bake for 25 to 30 minutes, until the center springs back when lightly touched.

Remove from the oven and cool before cutting into bars, 2 inches by 1 ½ inches. Enjoy right away warm or within a couple of days.

Vinegar Taffy, with Variations

Makes about ½ pound

Like vinegar pie, vinegar taffy is an old American tradition. It is fun to make and is a great activity to share with an older child. Once made, wrap the taffy individually and store in a tin that will protect it from moisture. You can find candy wrappers at party supply stores, baking supply stores, and at many Asian markets.

In the main recipe, I use balsamic vinegar because it pairs so well with vanilla. For other combinations of flavors, consult the Variations at the end of the recipe.

Confectioner's sugar
1 ¼ cup sugar
¼ cup good-quality balsamic vinegar
2 teaspoons butter, plus more for your hands
1 teaspoon pure vanilla extract

Have a marble slab, a platter, a candy thermometer, and a pair of kitchen shears nearby before you begin. Sprinkle sugar lightly over the platter and set it aside.

Heat the sugar, vinegar, and butter in a heavy saucepan set over low heat, stirring until the sugar is dissolved. Increase the heat and bring the temperature of the mixture to 265 degrees. Pour the candy onto the marble slab or buttered heat-proof platter and let it cool a bit.

When the taffy will hold a dent when pressed with a finger, sprinkle the vanilla over it. Rub butter over your hands and gather the taffy up into a ball.

Pull the taffy, using both hands to stretch it outwards and fold it over. This process will work best if you establish a steady rhythmic movement, stretching your hands about 18 inches apart, quickly folding the taffy back on itself, and repeating until the mass becomes a shiny, glistening ribbon.

Quickly gather the mass up into your hands. Stretch it into thin ropes, make cuts every inch, and let the pieces fall onto the sugared platter. Wrap the candy and store it in an airtight container.

Variations:

When you want to use other flavorings, these are the ones I think work best.

- Blueberry vinegar and ¼ teaspoon clove extract
- Raspberry vinegar and ¼ teaspoon lemon extract
- Cranberry vinegar and ¼ teaspoon orange extract
- Varietal red wine vinegar and ¼ teaspoon cinnamon extract
- Spice Vinegar (page 311) and ¼ teaspoon black pepper extract

Beverages

When it comes to oils, especially olive oil and toasted sesame oil, in beverages, especially cocktails, invention is the key. A new generation of bartenders—mixologists, as they are now—are experimenting with these ingredients, often with delicious results. Their concoctions can be as simple as swirling a bit of good olive oil in a cocktail shaker before mixing a Martini to as complex as brewing all manner of vinegar-based shrubs on the back bar. If you make cocktails at home, experiment. A float of toasted sesame oil on a mojito is absolutely delicious and a Bloody Mary with a shake of, say, cucumber vinegar and lime olive oil makes you want to come back for seconds.

The final recipes here are to perk us up when we are feeling poorly, from a cold or flu, a coffee-withdrawal headache, or simple malaise.

About Shrubs

File shrubs under "everything old is new again." Vinegar-based drinks were ubiquitous in early America and for decades were common in both homes and bars. They all but vanished but are now enjoying a renaissance, especially in bars and restaurants. Shrubs are very easy to make at home, they keep well, and are a refreshing hedge against summer heat. The basic formula is simple: Combine fruit or fruit juice with vinegar and, if needed, a bit of sweetener. Serve over ice, diluted with sparkling water or sparkling wine. You don't really need a recipe, especially if you are a comfortable cook, but I offer these as my favorite combinations.

Stone Fruit Shrub

Makes about 1 quart

4 cups sliced fresh stone fruit, from about 2 to 2 ½ pounds of fruit (see Note on next page)
1 to 2 cups sugar, plus more to taste
1 tablespoon grated ginger
2 cups apple cider vinegar, preferably organic
Sparkling water, ginger beer, or sparkling wine, to serve

Put the apricots into a large glass container, add 1 cup of the sugar and, if using, the ginger and crush together lightly with wooden pestle, wooden spoon, or vegetable masher. Taste and add more sugar until the mixture pleases you. Cover and refrigerate for 2 to 3 days.

Remove from the refrigerator and stir in the vinegar. Let rest for about 15 minutes and then strain through a fine sieve into a clean jar or bottle.

Chill thoroughly.

To enjoy, fill a glass with ice, add shrub to come about ⅓ of the way up the glass and then finish with sparkling water, ginger beer, or sparkling wine.

The shrub will keep for weeks in the refrigerator.

NOTE

Make apricot shrub in June, during the fruit's brief season. Peach shrub and nectarine shrub are best made from about late June through September. If you have access to Santa Rosa Plums, make it in July, when they are at their peak.

Berry Shrub

Makes about 1 quart

The best time to make berry shrub is when you have a lot of berries. If you do, you can also make berry vinegar, page 306, and pair it with the berry in the shrub. Although you can make a berry shrub quickly, letting the fruit macerate in the vinegar for just a few hours, I find the flavors blossom when allowed to rest for a few days.

4 cups berries
4 cups vinegar (see Note below)
Simple syrup, to taste
Sparkling water or sparkling wine

Put the berries into a large glass or stainless steel bowl, add the vinegar, cover and refrigerate for 3 to 4 days.

Set a strainer over a deep bowl, pour the mixture into it and press the berries to release as much juice as possible. Add simple syrup to taste.

Pour into glass bottles, seal with a cork and enjoy over ice with sparkling water or sparkling wine.

NOTE

Choose your vinegar based on compatibility with whatever berry you are using. I recommend these combinations:

- Blueberries, red wine vinegar or Spice Vinegar, page 311
- Blackberries and their cousins, red wine vinegar
- Golden, orange, red or purple raspberries, white wine or Champagne vinegar
- Pomegranate or cranberry, white wine vinegar

Cucumber Shrub

Makes about 1 quart

Cucumbers are so refreshing. If your eyelids itch and swell from allergies, as mine do, chilled cucumber slices are as helpful a treatment as any eye drop I've ever used. A few slices in water makes it more refreshing. When you want something more elaborate, try this shrub. I prefer it unsweetened but it is also good with a bit of simple syrup. You can also add a float of rum, about half a shot.

2 large cucumbers, peeled and chopped
Generous pinch of kosher salt
Zest of 1 or 2 limes
Juice of 1 or 2 limes
2 sprigs of mint
3 cups white wine vinegar
Simple syrup, optional
Sparkling water
Toasted sesame oil
Lime wedges and small mint sprigs, to serve

Put the cucumbers into a large glass or stainless steel bowl, add the salt, lime zest, lime juice, mint sprigs, and vinegar and stir. Cover and refrigerate for 1 to 2 days, stirring now and then.

Set a strainer lined with cheesecloth over a deep bowl, tip the mixture into the strainer and press to release as much juice as possible from the cucumbers. Sweeten to taste with simple syrup, if you prefer it that way.

Serve over crushed ice, diluted with sparkling water in a ratio of 1 part shrub to 2 parts water. Add a few drops of toasted sesame oil, garnish with a lime wedge and small sprig of mint and enjoy right away.

Shrubs with Fruit Juice

Serves 2

You can make a shrub on the spot using good vinegar and fruit juice and you can make as little or as much as you want. It's a perfect beverage for a summer party, as it is so refreshing.

Crushed ice
½ cup fruit juice of choice
½ cup vinegar of choice
Sparkling water or sparkling wine
Garnishes

Fill two tall glasses with ice, add fruit juice and vinegar and top off with sparkling water or sparkling wine. Add appropriate garnishes and enjoy right away.

Recommended Combinations:

- Orange juice or grapefruit juice with white wine vinegar or rice wine vinegar, garnish with a slice of the fruit
- Lemon juice or lime juice with yuzu vinegar or Champagne vinegar, along with a generous splash of simple syrup; garnish with a slice of the fruit
- Cranberry juice or pomegranate juice with a varietal red wine vinegar; add a splash of pomegranate molasses for a sweeter drink; garnish with a mint sprig or a few fresh cranberries or pomegranate arils
- Apple juice with apple cider vinegar
- Pear juice with pear vinegar or ginger vinegar

About Tonics & Elixirs

Humans have relied on tonics and elixirs for centuries and, for a time, it seemed like we might lose this art, so dependent did we become on doctors and the drugs they dispense. But no one has yet succeed in curing the common cold and the best advice is what it has always been: chicken soup. This is a tonic at its most basic, and its various nicknames, especially "Jewish Penicillin," highlight its healing qualities.

Here I offer a few of my favorites, the ones that get me through winter viruses, summer colds, and the occasion patch of unexplained malaise.

John's Cold Cure

Makes about 1 quart

My friend and colleague, writer and artist L. John Harris, who published my first two books including the original edition of this one, swears by this fiery tonic as a cure for colds. It has the benefit of being absolutely delicious, too. All medicine should taste this good!

4 cups homemade chicken broth or stock
¼ to ½ cup organic apple cider vinegar
6 large garlic cloves, pressed
Black pepper in a mill
Tabasco, Crystal, or other vinegar-based hot sauce

Pour the broth or stock into a saucepan, add the vinegar, garlic, and several generous turns of black pepper. When it is hot, remove it from the stove. Pour into a mug, add several shakes of hot sauce and sip. Repeat as needed until you feel better.

Hot Ginger Tonic

Makes 1 quart

During cold weather, flu season, and any time you have a cold, this tonic will warm you and make you feel at least a bit better. It is easily doubled and can be stored in the refrigerator for weeks without any deterioration in flavor.

4 ounces fresh ginger root, chopped or grated
Juice of 2 to 3 lemons, strained
¼ cup organic apple cider vinegar
Maple syrup, honey, or simple syrup, to taste
Whiskey, Scotch, or brandy, optional

Put the ginger into a saucepan and add about 2 cups of water. Bring to a boil, cover, remove from the heat and let steep for 30 to 60 minutes.

Strain the water into a clean pitcher or quart jar and discard the ginger. Add the lemon juice, vinegar, and enough water to make 4 cups. Taste and adjust for sweetness.

Serve warm, with or without a float of Whiskey, Scotch, or brandy.

Sip as needed until you feel better.

Coffee Headache Elixir

Makes 4 cups

If you drink a lot of coffee, you may experience headaches when you stop abruptly, such as when you lose your appetite for it when you have the flu or a bad cold. These symptoms last about five days. This tonic should help mitigate the symptoms.

4 cups spring water
1 tablespoon white willow bark
1 tablespoon fresh sage leaves
1 teaspoon chamomile flowers
Zest of 1 lemon or orange
3 tablespoons organic apple cider vinegar, yuzu vinegar, or any citrus vinegar
2 tablespoons maple syrup, or more to taste

Bring the water to a boil in a small saucepan, add the willow bar, sage, and chamomile, cover, and set aside to steep for 20 minutes. Strain and stir in the lemon juice and honey. Drink 1 to 2 cups in the morning, and again if the headache returns. Store in the refrigerator and reheat as necessary.

Sweet Potato Tonic

Makes about 1 quart

Sweet potatoes are full of good nutrients, including Vitamins A, B, and C. Chilies are good when you're down with a cold, too, as they've been proven as effective as most decongestants. Beef broth is healing as well, but if you don't feel up to making it and don't have it on hand, you can make a soothing, healthful tonic with water.

1 medium sweet potato, peeled and cut into chunks
Kosher salt
Black pepper in a mill
1 to 2 teaspoons ground cayenne or chipotle powder
4 cups beef broth, preferably homemade, or water
3 to 4 tablespoons apple cider vinegar, to taste
¼ cup fresh cilantro leaves

Put the sweet potatoes into a medium saucepan, season with salt, pepper, and cayenne or chipotle. Add the beef broth and vinegar. Bring to a boil over high heat, reduce the heat to very low and simmer gently until the sweet potato is fully tender, about 15 to 20 minutes.

Puree with an immersion blender or pass through a food mill. Taste and correct for salt and pepper.

To serve, ladle into a mug and top with cilantro leaves. Sip until you feel better.

Lagniappe

Lagniappe: a little something extra, an unexpected treat to nibble or to ponder, a small unexpected gift. Few foods offer as diverse and extensive an array of non-food uses as oils and vinegars. Only salt rivals this culinary duo.

Of hundreds of recommended uses, I can vouch for these and so I am happy to share them.

Olive Oil

When using olive oil in contexts other than cooking and eating, don't squander an ultra-premium or premium olive oil, which are made for their flavor and belong at the table, not on a sponge or cotton ball.

- A bit of olive oil on a cotton ball is an effective make-up remover and moisturizes skin as it cleans.
- For an inexpensive hair treatment, rub olive oil all over, including on the scalp, and leave on at least an hour before shampooing.
- Adding ¼ teaspoon, daily, to your kitty's food will help discourage hairballs.
- As we know from the story of Chanukah, olive oil can be used as fuel to produce light. It is easy to make your own "candle" by filling a glass jar—small Mason jars work well—with water, adding a ¼ inch or so of olive oil (oil floats on water) and setting a small wick (available at craft shops) on top.
- Can't stand the smell of shoe polish? Pour a little olive oil on a clean rag, rub on leather (not suede!) shoes or boots and buff.
- You can make your own soap using olive oil as the base. The best way to learn how to do this is to watch a tutorial on the Internet.

It is not difficult, and images help make sense of it if you've never done it before. Recommended sites include candleandsoap.about.com and sierraclub.typepad.com.

Coconut Oil

Once scorned as unhealthy and nearly impossible to find, coconut oil is now acknowledged as a very healthy fat. It is widely available in retail markets and there are a number of organic options. Trader Joe's is reliably excellent.

- Coconut oil makes an excellent body lotion and all-over moisturizer and has the added advantage of stopping itching.
- Add a bit of pennyroyal oil or peppermint oil to coconut oil to discourage mosquitos and other insects, including fleas.
- Massage a little coconut oil into the tips of your hair before washing it. This is particularly recommended for fine hair and curly hair, which are more fragile and prone to breakage than coarse hair and straight hair.
- If your feet are dry and cracked from dancing barefoot (or for any other reason), massage coconut oil into them before going to bed.
- Coconut oil can help keep your pup's coat and kitty's coat slick and shiny. Add a ¼ teaspoon per 10 pounds of weight to each meal.
- A little coconut oil will remove rust, loosen stuck hinges and zippers, and help you remove chewing gum from your kid's hair.

Vinegar

It's a good idea to keep a large bottle of distilled vinegar on hand, not in your pantry but under your sink, with other cleaning materials. Apple cider vinegar is helpful, too, but should be in the pantry.

- Fill a spray bottle half full with distilled or apple cider vinegar, top off with water, and use as an all-purpose cleaner.
- 2 tablespoons of apple cider vinegar in a cup of warm water makes an excellent hair rinse after shampooing.
- Skunk problems? If your pet gets sprayed, make an effective skunk dunk by mixing apple cider vinegar and water in a 1:1 ratio.
- Adding a teaspoon of vinegar to poaching water will keep egg whites tight and compact.
- Drinking a glass of warm water with a teaspoon of apple cider vinegar in it daily is said to encourage a flat tummy.
- Vinegar is an effective deodorizer. A bowl set in a room where someone has smoked will diminish the smell. An unpleasantly aromatic lunch box can be de-scented by soaking a sponge in vinegar and leaving it in the lunch box for a few hours. It will eliminate unpleasant odors from refrigerators, garbage disposals, and trash cans. Do not use it to clean a littler box, as cats avoid it.

PART 5
Appendices

Tasting Notes

Extra Virgin Olive Oil
California • Italy • Sicily • Spain • France • Greece • Tunisia • Chile • Israel

Professional olive oil tasters undergo extensive training and study international guidelines that determine what olive oils can legally use the "extra virgin" designation. Much of this tasting has to do with detecting defects; certification declares, in part, that an oil is defect-free. The oils must also meet certain chemical guidelines. Casual tasters explore for different reasons, to educate their palates and to find pleasing oils. The best olive oils change from year to year, as they are an expression of their environment, of the land itself, the changing weather, the light and even the temperament of the producer.

Producer________________________Country__________________
Region__________________

Date of Production______________Purveyor__________________
Price__________________

Varieties of Olives____

____

Color & Appearance

____

____

Aroma ____

Taste ____

____

Texture/Consistency______________Balance_________________
Finish___________________

NOTES ______________________________

____

Overall Opinion______________________________

Will Purchase Again ________

Producer______________________Country________________

Region________________

Date of Production______________Purveyor________________

Price________________

Varieties of Olives______________________________

____

Color & Appearance

____

____

Aroma ______________________________

Taste ______________________________

____

Texture/Consistency______________Balance________________

Finish________________

NOTES ______________________________

____

Overall Opinion______________________________

Will Purchase Again ________

Other Oils

Nut Oils • Flavored Oils • Seed Oils

Type_______________________Producer___________________
Country___________________

Date of Production_______________Purveyor____________________
Price__________________

Color & Appearance ____

Aroma ____

Taste ____

____

Texture/Consistency_______________Balance__________________
Finish____________________

NOTES ____

____

Overall Opinion____

Will Purchase Again __________

Type_______________________Producer___________________
Country___________________

Date of Production_______________Purveyor____________________
Price__________________

Color & Appearance ____

Aroma ____

Taste ____

____

Texture/Consistency ____________Balance______________
Finish_______________

NOTES ____

____

Overall Opinion____
Will Purchase Again ________

Type__________________Producer______________
Country_______________

Date of Production____________Purveyor______________
Price

Color & Appearance ___________________________________

Aroma ____

Taste ____

____

Texture/Consistency ____________Balance______________
Finish_______________

NOTES ____

____

Overall Opinion____
Will Purchase Again ________

Vinegar

Red Wine • White Wine • Champagne • Sherry • Varietal • Fruit • Flavored • Malt • Cider • Balsamic • Rice • Black

Type____________________Producer________________
Country________________

Purveyor________________Price_______________
Acidity______________________

Color & Appearance ______________________________________

Aroma ____

Taste ____

____

Best Uses ____

NOTES ____

____

Overall Opinion____
Will Purchase Again ________

Type____________________Producer________________
Country________________

Purveyor________________Price_______________
Acidity______________________

Color & Appearance ______________________________________

Aroma ____

Taste ____

____

Best Uses ____

NOTES ____

____

Overall Opinion _____________________________________

Will Purchase Again ________

Type______________________Producer__________________

Country____________________

Purveyor___________________Price__________________

Acidity_________________________

Color & Appearance __________________________________

Aroma ____

Taste ____

____

Best Uses ____

NOTES ____

____

Overall Opinion _____________________________________

Will Purchase Again ________

Resources

This list highlights pioneers in the world of olive oil and vinegar, informational organizations, and reliable mail order sources.

Buon Italia
75 9th Ave., New York City, 10011, (212) 633-9090, buonitalia.com

Purveyors of a vast array of Italian products, including the extraordinary Ardoino's Biancardo Late Harvest Olive Oil from Liguria, which is nearly impossible to find.

California Olive Oil Council
801 Camelia St., #D, Berkeley
CA 94710, (510) 524-4523,
cooc.com

Information and assistance for growers, producers; list of member producers with website links.

California Olive Ranch
1367 East Lassen Ave., Suite A-1, Chico, CA 95973, (866) 972-6879, californiaoliveranch.com

California's largest producer of olive oil; widely distributed.

B. R. Cohn
15000 Sonoma Highway, Glen Ellen, CA (800) 330-4064, brcohn.com

Estate olive oil from Picholine trees planted in the mid 1800s; other olive oils; outstanding vinegars; located at the B. R. Cohn Olive Hill Estate Vineyard.

Corti Brothers
5810 Folsom Boulevard Sacramento, CA 95819 (916) 736-3800, corti-brothers.com

Excellent array of extra virgin olive oils, authentic balsamic vinegars, specialty salt, wine, and many other products; will ship.

DaVero
766 Westside Road Healdsburg,
CA 95448, (707) 431-8000,
davero.com

Pioneers in the California olive oil renaissance. Producers of ultra-premium estate olive oil, Italian varietal wines, and more. Tasting room open daily. Mail order. No distribution; direct-to-consumer sales only.

International Olive Oil Council
internationaloliveoil.org

Information, primarily for producers.

Market Hall Foods
5655 College Ave., Oakland CA
(888) 952-4005,
markethallfoods.com

Landmark store in Oakland's Rockridge district, with an outstanding collection of vinegars including Vinaigre de Banyuls; olive oils, nut oils (including pistachio oil); cheese and charcuterie and more. Online sales.

McEvoy Ranch
5935 Red Hill Rd., Petaluma CA
94952, (707) 778-2307,
mcevoyranch.com

Nan McEvoy's spectacular 550–acre ranch, with thousands of Italian varietal olive trees producing ultra-premium olive oil in the estate mill. Body care products, wine, and more; open for tours by appointment; workshops. A retail store is located in the San Francisco Ferry Plaza Building.

O Olive Oils & Vinegars
1997 S. McDowell Blvd., Petaluma,
CA 94954, (888) 827-7148,
ooliveoil.com

Producers of premium olive oil and vinegars, including citrus olive oils and varietal vinegars. Widely distributed; online store.

The Olive Press
24724 Arnold Dr., Sonoma CA
95476, (707) 939-8900,
theolivepress.com

On-location olive oil production facility (horizontal decanter method), large selection of olive oils, vinegars, accessories, and more; community pressing days; open to visitors; located within the Jacuzzi Family Winery.

Round Pond Estate Olive Mill
886 Rutherford Rd., Rutherford,
CA 94573, (707) 302-2575,
roundpond.com

Producers of estate olive oils, vinegars, and artisan citrus syrups; estate olive mill, with tour and tastings during harvest season, typically November and December; adjacent to Round Pond Winery.

Sciabica's California Olive Oil
2150 Yosemite Blvd., Modesto, CA
95354, (800) 551-9612,
sunshineinabottle.com

Pioneers in California olive oil; wide selection of products, including olive oil, vinegar, tomato sauces, and more. Widely distributed; open to visitors.

The Spanish Table
1426 Western Ave., Seattle, WA
98101, (206) 682-98101,
spanishtable.com

The original store in Seattle opened in 1995, a Berkeley store in 2001 and a Mill Valley, CA, location in 2006. Wide selection of products, including olive oils, cured meats, cheese, rice, pasta, spices, and more. Emphasis on Spanish products but not exclusively. Excellent line of clay cookware.

Spectrum Naturals
Spectrum Customer Care, The Hain Celestial Group, 4600 Sleepytime Dr., Boulder CO 80301, (800) 434-4246, spectrumorganics.com

Producers of organic, unrefined cooking oils, including almond, avocado, coconut, grape seed, peanut, sesame, and walnut. Widely distributed.

Terra Savia/Olivino
14160 Mountain House Rd., Hopland CA 95449, (707) 744-1114, terrasavia.com

Estate wines, estate olive oils, olive oil products; traditional olive oil production facility; open to visitors.

The Vinegar Institute
versatilevinegar.org

Consumer information

The Vinegar Man

Lawrence Diggs's work of passion, "The Grand Central Station for Vinegar Information," as he puts it. vinegarman.com

Zingerman's Deli
422 Detroit St., Ann Arbor, MI
(888) 636-8162, zingermans.com

Purveyors of a an oustanding selection of quality vinegars, including Vinagire de Banyuls, and premium olive oils from France, Spain, and Italy, including the lovely and nearly impossible to find Poggio Lamentano; nut oil, including the rare Butternut Squash Seed Oil; several monthly clubs, including an Artisan Vinegar Club and Rare Olive Oil Club

Glossary

For descriptions of specific ingredients, see the Glossary of Oils and Vinegars, page 64.

Acetic acid: A colorless, organic acid (CH_3 COOH) produced in fermented liquids by acetobacters

Acetobacter: The classification of a group of bacteria that digest alcohol and produce acetic acid in the process

Acidity: The state or degree of the presence of acetic acid

Aroma: A characteristic and pleasant odor

Batteria: Italian name for a series of twelve wooden casks of descending size used to produce *aceto balsamico tradizionale*

Cholesterol: A chemical constituent ($Q_{27}H_{45}OH$) of all animals and animal tissue

Cold-pressed: The name by which the juice of the olive (the oil) is extracted mechanically, without recourse to heat or chemicals; it is applied to other oils, as well, somewhat inaccurately, as seeds and nuts must be warmed to release their oils

Demijohn: A large glass or earthenware bottle with a narrow neck, frequently encased in wicker

Esters: Aromatic molecules produced by the interaction of alcohol and acids and contributing subtle elements of flavor to wine and vinegar

Expeller-pressed: A mechanical process by which oil is extracted from raw material; no chemicals are used in the process, but the seed, nut, or grain may be heated before extraction

Extra-virgin: The designation given to olive oil from the first pressing of olives that meet certain chemical standards and have no defects

Fatty acid: A large group of acids forming the major building blocks of fats in plant, animal, and human cells; major component of membranes surrounding cells, the most common include palmitic, linoleic, stearic, and oleic acids

Fermention: A group of chemical reactions that convert organic compounds into simple substances, as in yeast's anaerobic conversion of sugar into alcohol and carbon dioxide

First press: The initial, mechanical pressing, generally of olives, that releases the first and the best of a the fruit's juices

HDL: High-density lipoprotein, considered the beneficial form of cholesterol

Horizontal decanter: The name of a machine that extracts oil from olives

LDL: Low-density lipoprotein, considered the harmful form of cholesterol

Malaxation: The mixing of crushed olives, during which tiny droplets of oil gradually coalesce into large droplets and pools, which in turn facilitates separation

Monounsaturated fatty acid: A fatty acid with only one double carbon bond

Mother: The gelatinous mat of bacteria that forms across the top of a liquid as acetobacters convert it to vinegar

Must: The cooked juice of grapes before fermentation has begun

Oleic acid: A highly fluid, monounsaturated fatty acid found in olive, almond, and other seed oils and the membranes of the cells of most plants and animals, including humans

Orleans method: The slow process of vinegar production by which the substrate, inoculated with acetobacters, is placed in tanks or barrels so that only a small surface area is exposed to oxygen

Oxidize: To combine with oxygen, a process that speeds the spoilage and discoloration of foods, including oils

Polyunsaturated: A fatty acid, with two or more double carbon bonds

Rancidity: Decomposition of an oil, generally through excessive exposure to heat, light, or oxygen, and resulting in a harsh, unpleasant taste and smell; unrefined oils are susceptible to rancidity and should be stored in a cool, dry, dark place and used within a reasonable time

Saturated: A fatty acid, the molecules of which are completely filled with hydrogen bonds

Sinolea method: A fairly new method of olive oil extraction in which hundreds of small metal knives are continuously dipped into olive paste; it is considered the most gentle method and generates no heat; however, the paste and the oil are exposed to oxygen during the process

Substrate: The original liquid—wine, apple cider, beer, for example—upon which acetobacters feed to produce acetic acid and, thereby, vinegar

Viscosity: Informally, refers to the degree of oiliness or thickness of an oil; technically, refers, in a liquid, to the degree of resistance to flow

Bibliography

Ackerman, Diane. *A Natural History of the Senses*. New York: Random House, 1990.

Anderson, Burton. "The Balmy Realm of Aceto Balsamico." Journal of Gastronomy 4 no. 4 (Winter 1988–1989).

Andrews, Glenn. *Making Flavored Oils & Vinegars*. Pownal, Vt.: Garden Way Publishing, 1989.

Barbee, Michael. *Politically Incorrect Nutrition: Finding Reality in the Mire of Food Industry Propaganda*. South Salem, New York: Vital Health Publishing, 2004.

Bittman, Mark. "Vinegar Vignettes." The Gourmet Retailer; February 1991.

Brooks, Jeffree Sapp. *The Art of Accompaniment*. San Francisco: North Point Press, 1988.

"Can Olive Oil Help the Heart?" Consumer Reports, October 1991.

Composition of Foods. Agricultural Handbook no. 8, USDA, 1963.

Chibois, Jacques, and Olivier Baussan. *Olive Oil*. Paris, France: Flammarion, 2001.

Cruess, W.V., and M. A. Joslyn. "Home and Farm Preparation of Vinegar." United States Department of Agriculture, circular no. 332, January 1934.

de Groot, Roy Andries. *The Auberge of the Flowering Hearth*. New York: Ballantine, 1973.

Diggs, L. J. *Vinegar*. San Francisco: Quiet Storm Trading Company, 1989.

Dolamore, Anne. *The Essential Olive Oil Companion*. Topsfield, Mass.: Salem House Publishers, 1989.

Dolnick, Edward. "The Mystery of the Healthy French Heart." In Health, May/June 1990.

Erasmus, Udo. *Fats and Oils.* Vancouver: Alive Books, 1986.
Field, Carol. *Celebrating Italy.* New York: William Morrow, 1991.
Foods & Nutrition Encyclopedia, 1st ed. Vols. 1 & 2. Clovis, Calif.: Pegus Press, 1983.
Gage, Fran. *The New American Olive Oil.* New York: Stewart, Tabori & Chang, 2009.
Gunstone, F. D., et al., eds. *The Lipid Handbook.* Vol. 4. London: Chapman and Hall, 1986.
Harris, Lloyd J. *The Book of Garlic.* Reading, Mass.: Aris Books/Ad- dison-Wesley, 1974.
Johnson, Marsha Peters. *Gourmet Vinegars.* Lake Oswego, Oreg.: n.d.
Jenkins, Nancy Harmon. *Virgin Territory: Exploring the World of Olive Oil.* Boston: Houghton Mifflin Harcourt, 2015.
Kamman, Madeleine. *The Making of a Cook.* New York: Atheneum, 1971.
——. *In Madeleine's Kitchen.* New York: Atheneum, 1984.
Kapp, Cornelia. "Time in a Bottle." Food Arts, November 1990.
Karoff, Barbara. *South American Cooking.* Reading, Mass.: Aris Books/ Addison-Wesley, 1989.
Klein, Maggie Blyth. *The Feast of the Olive.* Reading, Mass.: Aris Books/ Addison-Wesley, 1983.
Knickerbocker, Peggy. *Olive Oil: From Tree to Table.* San Francisco: Chronicle Books, 2007.
Lake, Mark, and Judy Ridgway. *Oils, Vinegars, and Seasonings.* New York: Simon and Schuster, 1989.
McGee, Harold. *On Food and Cooking.* New York: Charles Scribner's Sons, 1984.
——. *The Curious Cook.* San Francisco: North Point Press, 1990.
Ornstein, Robert, Ph.D., and David Sobel, M.D. *Healthy Pleasures.* Reading, Mass.: Addison-Wesley, 1989.
Pellegrini, Angelo. *The Unprejudiced Palate.* San Francisco: North Point Press, 1984.

Plagemann, Catherine, and M. F K. Fisher. *Fine Preserving*. Reading, Mass.: Aris Books/Addison-Wesley, 1986.

Rombauer, Irma, and Marion Rombauer Becker. *The Joy of Cooking*. New York: Bobbs-Merrill, 1976.

Root, Wavedy. *The Food of Italy*. New York: Vintage Books, 1977.

—— *Food*. New York: Simon and Schuster, 1980.

Rosenblum, Mort. Olives: *The Life and Lore of a Noble Fruit*. New York: North Point Press, 1996.

Simeti, Mary Taylor. *Pomp and Sustenance*. New York: Alfred A. Knopf, 1989.

Stapleton, Michael. *The Illustrated Dictionary of Greek and Roman Mythology*. New York: Peter Bedrick Books, 1978.

Swern, Daniel, ed. *Bailey's Industrial Oil and Fat Products*, 4th ed. Vols. 1 & 2. New York: John Wiley and Sons, 1979.

Taylor, M. D., Judith M., *The Olive in California: History of an Immigrant Tree*. Berkeley: Ten Speed Press, 2000.

Wolfert, Paula. *The Cooking of South-West France*. New York: Dial Press, 1983.

Index

Note: A 'b' after a page number indicates a box on that page.

C

Q

R

T

U

V

W